INFORMATION FOR MANAGEMENT DECISIONS

A System for Economic Analysis and Accounting Procedures

Information for Management Decisions

A SYSTEM FOR ECONOMIC ANALYSIS AND ACCOUNTING PROCEDURES

Yaaqov Goldschmidt

CORNELL UNIVERSITY PRESS
Ithaca and London

First published 1970

Standard Book Number 8014-0541-6
Library of Congress Catalog Card Number 72-87017

Printed in the United States of America
by The Colonial Press Inc.

PREFACE

One of the most important inputs in a decision-making process is information. This study deals with the type of information that is required for making decisions on resource allocation in a business firm. In particular, it develops a new accounting system, based on both economic concepts and accounting practices, that directly provides the necessary financial data. Since conventional accounting systems are not designed to provide, and therefore often fail to provide, the required data for allocation decisions, such a system has long been needed. In a series of meetings held in 1962, K. Admon, J. Freeman, and I discussed the need for a new type of accounting system for use in management decisions on Israeli farms. We went on to consider the possibility of preparing appropriate cost-accounting statements that would be consistent with economic principles. These discussions can be viewed as the embryo of the accounting system outlined in Part One of this book.

The book itself was written while I was studying and working in the Department of Agricultural Economics and the Graduate School of Business and Public Administration, Cornell University. The environment of the university enabled me to pursue a subject that draws material from several academic disciplines and tries to synthesize their insights and the practices of nonacademicians. The study also draws on my personal experience in advising large farms and manufacturing firms in Israel on management and economic problems, on my research into the application of managerial techniques to practical business use, on an extensive review of the literature, and on studies of economics and related disciplines at the University of Arizona.

During my work I have often been struck by apparent errors in decisions on resource allocation, even in well-managed firms. Although the managers tried to make rational decisions based on the available data, these decisions often turned out to be incorrect. For example, I observed many situations where a production line was discontinued because it produced an accounting loss. But post-mortem analysis indicated that this line had provided a considerable margin between revenue and variable costs and that the released fixed facilities did not have a better use.

Experience in the practical application of linear programing and other decision-making techniques in managing firms indicates that the existing cost-accounting and budgeting systems are often at variance with economic concepts and operations research techniques. The only way to introduce these management tools is to ignore at least some of the conventional procedures. To reconcile these differences, I hypothesized (while carrying out these applications) that a managerial information system based on principles of production economics and accounting techniques could be constructed. The hypothesis was informally tested in Israel, where I was fortunate to have the experience of working with the managers of a number of large kibbutz farms. These men were willing to test new managerial techniques if the meanings and implications were explained to them, and I owe them special thanks for their cooperation. This study tries to formalize the hypothesis we tested and to generalize the experience.

I also had the opportunity to work with the managers of a large farm in New York State. It was here that I obtained the data and information necessary for testing the new accounting system reported in Chapter VI, a task that could not have been accomplished without the kind cooperation of the managers.

Parts of this book are based on two published papers: Y. Goldschmidt, "Cost Analysis and Profitability of a Service with Seasonal Character," *American Journal of Agricultural Economics,* December 1968, and Y. Goldschmidt and S. Smidt, "Valuing the Firm's Durable

Assets for Managerial Information," *Accounting Review,* April 1969. I am indebted to the *American Journal of Agricultural Economics* and the *Accounting Review* for permission to use these articles.

I am deeply grateful for the encouragement and criticisms offered by B. F. Stanton, T. R. Dyckman, L. M. Falkson, and S. Smidt. Without their active help this book would not have been possible. The greatest debt is due Professor Dyckman for his insightful comments, as well as for the time he spent in improving my thinking about accounting, and to Professor Stanton for his encouragement in seeking new ideas and his help in presenting them. Professor Smidt gave me invaluable support and assistance in revising the manuscript for publication. I am also indebted to Professor Smidt, as co-author of a paper used in this study, for allowing me to reproduce it in this book.

Several other persons also deserve special thanks. K. Admon played an important role in the initial development of some of the ideas presented here. During the work I benefited from the comments of L. Shashua and J. H. E. Taplin on several subjects. Professor G. Shillinglaw was kind enough to read the manuscript and provide valuable comments that brought about important revisions in both content and form.

It is literally impossible to identify all those who have been kind enough to read parts or all of the manuscript at its various stages and who have contributed comments. Especially helpful were G. L. Casler, Dorothy C. Chase, G. J. Conneman, U. Gilead, W. H. Hausman, C. D. Kearl, A. K. McAdams, A. Melnik, and J. Vanek. I am indebted to Miss L. Wilcox for her excellent work in typing the preliminary and final manuscripts.

I also wish to take this opportunity to thank my parents, who influenced my way of thinking, especially in respect to the importance of combining academia with practice.

Last, but not least, my appreciation is due Rachel, for her indirect help, and Asaf, who enjoyed less of a father because of this book.

Yaaqov Goldschmidt

Tel-Aviv, Israel
April 1969

CONTENTS

FIGURES

TABLES

INTRODUCTION: THE PROBLEM, OBJECTIVES, APPROACH, AND ASSUMPTIONS

The manager of a business is influenced in the way he approaches his work by ideas and techniques of analysis developed in a number of academic disciplines, particularly economics, accounting, and operations research. Since each of these disciplines approaches problems from a specialized point of view, he often finds it difficult to integrate their basic findings into a workable whole. They may, in fact, give conflicting advice.

The economist provides a set of deductive, normative rules (that might be used by the management of a business) without much concern for estimating the necessary variables to make the rules operational. The accountant provides operational rules for recording and analyzing physical and economic data, often without much concern for the ultimate use of these data; his concern is to provide a clear routine so that all actual situations that may arise have been considered in an orderly and straightforward manner. It is generally assumed that the economist's basic notion of maximizing income (that is, revenue minus costs—often referred to as profit) appropriately describes the motivation behind many business decisions. Likewise, it is believed that decisions based on economic principles will lead to optimizing behavior if the conditions required for their operation are met. The real question is whether the information required to use these principles can be obtained or approximated in an operational manner by a functioning firm.

Given a set of data and assumptions pertaining to a firm, all economists or analysts can arrive at the same optimum plan of product mix and a set of shadow prices for the constraints and intermediate goods. On the other hand, given a set of data and assumptions, "equally competent accountants may arrive at different costs for the same product" (National Association of Accountants 1957, p. 4). But the economist, the analyst, and the firm's manager must use the accountant's cost data in their analysis. How should these cost data be specified and prepared so as to fit the economist's and analyst's needs?

Some way to bring together ideas from the related disciplines is necessary. Assuming that the objective of the firm is to maximize the present value of future income (revenue minus cost), a firm's resources should be allocated according to the dictates of accepted economic principles. Since accounting techniques provide much of the data required for making these decisions, the firm's accounts should be consistent with the demands of economics. It is the intention of this study to establish the basic elements of the type of information that management needs and can use in allocating its firm's resources.

Presumably, an information system is essential to any firm, and accounting constitutes an important part of it. As such, the accounting system plays a significant role in management activities, and improvements in the accounting system will certainly lead to improvements in some of these activities. The kinds and forms of data that the system generates should be specified by management needs, and as methods of analysis are improved, the system should be adjusted to provide the required data. The information generated must effectively describe the results of past decisions, provide a basis for evaluating these decisions, and allow the development of estimates of results that may be expected from alternative courses of action in the future. It should facilitate the various planning activities (that is, make economic decision rules operational) and enable management to evaluate these activities.

The main part of this study is devoted to the development of such a system. Termed the "Operational Accounting and Analysis System" (OAAS), it is designed to provide internal data for management decisions and simultaneously to allow management to act and decide in line with the firm's primary objective. Practical problems such as asset valuation, cost distribution, and pricing of intermediate goods must be solved, and costs and income must be estimated. The price mechanism should also be incorporated into the management process. By way of analogy, the OAAS considers the individual segments (departments, production lines) of a so-called centralized firm to be similar to independent firms in the economy. So that price-based decisions concerning each segment can be made, the OAAS provides internal prices for directing resource use.

There is no one "best way" to solve all management problems, and in some instances there is no single solution to a particular problem. It seems better to arrive at a suboptimum than to seek the remote (or practically unattainable) optimum optimorum and to be frustrated in the process. The emphasis is therefore placed on concepts and on the type of data, rather than on such specifics as methods of recording and handling the data.

Linear programing as a model and as a managerial tool has had an important influence on the development of this study. Using linear programing as a device for determining how resources should be allocated in a multiproduct firm automatically assumes the use of a number of principles from economic production theory. The economic model for a firm assumed by the linear-programing technique is also implied. Practical application of linear programing provides evidence that a sophisticated technique, based on the assumption of marginal analysis and income maximization, is applicable for solving actual management problems. Moreover, business managers are willing to substitute the technique for existing procedures. Inference from this experience indicates the need for, and the applicability of, the techniques suggested in this book. But although the debt to linear programing should be clearly acknowledged, the OAAS can stand on its own. The various concepts, procedures, and rules developed for the OAAS should meet the requirements of both linear programing and many other types of analysis for financial data.

Throughout the study the existence of a viable, operating firm is assumed. In general, it is assumed that any firm may use the system, procedures, and techniques proposed in this book. The following points are assumed to be valid:

1. The firm's objective is to maximize the present value of income or, more accurately, to maximize the firm's present value. This assumption is quite reasonable in applying managerial techniques and holds even in the case of multiplicity of goals (see Chapter XI).

2. The firm is a "going concern"; that is, a firm with an established set of assets and production processes will continue to operate beyond the planning horizon. This assumption does not preclude liquidation of any part of the firm.

3. The firm confronts a completely elastic demand function for its products and a completely elastic supply function for its inputs; the prices of inputs and outputs are treated generally as given. At times, this assumption is relaxed, particularly in Chapter VII.

4. The firm is centralized in organization, but its several departments or segments may take individual action within the frame of reference of the larger organization. In this sense the firm is quasi-decentralized (see Chapter XII).

5. The firm is an integrated, multiproduct business organization. Hence the firm is viewed as a conglomeration of segments.

6. The firm is large enough so that an information system is needed to manage it efficiently. The accounting system constitutes the center of the information system (see Chapter XIII).

7. In order to limit the scope of the discussion, only the production process of the firm is considered.

8. The firm confronts only a "short-run" situation. This assumption holds, since in any decision framework it confronts some former commitments (see Chapter XIV). This does not exclude the need for long-range planning (see Chapters XIII and XIV).

9. The firm is composed of many activities (in a linear-programing sense), each having a linear production function over a designated range. Each activity uses two types of factors of production: unlimited variable inputs which have a constant unit price, and limited resources.

10. Each segment of the firm is considered to be composed of one or more activities (in a linear-programing sense). Accordingly, the total variable cost function for a segment is composed of one or several

linear sections (see Chapter V). However, much of the discussion assumes implicitly that a segment is composed of only one section and thus the marginal cost curve is horizontal.

11. Income is generated concurrently with the production process. Hence, period income is generated by each segment (see Chapters XII and XV).

Part One
The Operational Accounting and Analysis System

I
SUMMARY OF THE SYSTEM

The operational accounting and analysis system (OAAS)[1] is designed to serve the decision maker by providing correctly specified internal financial data, mainly cost and income figures. It provides the information required for two purposes: for facilitating decisions on resource allocation and internal pricing[2] and for directing and motivating the decision maker. Unfortunately, conventional accounting systems do not provide correctly specified cost and income data for many types of internal decisions. The wide use of conventional accounting in business may therefore bring about one of the two following consequences: the accounting data may be used as the primary source of information in decision making, or managers may ignore the accounting information and look for other sources of data.[3] Either of these alternatives is bad.

[1] The term "operational accounting" is borrowed from Churchman and Ackoff (1955) and is also suggested by Ijiri (1967, p. 67).

[2] Also to facilitate pricing decisions in a firm that sells its products in a non-perfect market.

[3] The results of using conventional accounting data as a basis for decisions might follow the "gigo principle"—that is, garbage in, garbage out (Boulding 1966, p. 10). Thus, for example, "management had been led to make erroneous decisions by reliance upon profit figures determined by absorption costing" (National Association of Accountants 1961, p. 82). The possibility of using inappropriate accounting data in decision making may be increased because of the rise in management services provided by certified public accounting firms in the U.S. (for data see Buckley 1966).

Simon *et al.* (1954), in a study of seven decentralized firms and after inter-

A different accounting system, or improvements in existing systems, must be installed to provide the required data.

1. Characteristics of the OAAS

The OAAS provides data pertinent to the past. Hence, it is considered as an accounting system. On the other hand, being designed to provide data for management decisions, the OAAS is partially based on such production economic concepts as marginal analysis and opportunity cost. Since such a procedure is contrary to accepted accounting principles, some accountants may not accept the classification of the OAAS as an accounting system. The OAAS may therefore be considered as a procedure for a cost and income analysis.

The OAAS is considered to be a part of a firm's information system, as will be outlined in Chapter XIII. More specifically, it constitutes the reporting phase in the programing control system described in that chapter. As "subsets" of a system, the three phases—programing, reporting, and analysis of results—should be compatible with each other, especially reporting (based on accounting techniques) and programing (based on economic principles). This can be accomplished by making sure that the accounting data are relevant for economic analysis. The method of analysis determines the type of reporting, and the results from the report are an important part of the analysis.

The discussion above implies that the conventional distinction between ex post and ex ante analysis is ignored. Thus, in the OAAS, ex post operations are analyzed in terms similar to those used while planning these operations. This analysis, in turn, serves for ex ante decisions.

The use of the information should dictate the type of data provided by the accounting system. Hence, it is not necessary to reproduce the history of the firm in objective terms or to provide exact measurements of events in order for the system to be useful in decision making. Although this approach is in contrast to much of conventional historical

---

viewing more than four hundred executives, found both that conventional accounting data are used for internal decisions (pp. 36, 37) and that managers claimed that "the profit and loss statements were not considered important management tools" (p. 42). Evidence on the first point can also be found in Eiteman and Guthrie (1952), Gibson (1963), Shillinglaw (1967), and Vatter (1967).

accounting, it fits the following statement by a committee of the American Accounting Association (1966, p. 63): "A possible structure of future accounting theory will be more normative and less descriptive than in the past."

Most of the data input into the OAAS consists of the same data used in conventional accounting. The rest of the data has to be searched for and prepared before being used in the system. The data are organized so as to fit internal management purposes. The emphasis is on providing the data in a form that best represents the actual situation confronting management in the period for which the accounting report is prepared.

In any business concern, the requirements for data are quite diversified, and information that suits one purpose may be worse than useless for another purpose. In a large business the problem can be solved by computerizing the information system; when a certain type of data is required, it is recalled by means of the computer. When computer service is not available, one set of books must be enough even though more than one summary and analysis is made. Here conventional accounting and the OAAS must be related in an effective manner.

The OAAS is designed neither to provide information for decisions on financing the firm and dividends nor to serve for tax and stewardship purposes.[4] By no means is it meant to substitute for the conventional financial accounting for external reporting or for standard cost accounting for internal control. However, the OAAS has important implications for conventional accounting practices used in both areas. The OAAS procedures and rules are applicable to a broader range of situations than simple accounting. Some situations or instances which may also be studied using some of the OAAS procedures are production economics and operations research studies of firms, cost specifications for data collection, setting transfer prices in a decentralized firm, setting prices in a vertically integrated group of firms, assets valuation

[4] Solomons' opinion (1965, p. x) on the matter of tax accounting is worth considering: "Though the needs of tax accounting and management accounting are widely recognized to be different, it is perhaps not so widely recognized that many companies are paying a substantial, though concealed, price for tax savings, when in the pursuit of these savings, they adopt accounting methods which do not serve the needs of management and may even positively mislead it."

for appraisal purposes, and calculating and stating costs of production for a product.

In developing the OAAS procedures, emphasis is given to the method of analysis rather than to the details of carrying out the accounts or to the compatibility of the system with organizational lines of management responsibility. The discussion indicates only how to provide correctly specified data for decisions. For this purpose, information is required on individual segments of the firm. Since the various procedures are interconnected, it is almost impossible to consider one without referring to another. The discussion provides a framework that can serve to focus and channel the discussion in later chapters. The interrelations between the OAAS and conventional accounting are indicated at the end of the chapter, together with a summary in tabular form of the pricing and costing rules in the framework of the OAAS, conventional accounting, and economic decision making.

2. The Requirements for Cost and Income Figures

For managing a firm—that is, for decision making and control—the cost and income (revenue minus costs) for each segment of the business must be measured or estimated in every period. A segment is defined as a part of a firm that is considered as a unit in the analytical framework (department, production line). The OAAS is designed to measure the cost and income of the individual segments. To suggest a method for estimating cost and income, the ultimate use of these figures must be specified. The main purposes for which cost and income of a segment are required are allocation decisions, pricing decisions, and performance measurements.

Allocation decisions are those decisions pertaining to resource allocation and thus to the production level and mix in a given period. There are two types: decisions pertaining to the scale of operations, for which marginal costs must be estimated; and decisions as to whether to keep or liquidate a segment, for which the contribution of the segment to the objective of the firm must be estimated.

By relaxing the assumption that the firm confronts a completely elastic demand function for its products, we may define pricing decisions as those decisions pertaining to the price level of a product sold in a nonperfect market. Economic theory teaches that marginal costs are required for these decisions; however, many studies claim that, in practice, businessmen use total-cost data (see Chapter VII). Hence both marginal and total costs should be estimated for pricing decisions.

Performance measurements estimate the actual results in terms of income. These estimates for each segment are required for two purposes. First, they are used to motivate managers at various levels to decide and to act in line with the firm's primary objective. To this end, the contribution of each segment to the firm's objective must be estimated. (This measure is compatible with the income measure used for allocation decisions.) Second, the estimates are used for making comparisons between income figures so as to detect both weak and strong spots in the production process and thus to call attention to further decisions. The comparisons may be between the period income and the income in former periods (that is, measuring the trend of income), or between one segment's income and that of another in a given period.

In short, the following data are required for each segment: two cost figures (marginal and total) and two income figures (for decisions and comparisons). The OAAS is designed to provide estimates that surrogate these figures. To arrive at meaningful figures, of course, the firm's operations must be decomposed in the analytical framework.

3. Main Features of the OAAS

The main features of the OAAS can be summarized as follows:

The continuous operations of an integrated firm are decomposed. The decomposition takes place in both a temporal and a spatial context; that is, the operations are decomposed into periods and segments.

Values (transfer prices) are assigned to assets (durables, inventories) that are transferred among periods and to intermediate goods and services that are transferred among segments. The market price of the assets and intermediate goods provide the basis for the valuation.

Two kinds of transfer prices are used: market prices, when a market for the goods exists; and "determined values," when an active market does not exist.

Contrary to conventional accounting practices, indirect costs are not allocated to either periods or segments. Acquisition costs of durable assets are not distributed to periods (by means of depreciation accounting), and overhead and common costs are not distributed to segments or units of product. This implies that the overhead costs are kept in the aggregate.

Only traceable costs, which are classified into avoidable and nonavoidable costs, are charged to the segments.

A distinction is made between liquid and nonliquid durable assets. The costs associated with these assets are included, respectively, in the avoidable and nonavoidable costs of the segment.

Contrary to accepted accounting principles, implicit costs, such as the market value of intermediate goods or the interest on capital, as well as explicit costs, are charged to the segments. Similarly, implicit revenue items, such as the market value of intermediate goods, as well as explicit revenue items, are credited to the segments. This procedure implies that each segment (service as well as productive activity) is considered as a "contribution center."

Both marginal and opportunity costs are estimated in an operational manner for a given production level.

A distinction is made between two types of opportunity cost: external and internal. The former is considered as a cost item, and thus serves as an "input" to the system. The latter represents an "output" of the system.

An unequivocal income measure does not exist. Two kinds of contribution margins (revenue minus relevant costs) pertaining to a segment are suggested: one for decisions on resource allocation, the other for evaluation of performance.

4. Decomposing the Firm's Operations and Transfer Pricing

If the price mechanism is to be incorporated into the process of managing a firm, the operations of the integrated going concern should be decomposed in the analytical framework. The decomposition takes place in both a spatial and a temporal context; that is, the operations are decomposed into segments and periods.

In the spatial context, the firm's operations are decomposed into segments resembling activities in a linear-programing formulation. Each segment of a centralized firm is viewed in the analytical framework as a contribution center, similar to a profit center (division) in a decentralized firm. Any firm can be viewed as having the characteristics of both centralized and decentralized forms of organization. Therefore, the firm is considered in the analytical framework as quasi-decentralized.[5] On the one hand, income for each segment is measured similarly to the procedures used in an independent firm. On the other hand, the segment is an integrated part of the firm at large, and thus not independent.

Operations over time are decomposed into periods in a method analogous to spatial decomposition. This decomposition is necessary if each period's income is to be measured, whereas the spatial decomposition is desirable but not essential.

The objective of the firm can now be stated as the maximizing of period income for each segment, subject to long-range considerations and to the firm's constraints.

The decomposition of the firm's operations is made possible by assigning transfer prices to the goods that are transferred among segments and periods. Pricing based on conventional accounting rules often causes inappropriate transfers of income from one segment and/or period to another, and the resulting information is likely to bias decision making. The criterion for pricing a good is based on the opportunity the firm confronts. When an external market exists, the market price serves as a transfer price.[6] When an external market does not exist, determined value is used. Determined value is an analyst's estimate of the value of a good (intermediate good, service, or asset), an estimate that is based on market considerations.

Pricing Spatial Transfers. The problem of pricing intermediate goods that are transferred between segments of an integrated firm may be thought of as similar to the economic problem of price formation in a market. The price mechanism enables each unit in the economy to function independently and efficiently; similarly, the transfer prices in a decentralized firm enable each division to function independently. Continuing this analogy, transfer prices in a centralized firm enable

[5] The term "quasi-decentralized" is borrowed from Whinston (1964*a*, p. 441).

[6] An external market is said to exist if it is possible to estimate prices at which the good could actually be bought or sold.

each segment to be analyzed as if it functioned independently. This is the procedure followed in the OAAS.

The use of transfer prices to value transfers between segments (material goods and services) enables the analyst to consider each segment of the firm as a contribution center. When determined values are used to enable further decomposition beyond that achieved by the use of market prices alone, an "artificial contribution center" emerges. This is because the determined values do not represent prices of actual opportunities, but rather figures arrived at by "artificial" means.

Valuing Assets. Valuing capital assets (durables, inventories) is, in fact, the process of assigning transfer prices to "temporal intermediate goods," which are transferred from one period to another. As with "spatial intermediate goods," which are transferred between segments, the type of transfer price depends on whether there is a market for the goods.

A corresponding distinction is made between liquid and nonliquid assets. When a market exists and the asset can be sold with relative ease on the market, the asset is considered as liquid (durable liquid assets such as livestock or trucks, raw material, finished goods) and its value is determined by the market price. When an active market for the asset does not exist, the asset is considered as nonliquid (durable nonliquid assets such as buildings or roads, goods in process) and its value must be determined by an analyst. The determined value for the durable nonliquid asset is based on its replacement costs.

The distinctions discussed in this section may be summarized as follows:

Market situation	*Basis for transfer pricing*	*Classification of assets*	*Classification of contribution centers*
Existing	Market price	Liquid	Regular
Nonexistent	Determined value	Nonliquid	Artificial

5. Costs of Production

Costs may be classified in two ways: by the ability to trace a cost to a specific segment, and by the ability to control a specific cost. Only traceable costs are charged or distributed to segments. Nontraceable costs, mainly overhead costs, are not distributed to segments but are kept in the aggregate. The ability to control a segment cost is of major importance—where "ability to control" means that management can avoid incurring the cost. Accordingly, traceable costs are classified into avoidable and nonavoidable costs. This classification differs considerably from the conventional classification of variable and fixed costs, as the discussion below implies (see Figure 1 at the end of this chapter). The corresponding specification of these cost items is as follows:

Character of cost	*Type of cost*	*Main use*
Controllable by a segment	Avoidable	Allocation decisions
Traceable to a segment	Avoidable, nonavoidable	Evaluating performance, pricing decisions
Actual to the firm	Traceable to segments, overhead	

Opportunity Costs. A distinction is made between external and internal opportunity costs. External opportunity cost is defined as the market price of a commodity (goods, service, asset) that is used in production rather than sold or bought. Internal opportunity cost is defined as the contribution (revenue minus avoidable costs) that a limited and versatile resource or facility could earn in its best feasible use within the firm. Self-owned capital, if lending or borrowing is permissible, has an external opportunity cost; if the amount of capital is limited and scarce, it will also have an internal opportunity cost.

Marginal Costs. Marginal costs, pertaining to a given level of production, are approximated by a surrogate avoidable cost. The avoidable cost in a particular situation is measured by the variable costs plus the external opportunity costs. When avoidable costs that hold on the margin differ from average costs, the former is reported. This cost figure is crucial in the OAAS.

The avoidable-cost figure is related to the opportunity costs. On the one hand, avoidable costs include external opportunity costs; on the other hand, revenue minus avoidable costs, when imputed to a limited resource or facility, provides for the internal opportunity cost. Suppose warehouse space can be hired. The hiring rate provides the basis for the external opportunity cost. This cost item is included in the avoidable costs. But plant space cannot be hired. The internal opportunity cost of plant space is calculated by subtracting the avoidable costs from the revenue of an alternative segment using plant space (see Section 6). It should be noted that while the external opportunity cost serves as an input in the OAAS, the internal opportunity cost represents an output.

Capital Charges. The cost of capital (implicit interest) is charged to the users of capital.[7] This procedure, just as in calculating avoidable costs, is contrary to accepted accounting principles. The costs related to the holding of capital assets are composed of implicit costs, such as interest and change in the asset's value (depreciation and obsolescence), and explicit costs, such as maintenance, insurance, and taxes. These costs are charged to the users of the asset's services unless an asset or a group of assets is considered as a contribution center, when there is a market for the asset's services.

The implicit costs associated with liquid assets (interest and change in value) are considered as avoidable costs. On the other hand, the implicit costs of nonliquid assets are considered nonavoidable.

Overhead and Common Costs. Overhead costs are not distributed to the segments since these costs are not traceable and any distribution is arbitrary or discretionary in nature. These costs are recorded and kept in the aggregate, and thus the corresponding segment is considered as a cost center.

Some cost items incurred by a segment are not influenced by the scale of production. These are included in the category of common costs of the segment. Just as overhead costs are not distributed to segments, common costs are not distributed to units of product. Since the OAAS is designed to provide data that are relevant for marginal analysis, the common costs are considered nonavoidable.

[7] Because of its serious shortcomings, the conventional procedure of computing the rate of return is not used in the OAAS (see Chapter II).

6. Income Measurements

Since it is assumed that the primary objective of the firm is to maximize income, income should be used as a criterion for management decisions and control. Thus it is necessary to measure the income of each segment. Income of individual segments should serve two purposes: decisions on resource allocation, by measuring the contribution of the segment to the firm's objective, and evaluation of performance, by using an income measure that is comparable to income in former periods and in other segments. Accordingly, two income measures are suggested for the respective purposes: attainable contribution and contribution to overhead. Income for the firm at large is measured as well. The corresponding specification of the contribution margins is as follows:

Type of contribution	*Cost items deducted*	*Main use*
For a segment:		
Attainable contribution	Avoidable	Decisions, motivation
Contribution to overhead	Avoidable, nonavoidable	Evaluating performance
For the firm:		
Net contribution	Total costs	

Attainable contribution is calculated by subtracting avoidable costs from the segment's revenue. Contribution to overhead is calculated by subtracting from the revenue all the traceable costs (avoidable and nonavoidable) or by subtracting nonavoidable costs from the attainable contribution.

In the OAAS, attainable contribution is the main income measure for segments. It is used for allocation decisions and for motivation of managers. For example, the attainable contribution provides a surrogate for the objective function coefficient (Cj) of an activity in a linear-programing formulation. Imputing this contribution to a limited resource provides for the internal opportunity cost (shadow price). On the other hand, the goal of a segment is to maximize the attainable contribution, while observing the relevant restrictions. The contribution to overhead includes all costs traceable to a segment. It can thus be used for comparing the period income of a segment to income in former periods and in other segments, and thus can serve for evaluating performance. The attainable contribution cannot be used for comparisons.

A list of cost and revenue items follows:

Cost and revenue items	*Basis for costing or pricing*
Avoidable costs	
Variable inputs:	
Purchased directly	Actual costs
Inventoried materials	Replacement costs plus holding costs
Goods in process	Determined values (or market prices when available)
Intermediate goods	Market prices (or determined values)
Durable, liquid assets:	
Depreciation	Change in market value
Interest	Market rate
Explicit costs (insurance)	Actual costs
Miscellaneous	Actual costs
Nonavoidable costs	
Durable, nonliquid assets:	
Depreciation	Change in determined value
Interest	Cost of capital
Explicit costs	Actual costs
Common Costs	Actual costs
Miscellaneous	Actual costs
Revenue	
Realized	Actual revenue
Realizable:	
Intermediate goods	Market prices (or determined values)
Finished goods	Net sale price or total avoidable costs
Goods in process	Determined values (or market prices when available)

There is no unequivocal solution to the problem of how to measure income, performance, and efficiency and which criterion to use. The use of a single income or performance criterion cannot suffice, since it would not necessarily indicate the degree of overall income goal attainment.

7. Types of Segments

The segments of a firm are classified into regular or artificial contribution centers, rent centers, and cost centers.

Regular Contribution Centers. By using market prices for valuing intermediate goods, an integrated production process is decomposed into segments, and each segment is considered as a contribution center. This means that the various stages of the production process are "exposed" to the "market forces." Under conventional accounting practices, on the other hand, the individual stages are "protected" from the "market forces." The contribution margin of each segment should be used for decisions, motivation, and evaluation purposes.

Artificial Contribution Centers. Some of the contribution centers are "artificial" because determined values rather than market prices are used as transfer prices for the intermediate goods (or services) "bought" and "sold" by the artificial contribution center. An artificial contribution center is established so as to enable further decomposition of a regular contribution center when a market for the intermediate good does not exist or when selling or buying the intermediate good on the market is not a relevant opportunity. The contribution margin pertaining to an artificial contribution center cannot therefore be used directly for allocation decisions. But it should be used for motivation and evaluation purposes. Consolidating the data pertaining to related artificial contribution centers provides data pertaining to a regular contribution center.

The procedure of establishing artificial contribution centers is of special importance for analyzing service departments, since in this way the service activity is analyzed similarly to a regular productive activity.

Rent Centers. The procedure of charging to the segments implicit costs (interest) may cause some complications in accounting. Special accounts, termed rent centers, must be established to balance these charges. The contribution of such an account stands for the economic rent of the factor for which the account stands (capital). When cost on the margin differs from average cost, the former is charged to the segment. This procedure also requires a special account (rent center) to absorb extra charges when marginal costs increase, or missing charges when marginal costs decrease while the volume of production increases.

Cost Centers. The administrative activities of the firm are considered as cost centers, since the amount of service rendered by these activities to the individual segments cannot be traced, and since there is usually no way to determine a price for these services. Hence, the costs incurred by these activities are not distributed to the contribution centers.

To evaluate the cost centers, costs are categorized as avoidable and nonavoidable. Thus, from the costing point of view, all centers are treated alike. The difference lies in the revenue. While revenue is credited to contribution centers, it is not credited to cost centers.

8. The OAAS and Conventional Accounting

After reading the preceding sections, one might ask: What does the OAAS have to do with conventional accounting? The need for an accounting system that serves for management decisions is well recognized. A committee of the American Accounting Association (1966, p. 37), for example, states: "Management accounting is less well developed and the foundations for it are less well understood than is the case with externally oriented accounting theory." In developing the OAAS, an effort is made to provide for a missing accounting system.

Any accounting system provides some specific information according to its task, and thus digresses from textbook, financial accounting; but still it is connected to it. This is the case with standard cost accounting and variable costing, and the same holds here.[8] It should be borne in mind that even conventional financial accounting is far from perfect in regard to its task and its stated objective. The literature is filled with criticisms of existing accounting procedures[9] and suggestions for

[8] It should be noted that "cost accounting was the domain of the engineer until late in the 1800's, and that the integration problem arose only when accountants began to 'audit' cost records, and then eventually took them over" (Anton 1966, p. 520).

[9] Let us quote some extreme statements: "Accounting is plagued with fetishes and sacred cows" (W. A. Paton, reproduced in Taggart 1953, p. 313). "It is . . .

changes. It is not possible for one accounting system to serve all purposes. Rather, the accounting system has to be tailored to the purpose at hand. The OAAS is tailored to the purposes of decision making.

Since the OAAS can be considered as a method for analyzing accounting data, some relevant procedures or rules from the OAAS can be applied to the raw data of the accounting department whenever an analysis is required. But constructing an accounting system using some (or all) of the OAAS procedures should be much more effective and meaningful to management. Some of the procedures and rules (Figure 1) may not appear at first as applicable to business concerns. It is not meant, however, that all the rules have to be incorporated into an accounting system. Presumably, if only some of the major procedures are incorporated, an important improvement regarding the kinds of data supplied for decision making may be achieved. Some rules may be used sporadically or as a basis for approximations rather than for detailed or accurate computations.

For efficiency and effectiveness, the various parts of the information system should be interconnected (see Chapter XIII). Although the OAAS is constructed assuming the use of economic principles in decision making, many items of the basic data are used by both the OAAS and conventional accounting. There is a possibility of bridging over the differences between the OAAS and the conventional accounting system so that both will be considered as subsystems of the firm's information system. Accountants are ingenious in manipulating figures and in overcoming complicated problems which arise at times. This capacity can be used successfully to bridge the gap between the two systems, given the will to do it. (An experiment of this kind is reported in Chapter VI, Sections 3 and 4.)[10]

---

instructive to watch the accountant endeavor to support illogical procedures with logic" (Husband 1954, p. 13). "Accounting has not been the real interpreter of and to business that it should be" (Knowpole and Seybold, reproduced in Evans 1955, p. 1739). "Accounting theory needs a drastic house cleaning" (Philips 1963*b*, p. 699).

[10] An M.B.A. thesis by J. Dickerson, reported by Mattessich (1964, pp. 170–175), demonstrates that it is possible to amend inexpensively the data of traditional accounting so as to provide a financial statement in conformity with the proposal made by Edwards and Bell (1961).

Figure 1. A summary of pricing and costing rules in the framework of conventional accounting, OAAS, and economic decision making

Price or cost item	*Conventional accounting*	*OAAS*	*Economic decision making*
Temporal transfer price			
Inventories:			
Raw material	Acquisition cost	Replacement cost	Replacement cost
Finished goods	Cost of production	Realizable value	Present value of future cash flow
Goods in process	Cost of production	Determined value	(Present value of future cash flow)
Durable assets:			
Liquid	Acquisition cost	Market price	Present value of future earnings or sale price
Nonliquid	Acquisition cost	Determined value based on replacement cost	(Present value of future earnings or sale price)
Spatial transfer price			
Intermediate goods:			
Market exists	Cost of production	Market price	Market price
Market nonexistent	Cost of production	Determined value	Shadow price
Service of self-owned resources and facilities:			
Market exists	Actual cost	Market price	Market price
Market nonexistent	Actual cost	None	Shadow price

Capital charges for durables			
Interest on:			
Liquid assets	None	Market rate	Shadow price
Nonliquid assets	None	None (allocation decisions) or cost of capital (pricing decisions)	None
Depreciation of:			
Liquid assets	Formula on acquisition cost	Change in value	Change in value
Nonliquid assets	Formula on acquisition cost	None (allocation decisions) or change in value (pricing decisions)	None
Cost and income			
Cost of production	Variable cost	Avoidable cost	Marginal cost
	Fixed cost	Nonavoidable cost and overhead	None
	Full cost	Total cost	Total cost
Revenue	Realized	Realized and realizable	Expected revenue
Income measurement	Revenue minus variable cost	Attainable contribution	Attainable contribution
	Profit	Net contribution	Net contribution plus assets' change in value

Introducing changes in an internal accounting system does not involve the same problems as when a change is proposed for the financial accounting system that serves external parties since these parties expect businesses to adhere to accepted accounting principles.[11]

[11] Consider the following statement by the Accounting Principle Board of the American Institute of Certified Public Accountants: "The Board believes, however, that while these studies are a valuable contribution to accounting thinking, they are too radically different from present generally accepted accounting principles for acceptance at this time" (*Journal of Accountancy,* May 1962, p. 10).

II
INCOME MEASUREMENT FOR DECISION MAKING AND CONTROL

A firm may be characterized as maximizing the present value of its income (net receipts) subject to certain constraints on its behavior. If the firm can be effectively segmented so that the contribution of each segment to the firm can be determined, these segments can serve as decision-making and control units. The objective of this chapter is to analyze the problems involved in measuring the income of these segments, assuming they can be established. In the process, several solutions to the measurement problem are examined. Because multiple solutions to the measurement problem can be developed, the relative advantages and shortcomings of the various alternatives are evaluated.

The difficulties in measuring income stem in large part from the necessity of imposing arbitrary time evaluations on a continuous process. For example, inventories, equipment, buildings, and other assets must be valued at discrete points in time if the process of income measurement is to be accomplished. There is no single accepted means, however, for determining the necessary values; many means are available and used in present practice. Since the final income figure is a product of the valuation method selected, several accountants acting independently could easily show a different final income figure for the same firm for the same time period.[1]

[1] Chang (1962, p. 637) quotes a statement made by J. B. Canning: "Income is simply . . . 'the figure that results when the accountant has finished applying the procedures which he adopts.' "

The problems in measuring the income of a segment are even more complex. This is true because intermediate goods that are transferred to and from the segment must be valued and because overhead and common costs must be allocated. Here again there are many valuation and allocation procedures that may be and indeed are used by accountants. The difficulty of achieving a meaningful income measure under these conditions moved one writer to comment that it is doubtful "whether any routine divisional net profit computation along traditional full-cost lines can ever mean anything useful to either the divisions or top management" (Dean 1958, p. 8).

1. The Requirements for an Income Measure

Income is generated by the continuous operations of the total firm. For decision making and control, however, the income for each segment of the firm must be measured or estimated every period. The problem is how to decompose the firm's operations in both a temporal context—measuring period income—and a spatial context—measuring the income of a segment—in order to support the required analysis. The period income of a segment must be measured in order to answer two questions: What has been achieved?—the answer can be used for future resource allocation decisions assuming that the future resembles the past. What was the level of achievement?—the answer can help management to detect and react to both weak and strong areas of performance.

The segment income measure should be chosen so that decisions made on the basis of the measure are compatible with the firm's objective. Furthermore, it is helpful in evaluating performance if the income measure for each segment is comparable to both the income measures of other segments and those of former periods. In this chapter two income measures are designed to facilitate these goals: attainable contribution and contribution to overhead.

The next section describes the difficulties associated with measuring income that arise from the need to have period measures and the necessity to measure the two ingredients of the income figure, namely costs and revenues. The attainable-contribution and contribution-to-overhead income measures are then defined and their merits and shortcomings discussed. For the sake of simplicity, a stable price level is assumed in this chapter.[2]

2. Period Income and the Firm's Objective

It has been argued that the measure of segment income must be consistent with the firm's primary objective of maximizing the present value of its income. Consider this problem first in an ex ante context.

Maximizing the income of a segment in a given period may be at odds with the firm's primary objective. For example, the costs associated with employee training or equipment maintenance would reduce the measured period income although the present value of the expected future additional income resulting from these actions could easily exceed the respective period costs.[3] This is the typical case, for example, with new investments.

This problem can be remedied, however, by imposing long-range considerations as restrictions on the program for any period. This procedure implies that employee training and other investment activities are undertaken in the framework of a long-range plan and may, therefore, be considered as "given" to or as restrictions imposed on any shorter-range plan.

For the period income to be meaningful, assets transferred to and from the period must also be valued. Furthermore, the implicit interest on the capital used in a given period must be recognized. If the valuation problem can be solved, if interest is charged for the use of capital, and if long-range considerations are incorporated in the restrictions, maximizing period income can be compatible with the firm's primary objective.

But to achieve maximum period income, an optimum production (or output) program, given resource availabilities, is required. This might be accomplished by applying a linear-programing analysis or some other planning technique. Any optimization method implies an

[2] Edwards and Bell (1961) partition income into two components, namely operating income and holding gains, even when the general price level is stable. The term "income" as used in this chapter includes both these components.

[3] Keeping up the period income of a segment by "milking" the business (Solomons 1965, p. 60) is induced especially when a manager is appointed for a relatively short period of time.

objective, which, it is assumed here, is a function of income. An optimum program can thus be established only if the proper income figures for the individual segments can be obtained. Income determination requires the measurement of both costs and revenues. In turn, in order to measure the income of a segment, the assets and intermediate goods must be valued.

The economic criterion for valuing assets and intermediate goods that are transferred to and from the period and the segment is a function of the opportunity that the firm confronts; that is, it is market oriented. Accordingly, the market price can be used as a basis for valuation and thereby can be used to determine costs. This subject will be discussed in Chapters III–V. The discussion in the rest of this chapter assumes that market prices can be estimated and values for both intermediate goods and assets can be determined (see Chapters III and IV). It also assumes that costs that are relevant to the analysis can be determined (see Chapter V).

3. Two Kinds of Contribution Margins as Income Measures

All income measures are subject to some shortcomings. It follows then that no income measure will be ideal for all management's needs. This chapter concentrates on two areas of management concern and suggests a different segment income measure for each. In the area of decision making (for example, in allocating resources), attainable contribution is the income measure suggested, while in the area of performance evaluation, the income measure suggested is contribution to overhead.

Attainable contribution is defined as the difference between revenue and avoidable costs. It is the result of subtracting only avoidable costs from revenues. This figure is used both for allocation decisions and for motivation of lower-level managers.

Contribution to overhead is obtained by subtracting all the traceable costs (avoidable and nonavoidable) from the segment's revenue. An identical result can be obtained by subtracting the nonavoidable costs from the attainable contribution.

The difference between these two types of contribution is nonavoidable costs. Perhaps the most important nonavoidable cost is represented by the capital charges for the services of durable nonliquid assets. These charges must be subjectively determined by an analyst.

4. Attainable Contribution as a Maximization Criterion

In order to maximize the period income for the whole firm, an optimum combination of products (recall that products may be treated as segments) is required. For the sake of simplicity, linear programing will be used as the optimization method. The firm's situation is formulated into a linear-programing model, which is used to determine the optimum product mix and resource use for a future period. The objective function of the model is to maximize the attainable contribution subject to a variety of constraints.[4]

The attainable contribution of each activity provides the coefficient (the value of Cj in technical terms) used in the linear-programing objective function. The optimum solution determines the activities to be included in the program. This program is then put into effect.

Once the program is in effect, however, changes may occur which render the previous solution no longer optimal. This situation essentially requires that the previous program be revised as often as is practical. In the meantime, segment managers may be given the authority to modify their portion of the solution. But even if segment managers are not given the authority to change the activities included in their segment or the level of the activity (the production level), they retain the authority to attempt to improve the actual, attainable contribution by reducing costs, improving employee morale, and so on. In other words, a higher contribution for an activity included in the program is preferable to a lower contribution. If an activity or group of activities is considered as a segment, any effort to maximize the attainable contribution of a segment, taking into account the relevant restrictions, is in line with the firm's overall objective. It should be noted that the discussion has now shifted from an ex ante analysis to an analysis of actual operations. Subsequently, the discussion turns to an ex post analysis.

[4] The constraints are due to physical and institutional restrictions on production, long-range considerations, intersegment relationships, and any additional goals, if such exist, at some predetermined level.

The previous discussion implies that lower-level managers should be induced to maximize the attainable contribution of the segments for which they are responsible, simultaneously taking into account the restrictions that apply to their segment. It is reasonable to expect the manager to act so as to improve his performance report, which is the criterion by which he is judged. In fact, there is evidence that he behaves in this manner.[5] Hence, attainable contribution can be used as a performance criterion. The fact that this income measure is used in the beginning of the period in the decision-making framework, and that all cost and revenue items included in the attainable contribution are controllable, except for the imposed restrictions, is an appropriate characteristic for a measure used for motivational purposes. Moreover, the attainable contribution can be used to measure the change in income that would have occurred if the scale of operations were changed, thereby providing important feedback information for future decisions. Attainable contribution is therefore suggested for two purposes: to measure performance in the former period and to serve as a surrogate for decisions pertaining to the next period.

Using attainable contribution as one yardstick for measuring a manager's performance has several merits, as indicated above, but it simultaneously also exhibits shortcomings. First, it is sometimes difficult to measure the degree to which certain constraints imposed on a segment are satisfied. Second, this measure does not indicate whether a maximum is achieved; that is, it does not tell just how high the performance is. These shortcomings can be eliminated, but not without introducing new limitations.

As was mentioned earlier, a manager should attempt to maximize a segment's contribution while observing the relevant constraints. However, it is easier to measure the attainable contribution than the degree to which the manager complies with the imposed constraints. One way to evaluate the use of resources in relation to the constraints is by means of their shadow prices. Indeed, some authors suggest that these prices

[5] Ridgway (1960) cites several reports that indicate that managers are motivated to maximize the performance measure used, even when this behavior is at odds with the firm's primary objective. This is also Dean's experience (1958, p. 5). Generalizations based on a survey of literature by Ammons (1956) suggest that a knowledge of performance affects motivation and the rate of learning.

be incorporated into the accounting system or into the ex post analysis.[6]

Consider an example. Suppose a firm has two pieces of equipment, one in reasonably good shape, the other in poor shape. Suppose further that the product produced by the former gets a premium price. Two departments presently are using this equipment up to its capacity. If the department's performance is measured by its attainable contribution, both managers will be reluctant to use the poorer piece of equipment, unless both pieces are priced at their respective shadow prices. But central management should allocate the equipment to the departments according to economic principles, and this allocation must be accepted by or imposed on the involved departments. (It becomes an imposed constraint on the segment.)

Whether the shadow price is charged or not, the managers should strive to maximize the contribution over the costs charged. This means that the manager does not have to maximize the absolute attainable contribution; he instead maximizes the contribution above that figure that is supplied by the budget. In other words, the manager should maximize the net receipts above the contribution that is figured in the budget, regardless of whether this contribution is calculated by subtracting avoidable costs or avoidable costs plus shadow prices from revenue.[7] The implication is that charging the shadow prices of the limited resources to the segments is not in and of itself crucial for motivating the manager. It is neither necessary nor sufficient to overcome the constraint problem.

Another possible solution is to use the actual attainable contribution (that is, ex post) as a performance measure by comparing it to the budgeted contribution, and thereby motivate the manager to maximize the positive variance between the two.[8] This solution might, however, induce a manager taking part in the budgeting process to suggest low contribution figures to be used in the budget. In order to mitigate this problem, the budget or the actual performance figures could be com-

[6] See Smith and Barnard (1960), Dopuch and Drake (1964), Samuels (1965), and Bernhard (1968).

[7] No attempt is made here to deal with the general problems of budgeting and motivation. For a discussion of this subject, see Stedry (1960), Benston (1963), and Caplan (1966)

[8] Shillinglaw (1962, 1964) suggests a similar solution.

pared to performance in earlier periods. Attainable contribution, however, cannot serve for such comparisons since it does not include all the traceable costs. For example, if an investment in nonliquid assets substitutes for labor, the attained contribution will increase (labor is an avoidable cost while the services of nonliquid assets are nonavoidable). The increased contribution does not necessarily indicate that operations are more efficient in an economic or even technical sense.

To summarize, measuring performance relative to that planned can be used to inform managers how well they have done. But the questions of whether the planned income level is optimal and whether or not there is a possibility for improving it must both be evaluated.[9]

5. Contribution to Overhead: A Comparable Performance Measure

In order to evaluate the level of income attained, the income measure should be comparable to other income measures. The comparison may be to income levels in former periods, to be discussed first, or to the income levels of other segments, to be discussed later.

Attainable contribution should be maximized. Hence, it is tempting to use this figure as a performance criterion by comparing it to the segment's results in former periods. But unfortunately, as was shown in the previous section, this measure cannot be compared since it does not include all traceable costs. This fact suggests that some other measure—for example, contribution to overhead—be examined.

The contribution to overhead is computed after all costs (avoidable and nonavoidable) incurred by the segment are subtracted from revenue. The subjective nature of substantial cost determinations in this area (primarily capital charges including depreciation and interest for the services of durable nonliquid assets) will, unfortunately, produce some undesired variability in these figures. Despite this limitation, the contribution-to-overhead figure perhaps still serves as a useful figure for general comparative purposes. This is especially true in light of the changing conditions prevailing in any period which reduces the relevance of any temporal comparisons.

[9] Horngren (1967) suggests measuring two types of variances in this regard: actual performance versus budget, and budget versus (practical) capacity.

Such comparisons, nevertheless, do enable management to study the change in income over time. The measurement of the contribution to overhead can serve as one performance measure, especially since it is calculated after all traceable costs are charged to the segment, including implicit interest on the use of capital.

The contribution to overhead of a segment can, if circumstances allow, be compared to that of similar segments in different firms. Such comparisons are limited in extent, since equivalent income data for segments in other firms are usually not available.[10] Perhaps the most common comparisons carried out in business are between income measurements of individual segments of a firm. These comparisons, however, are subject to several severe limitations.

6. Income Measurements as Performance Criteria

Typically, income measurements serve as the overall criterion of performance and efficiency. Thus, it is customary in business to consider low segment-income as an indication of inefficiency and a signal to search for its causes. Contrarily, if a segment generates income, it is considered to be functioning efficiently.[11] Moreover, a commonly held belief is that "it is usually easier to improve on a bad performance than on a good one" (Solomons 1965, p. 283). This, of course, may not necessarily be true. It is not difficult to conceive of situations where the opposite holds; that is, where a good performance can be improved more easily than a bad one. An illustration is supplied later.

The success of an activity, measured by the level of income achieved, does not depend only on the manager. External factors, such as the level of prices for the product and inputs, obsolescence of assets, and weather, all may have an important effect on the final income figure. Thus, high income may be achieved without the manager's efforts, although it may also indicate that he is able to take advantage of these favorable conditions. Internal factors also affect the income level (especially when the shadow prices are not included in the income report). As a result, high income does not necessarily indicate a good perform-

[10] This procedure is followed extensively in agriculture by the advisory services in several countries.

[11] For evidence see Simon *et al.* (1954, p. 22).

ance or high efficiency in production, nor does it indicate that income cannot be improved. Consider an example.

Suppose again that a firm has two pieces of equipment, one in good shape, the other in poorer shape, and that two departments use the equipment. If income is used as a performance measure, the managers will be reluctant to use the poor piece of equipment. Now suppose the poor piece is allocated by the central management to segment A because this is the best solution for the firm at large. The relatively low income of segment A is not an indication of bad performance or inefficient use of its resources. For a case illustrating the contrary, assume that segment A is technically efficient in the use of some or all inputs, and that the managers of this segment are performing as well as they can under the given conditions, yet income is low. The relatively high income of segment B does not indicate whether this is really the highest income attainable under the conditions given.[12] This situation can be partially corrected by means of charging the shadow prices of the constraints (imposing the use of this type of equipment) to the segments. But this raises another problem.

The shadow price of a constraint can be defined as the portion of the value (contribution) of an optimum program that is imputed to the corresponding constraint by a linear-programing solution. The sum of the shadow prices of the constraints therefore must equal the contribution of the optimum program. This implies that if the shadow prices are charged to the activities in the framework of a budget (which is based on the linear-programing solution), the income of the whole firm and each activity (segment) will be zero. The accounting reports can be designed accordingly. The shadow prices will be charged to the segments, and the deviation of the results from zero will provide a device for evaluating performance.

It can be concluded from the discussion in this section that income should not be used for comparing performance among the segments of a firm. This holds whether conventional profit or contribution-to-overhead measures are used.

[12] Moreover, favorable conditions bring about high income, which in turn may conceal inefficiencies in operations: there is enough income to allow for inefficiency.

Comparisons of the contribution to overhead made by the individual segments of the firm may, however, suggest potential opportunities that the firm should investigate further. For example, if product prices are given, a high contribution level suggests that the firm should consider the possibility of expansion. Alternatively, if prices are determined by the firm, relaxing the assumption that the firm confronts a completely elastic demand function for its products, a high contribution level may indicate the likelihood of increased competition through the entry of new firms into the market. In both cases the relevant information requires a market-based income figure. Contribution to overhead is a market-based income figure and is therefore able to provide the desired information.

Comparison of the attainable contribution of the individual segments is also useful in a decision-making context. But here it is the economic performance of the segments that is being compared, not the manager's performance. One way to measure the economic performance of a segment is to impute the attainable contribution of the segment to a limited resource in order to evaluate the latter's opportunity cost.[13] Still a different procedure of imputing income to limited resources is in general use by business concerns today—the rate of return.

7. Rate of Return: A Misleading Performance Criterion

The ratio of income per unit of the main resource employed by a firm is in wide use in business. Such ratios are used to measure the performance and efficiency of the whole firm, a segment of it, or even a venture. Thus, in this country it is quite common in business corporations to relate profit to invested capital by using the "rate of return on employed capital" or the returns on investment.[14] In agriculture,

[13] Suppose the attainable contribution of segment Y is $10,000 per period and it uses 5,000 square feet of the limited space of the factory. By dividing the first figure by the second, a cost figure of $2 per square foot is obtained that indicates the opportunity cost of utilizing the space by another segment. For further discussion, see Chapter XIV.

[14] See National Association of Accountants (1959). Du Pont, for example, has used the criterion of "returns on investment" since the 1920's (Kline and Hessler 1952). On the other hand, Simon *et al.* (1954, pp. 25–26) indicate that managers are not interested in ratio figures.

on the other hand, where the business is often owned and managed by one man, it is common to relate profits to the labor resource charging implicit interest on capital.

As a criterion to be maximized, the rate-of-return ratio can lead to mistakes.[15] First, the objectives of an operation are almost invariably to maximize some difference rather than some ratio.[16] Second, it assumes that the resource (capital) used in the ratio is the only scarce resource and encourages economizing it at the expense of all other resources. In addition to these limitations, there are also problems in calculating the income ratios.

Income ratios are based on two figures that are each the result of an estimate or appraisal: income measurement (profit in conventional accounting or contribution to overhead) and the volume of the resource employed by the segment. The fact that estimated figures are involved and that the estimates are often substantial (along with the other limitations of rate of return) suggests that it would be inappropriate to rely on one ratio alone as a sole criterion of performance. Furthermore, there are many problems as to which figures should be used in determining both the numerator and the denominator.[17]

With conventional accounting figures based on a set of rules and what one might describe as essentially "discretionary procedures," the ratio of returns on investment may be substantially in error. For example, suppose the bulk of the capital of a segment was invested a long time ago. Part of it has already been written off the books. The rest is carried at historical cost. This procedure implies, first, low depreciation charges and thereby high profits (a large numerator in the ratio) and, second, a low level of employed capital (a small denom-

[15] See Dorfman (1960, p. 613).

[16] Comparison of the rate of return at various periods fails to indicate whether there is a growth in income which is an important feature in measuring performance. See Bierman (1963, p. 87).

[17] Some of the alternative figures that might be used for the denominator are: total capital available or employed, or employed in operations (National Association of Accountants 1959, p. 3); book value or corrected value by price level changes; gross value or net of depreciation; if net of depreciation, using various depreciation methods; with or without retired assets (Davidson 1962, p. 10); total capital or equity (Vatter 1959); only items that are capitalized or also some items that conventionally are charged to expense (Bierman 1963, p. 81).

inator) in comparison to situations involving relatively new assets. The wide use of this yardstick in business implicitly assumes that the various biases will cancel one another, an assumption that seldom is valid in practice.

Ratios also ignore the absolute magnitudes of both numerator and denominator. Suppose the income per dollar invested for segments A and B are $5 and $0.5, respectively. Segment A seems superior to segment B. But suppose further that the invested capital is $100 and $10,000, respectively. Segment A then is earning only $500 while segment B is earning $5,000. This may indicate an essentially different evaluation of segment importance although not necessarily providing a valid performance measure.

Measuring performance by the ratio of return on investment will tend to cause the manager to act in such a way as to maximize this criterion. Thus, additional investment, although profitable, might be rejected if it reduces the average rate of return. For example, suppose a manager confronts two equally risky alternatives that will increase output. The first alternative is to hire equipment and the second is to borrow capital and buy the necessary equipment. Assuming that both alternatives portend the same output increase, under a rate-of-return criterion, the manager may be motivated to choose the first alternative even when the second has a higher net present value, because by adopting the former, the denominator of the ratio is not increased.

In Section 4 it was stated that the attainable contribution should be maximized subject to the relevant constraints. This statement is equivalent to saying that the attainable contribution, imputed to all the restrictions simultaneously, should be maximized in a manner similar to linear-programing formulation. When there is more than one restriction, trying to maximize the contribution per unit of one restriction would probably be at odds with the firm's objective. The two are compatible only if the firm confronts one primary restriction.

Suppose a firm is restricted only by one resource: capital. This means that maximizing the returns to capital maximizes the firm's income. But this situation never exists in a multiproduct firm. If it is assumed that the firm behaves rationally and strives to maximize its income, the very fact of producing more than one product implies a situation of more than one restriction.[18] If there were only one restriction (capital), management would have chosen the one production line that provides the highest rate of return to it.

On one hand, every firm has a set of restrictions on production, among them several limited resources. On the other hand, the limited resources often are not completely restricted, since more of the limited resource can usually be acquired at some price. This implies that if the criterion rate of returns is used, it should be computed to more than one resource.

To summarize, the income ratio as a performance criterion has some severe shortcomings. These are: lack of correspondence to the objective of maximization, the need for additional estimates, and the implicit assumptions that only one resource is restricted and that the production function is linear (see Chapter IX, note 4). These are in addition to the limitations that any income measure has as a performance criterion. The conclusion is that "rate of return on investment" should not be used as a single criterion to evaluate performance.

In an ex ante decision framework, nevertheless, when linear programing is not used, the decision maker should consider (1) the attainable contribution of each activity and (2) a small number of relevant restricted resources or facilities for the firm at large. Computing the ratio of (1) to (2) provides the internal opportunity cost of the resource, which is, in other words, the yardstick of economic efficiency of the resource in its alternative uses (see Chapter XIV).

In an ex post analysis framework, when management wants to learn about performance of various operations, a similar procedure can be followed. The contribution to overhead can serve as the numerator of the ratio. All the costs have been deducted to calculate this measure, including interest charges for the use of capital. Only when the ratio is computed for several resources can management make a judgment as to the efficiency of operations.

8. Summary and Conclusions

This chapter has discussed procedures for measuring the income of a segment. These measures are required for management decisions

[18] This is implied from a linear programing model. Because of uncertainty considerations, however, the firm may produce more than one product.

and control. We have assumed that segments can be established, intermediate goods and assets can be valued, and costs can be estimated—subjects to be discussed in the next three chapters.

Two income measures for a segment have been suggested. Attainable contribution is used mainly in the decision-making framework and for motivating managers. Contribution to overhead is compared for one segment over several periods to indicate income trends and to similar segments in the same firm and in other firms (if possible) to measure its absolute value.

We have examined several measurements of performance, including the absolute level of attainable contribution; the attainable contribution after shadow prices are charged; the variance between the actual attainable contribution (an ex post concept) and the budgeted contribution; contribution to overhead compared to the contribution in former years, similar segments in other firms, or other segments in the same firm; rate of income growth; and rate of returns. Other kinds of nonincome performance measurements are available in ratio or nonratio form, including the level of production, sales volume, the volume of input, or cost of production. These measurements are discussed in Chapter IX. They can and should be used under certain conditions to supplement the income measurements.

Every performance criterion has some shortcomings arising from either noncomparability or the inability to measure the degree of income goal attainment. Maximizing with respect to any one of the criteria may not be consistent with the firm's objective. If the manager of a segment maximizes that criterion by which he is judged, several performance criteria used simultaneously for measuring performance are probably better than a single measure.[19] This in turn implies that the ultimate measurement of performance of a segment must be based to some extent on judgment. Providing several performance criteria from the information system will perhaps cause this judgment process to be effective, but it will not necessarily make it efficient.

The conventional practice of providing one performance criterion—profit—although efficient and straightforward, may not necessarily convey the required information to make the system effective. The

[19] This may also reduce the incentive to distort figures.

right balance between effectiveness and efficiency in evaluating performance must be established separately in each case. Ridgway (1960, p. 374) notes: "The inadequacy of a single measure of performance is evident. . . . Recognition of the inadequacies of a single measure of success or performance leads organizations to develop several criteria. It is felt then that all aspects of the job will receive adequate attention and emphasis so that efforts of individuals will not be distorted."

In practice, many criteria cannot be measured. Only a few should be reported (for example, the two contribution margins in both absolute and ratio forms). The rest may be checked by means of sampling, if performance is to be evaluated. For decision-making purposes, before a decision is taken, several criteria may be checked.[20]

Since the figures for attainable contribution are necessary for decision making and the figures of contribution to overhead are valuable for comparison purposes, both are reported in the OAAS income statement (see Chapter VI).

[20] A manager's performance should be measured not only by the results achieved in operations, but also by evaluation of his expectations and reallocation decisions using appropriate diaries (see the discussion in Chapters XIII and XIV).

III
TRANSFER PRICING

Assuming that the primary objective of the firm is to maximize income, it is reasonable to use income as a criterion for management decisions and control. To make decisions and exercise control, in either a large or a small firm, it is necessary to know what contribution each segment is making to the firm's overall objective. Hence, the income of each segment should be measured. This can be done only if the firm's operations are decomposed into individual segments in the analytical framework. In dealing with a centralized firm, the ideal solution would be to consider each individual segment of the firm as similar to an independent division of a decentralized firm. Since this ideal cannot be fully achieved, it is suggested that each segment be viewed in the analytical framework as a "contribution center." [1]

Thinking of a firm as a conglomeration of contribution centers has merits from both economic and organizational points of view. Thus, in linear programing, each activity (segment) is formulated as a vector producing income (the coefficient for the objective function—Cj). No firm is completely centralized. Any so-called centralized firm, no matter what its scale, is decentralized to some extent (see Chapter XII). A manager, being responsible for a segment or a group of seg-

[1] Considering each department in a plant as a profit center for improving control was suggested as early as 1889 by G. P. Norton in England (Garner 1954, ch. 7).

ments, has some authority (explicitly or implicitly) to make decisions. The procedure of measuring the income of each segment may induce the manager to act in line with the firm's primary objective.

To consider each segment of the firm as a contribution center, all production must be valued, and transfer prices must be assigned to the intermediate goods transferred between segments. In addition, in order to measure the income of a period, transfer prices must be assigned to "temporal intermediate goods," those transferred from one period to another. The first case is discussed in this chapter; the second is discussed in Chapter IV.

A summary of the OAAS rules for establishing the transfer prices for both decisions and evaluation purposes follows. It is assumed here that the market is perfectly competitive in regard to the demand for or the supply of the intermediate goods.

Market situation	*Production-capacity situation (of supplying segment)*	*Transfer price for decisions*	*Transfer price for evaluation*
Existent	Excess	Marginal cost market price	Avoidable cost market price
Existent	No excess	Market price	Market price
Nonexistent	Excess	Marginal cost	Avoidable cost
Nonexistent	No excess	Shadow price	Shadow price
Nonexistent	Excess, no excess	None	Pseudo market price

There is an extensive literature on the subject of the kind of transfer prices to be used in various situations in a decentralized firm.[2] There is less literature, however, on the extent of their use and the bases used for transfer prices in business.[3] Suggested methods of determining

[2] A comprehensive review of the literature can be found in Ophir (1960, app. A) and a very short one in Gordon (1964). A discussion of the subject can be found in Shillinglaw (1961, ch. 22) and Solomons (1965, ch. 6). For a survey of problems and examples in business, see National Association of Accountants (1956).

[3] Stone (1957) carried out a survey in 1956, by means of a questionnaire, of the use of transfer prices in the largest corporations in the U.S. He found that

transfer prices, along with references to some of the authors who indicate the use of each method, may be summarized as follows: (1) full cost (in traditional accounting the problem of pricing transfers is viewed as a problem in pricing inventories, and cost is usually used for this purpose); (2) variable (direct) cost (Bierman 1963, p. 89); (3) standard costs (Shillinglaw 1961, pp. 731, 733); (4) full cost plus (Cook 1955; Dean 1955); (5) variable cost plus subsidy (Shillinglaw 1961, p. 743); (6) standard costs plus (Ophir 1960, ch. 7); (7) opportunity cost (Bliss 1922; Cook 1955); (8) marginal cost (Hirshleifer 1956, 1957, 1964; Gould 1964); (9) shadow prices (Koopmans 1951; Arrow 1959; Baumol and Fabian 1964); (10) market prices (Bliss 1922, Cook 1957); (11) market price minus (Stone 1957, p. 119); (12) negotiated prices (Cook 1955; Dean 1955); (13) formula prices (Heuser 1956; Dearden 1960); (14 and 15) equalization of returns on investment, and two-part tariffs (Ophir 1960, ch. 7).

Every type of transfer price has some limitations.[4] The philosophy taken here is that there is no one price or method of pricing that is best and suits all cases. Thus, the method that should be incorporated depends on which one fits the specific case at hand.[5]

To incorporate into the accounting system transfer prices that are not based on the cost of production is alien to traditional accounting. However, the very act of searching for these prices has advantages. It provides attention-directing information. The concern for these prices in the reports suggested by the OAAS emphasizes their role in decision making.

1. Transfer Prices for Allocation Decisions

The analogy between the economy as a whole and a decentralized

out of 332 replies, 236 do some kind of internal transfer pricing (p. 54). He also found (pp. 93–95) that out of 236 firms, 54 (23%) used only the cost base price, while 161 (68%) used it to some extent; 48 (20%) used only the market price, while 167 (71%) used it to some extent; and 6 (3%) used only the negotiated price, while 64 (27%) used it to some extent. Dean (1955) claims that full cost plus is the commonest cost base used by decentralized firms.

[4] Cook (1957) and Greer (1962) claim that none of the methods provides a satisfactory solution.

[5] Ophir (1960, p. 153) in his survey of 22 decentralized firms found that most of them used more than one method of pricing.

firm as is sometimes made in the literature (see Appendix D) can be extended to a centralized firm. Transfer prices in a decentralized firm, like prices in the economy at large, are an important device for achieving both coordination and efficiency (where efficiency is related to allocation decisions). In a centralized firm, the use of transfer prices should mainly promote efficiency. Furthermore, these prices should motivate lower-level managers, since every so-called centralized firm is to some extent decentralized.

If resources are to be allocated optimally, one of the following should be used as transfer price for the intermediate goods: marginal costs, shadow prices, or market prices. The purpose of this section is to indicate briefly why these prices (or costs) should be used as transfer prices and the situations in which each is relevant.

When an intermediate good is actually traded on the market, the market price serves as a transfer price. Where no market for the transferred intermediate good exists, the correct procedure is to transfer at marginal cost (for which avoidable cost is the surrogate). But when the capacity of the supplying segment is limited, and various products are or can be produced by this segment, each limited resource has an internal opportunity cost (that is, shadow price). This should be reflected in the transfer price of the intermediate good. That is, marginal cost is appropriate as a transfer price only when excess capacity exists. When capacity is limited, the shadow price is the correct transfer price for the intermediate good. The shadow price in this case is the dual figure corresponding to the constraint that is formulated (in the linear-programing tableau) to facilitate the transfer of the intermediate good from the supplying activity to the customer activity. This shadow price can be approximated by adding the relevant opportunity cost figures of the restrictions to the marginal cost, where only a few restrictions exist.[6]

[6] Let TP_k = transfer price for the intermediate good k; MC_k = marginal cost of producing a unit of k; n = limited sources used in producing k; a_{ik} = production coefficient (the requirement of a unit of k for the ith resource); and OC_i = opportunity cost (in a ceteris paribus sense) of the ith resource, then

$$TP_k = MC_k + \sum_{i=1}^{n} a_{ik} OC_i .$$

When n is (very) small, the TP will be (equal or) an approximation of the shadow price.

Consider a firm producing product A for sale and product B which is used as an intermediate good in producing product A. The firm's warehouse is needed in the production of B. The avoidable costs (the marginal costs) of producing B are $5 per unit. This figure can be used as a transfer price for B assuming that no market exists for product B and that an alternative product that requires warehouse space is not available (a situation of excess capacity). Suppose now that the firm can sell B at $7 per unit. This price should be used as a transfer price, whether the firm actually sells B or not.

Now assume the firm can also produce product C, which competes with B for the fixed limited warehouse space. Suppose the optimal linear programing solution includes the three products and indicates a shadow price of $8 per unit of B.[7] This means that if B is transferred at $8 per unit, its contribution per square foot of limited space equals the contribution of product C (on the margin). The very fact that B is included in the program implies that it is a "profitable" activity. Part of the income generated by A is imputed to B, to provide the shadow price. This outcome is in line with the assumption (which is taken in this book) that income is generated concurrently with and recognized at the various stages of the production process. If products A and B are both considered as segments, under the suggested procedure, both segments generate and earn income.

The use of the shadow price ($8) in the reports will motivate management to treat B as a profitable segment, similar to A. If product B were transferred at cost, management might consider the segment producing B as a service activity. Often, management attention is focused on "productive" activities and service activities are neglected.

The example illustrates the advantage of using shadow prices as transfer prices when a market does not exist for the intermediate good. Despite the complications of including shadow prices in the accounting system (see Chapter II), when a shadow price for an intermediate good

[7] This holds even if the opportunity to sell B still exists. In this case, however, $7 per unit should be used in the OAAS. Note that $7 per unit represents an external opportunity cost, whereas $8 per unit represents an internal opportunity cost. Note further that there is an opportunity only to sell B, not to buy it. If the opportunity to buy B were available, the solution would indicate buying B rather than producing it.

exists, it may be used in the OAAS. The shadow price in this case is a form of a determined value (see Section 5).

2. Market Prices

Whenever a market exists for an intermediate good, the market price should be used as a transfer price, since this price represents a real opportunity for the firm, even if the firm does not participate in this market. Strictly speaking, this statement is correct only if the market for the intermediate good is perfectly competitive, as assumed in this book. But even under market imperfections, the use of market prices still provides important information, as the discussion below implies.

If the contribution center were, in fact, an independent business, all the transfers of intermediate goods would require a market transaction. Since the contribution centers are segments of a firm, however, the intermediate goods are "traded" internally. An intermediate good is "sold" by one segment to another instead of on the external market. If the external market price is used as a transfer price, this is considered as a realizable revenue by the supplier segment, and as an (external) opportunity cost by the customer segment.

Including market prices (that is, the concepts of opportunity cost and realizable revenue) in an accounting system runs against such conventional principles of accounting as realization and objectivity.[8] But the aim of this study is to suggest an analytical framework that will serve managers in making decisions, regardless of existing accounting principles.

Published market prices or the price at which the latest transaction took place provides the information for setting transfer prices. The existence of imperfections in the market may cause some difficulties in using these prices. Volume of trade, product differentiation, timing, and location may produce some variability in the determination of

[8] Such a procedure was suggested as early as 1922 by J. H. Bliss in his description of cost methods in the meat-packing industry. Bliss states that a product is "worth to a department of an organization what the preceding department had the opportunity to get for it were it to sell it in an outside market" (p. 12). He suggests the use of these prices (which are the "full value" of the product) as internal transfer prices and calls this method "transfer at opportunity cost."

these market prices. These figures may be nominal prices rather than real transaction prices and therefore may require adjustment.

Most market prices are the result of some kind of negotiations between independent firms, so it is difficult to pinpoint a definite price. In many instances, if market prices are to be used, they must be estimated. Dearden (1960, pp. 121–122) for example, enumerates "methods that have been used successfully in obtaining or approximating competitive prices."

To summarize, the market prices provide an important guide to decision making. It is assumed that whenever a market exists, the market price can be ascertained or estimated and, as such, used in the analytical framework. This procedure is as near alibi-proof for segment income measurement as any transfer price can be.

The problem of whether the selling or the purchasing price should be used still has to be solved. But first let us see how the market prices can be incorporated into the accounting system.

3. An Example

Consider an ice cream manufacturer (firm A) consisting of two departments: a production department producing milk as an intermediate good, and a processing department that transforms the milk into ice cream. The milk is produced from a herd of 100 cows. (The herd is held constant by using home-produced heifers to replace the culled cows). Three by-products are sold: steers and culled cows, originating in the first department, and skim milk, originating in the second. Only the by-product "steers" requires additional processing, hence it is considered as a separate segment.

Three contribution centers are distinguished in the framework of the OAAS: "ice cream," "cows," and "steers." This distinction can be made since there are (perfectly competitive) markets for both milk and bull calves where the selling prices are $0.12 and $50 per unit respectively. Suppose that 500,000 units of milk are produced and processed and 50 bull calves are born, raised, and sold in a year (for simplicity, no mortality is assumed). A partial income statement for the whole firm and for each segment, using conventional and suggested (OAAS) procedures, is presented in Table 1 by means of simplified figures. The table distinguishes two kinds of revenue: realized and realizable. Realized revenue is that realized during the accounting period; realizable revenue means revenue that can be realized during the accounting period—for example, the milk that can be sold rather than transferred internally.

Six points can be made about the example:

1. With the aid of the transfer price, the profitability of each segment can be measured. Each segment is viewed as a contribution center similarly to the conventional notion of a profit center. This provides important, eye-opening information, even if the market price is not a wholly accurate figure. Thus, for example, the contribution margin for cows is higher than for ice cream—information that is concealed under traditional procedures.

2. The contribution of each segment can be measured more objectively. The bull calves are considered a by-product of cows. If this by-product is transferred at zero price, as some conventional practices imply, the contribution of steers is considered to be $4,000 rather than the more correct figure of $1,500. Since management can sell the bull calves for $2,500, this figure is considered as a cost for steers.

3. Considering each segment as a contribution center, and crediting and debiting the prices of intermediate goods, will cause the income statement (both cost and revenue) to be inflated. Thus, the total revenue of the three segments is $152,500 under the suggested procedure and $90,000 under the traditional procedure.[9]

4. One could view steers and ice cream as joint products produced from a common process—cows, in which case the total income could be imputed to the common process. But since there are markets for milk and bull calves, the three segments (ice cream, steers, cows) can be considered as contribution centers and analyzed as such.

5. It is possible also to illustrate an externality (external diseconomy) between segments. Suppose the odor from the barn has some effect on the quality of ice cream, depending on the wind direction. Hence, part of the ice cream is sold as a lower grade, causing an annual reduction

[9] A similar problem exists in measuring the national product, where the production of intermediate goods usually is not included.

Table 1. A partial income statement for firm A (in U.S. dollars)

Item in analysis	Conventional procedure: total of segments	OAAS procedure			
		Total of segments	Ice cream	Steers	Cows (and heifers)
Revenue					
Realized:					
Ice cream	65,000		65,000		
Skim milk	5,000		5,000		
Steers	15,000			15,000	
Culled cows and heifers	5,000				5,000
Realizable:					
Milk (transferred)					60,000
Bull calves (transferred)					2,500
Total revenue	90,000	152,500	70,000	15,000	67,500
Cost					
Variable inputs	55,000		4,000	11,000	40,000
Intermediate goods:					
Milk			60,000		
Bull calves				2,500	
Total cost	55,000	117,500	64,000	13,500	40,000
Contribution	35,000	35,000	6,000	1,500	27,500

of $2,000 in income. This effect should be specified and reported. It can be said that odor is transferred at negative price from cows to ice cream; that is, the reduction in income due to the odor is charged to cows. The revised contribution figures are $25,500 and $8,000, respectively. The steers segment is not charged for the odor since, even if that segment is liquidated, the odor will continue; if the cows are liquidated, the steers are liquidated as well.[10]

6. The suggested report may indicate that a segment has a loss that conventional accounting will not indicate. This means that the suggested reporting system uncovers implicit subsidies given in such a case by the firm, or other segments in the firm, to the inefficient segment. Suppose the revenue for steers is $13,000 rather than $15,000 as indicated in Table 1. A negative contribution of $500 is then reported under the suggested procedure. Assuming that the firm tries to maximize income, the steers would be liquidated. Under conventional procedures, the loss is not recognized and the steers are not liquidated. Thus, cows and ice cream "grant" a subsidy of $500 per period for keeping the steers.

There are situations when a market and a market price for an intermediate good exists, but selling or buying the intermediate good is not a relevant opportunity. Two examples illustrate this situation: management decides that the intermediate good should not be sold for some specific reasons;[11] or the market is too small to be significant to the firm or too far away to provide an actual opportunity. Consider for example, a firm having a warehouse. Although leasing warehouse space is a common transaction in the market, it might be that this particular firm is located in advantageously to lease its warehouse space. In this case the market place should be treated as a determined value (see Section 5).

In the preceding discussion, the market (selling) price has been used for computing the realizable revenue of the supplier segment and the

[10] The odor might cause an externality between independent entities as well. For example, it might affect a neighbor, so that firm A must pay compensation to him. This payment should be charged as costs to "cows."

[11] See, for example, Goetz (1967).

avoidable cost of the customer segment, assuming that the intermediate good can be sold on the market. The customer segment, however, might buy the intermediate good in the market. Thus, the purchasing price is relevant here.

4. Selling or Buying Price and Gains of Integration

In a producing business, there is usually a difference between buying and selling prices. This difference is due to the middleman's expenses and profits, access to market, transportation costs, and so forth. Therefore, the buying price as an input exceeds the selling price as an output. A consumer segment, if charged the realizable selling price of the intermediate good, gets a "subsidy," since the opportunity cost for this segment is the purchasing price in the market. Therefore, when the profitability of a segment in an integrated firm is analyzed, the relevant price (buying or selling price) should be used.

The price to be used depends on the opportunity on hand. When the volume of sales is at stake, the selling price is relevant. When the volume of purchasing is at stake, the buying price should be used.[12] The very existence of a divergence between buying and selling prices often provides the reason for integration of various activities in a firm.

In an analytical framework, the aim is to view each activity as standing independent of the others. This can be done by assigning the selling price to the intermediate good provided by the supplier segment and the

[12] Gould (1964) analyzes this subject in terms of the transfer price that will lead towards an optimum level of production—that is, the situation where marginal revenue equals marginal cost for the entire firm. He indicates three sets of conditions with respect to the transferred good, for which the conclusions are as follows: (1) The amount produced exceeds the amount processed and the extra intermediate good is sold on the market. The selling price is used in this case. This price applies to both supplier and customer segments. (2) The amount produced is less than the amount processed and the needed intermediate good is bought on the market. In this case, the buying price is used. (3) The amount produced equals the amount processed. In this case, the transfer price is between the two market prices. Note that in case 3, the divergence between the prices provides a leeway for price negotiation between the involved divisions in a decentralized firm. Stone (1957, p. 119), for example, indicates that some firms discount the market price when it is used as a transfer price to represent savings in selling costs.

buying price to the same good when consumed by the consumer segment. Gains of integration will result from the use of two prices. This point is illustrated by extending the former example.

Suppose both departments, cows and ice cream, are considered as independent units. Let us assume that the former sells the milk on the market at $0.12 per unit, and the latter buys it from the market, at $0.13 per unit. The use of selling and buying prices will reduce the contribution of ice cream by $5,000 (500,000 units at $0.01 per unit). The reduction in contribution is still income to the firm, which can be termed "gains of integration." This point is illustrated numerically in Table 2.

Table 2. Gains of integration in firm A (in U.S. dollars)

Contribution	Ice cream	Steers	Cows	Gains of integration	Total
Contribution from Table 1	6,000	1,500	27,500		35,000
Revised contribution	1,000	1,500	27,500	5,000	35,000

This kind of analysis and reporting provides the following information: (1) It gives an objective score card for each segment, putting an integrated segment in the same position as a nonintegrated unit. This is also important when interfirm comparisons are made. Thus, a specialized firm that produces only ice cream can be compared to the ice-cream-producing segment of an integrated firm. (2) Attention-directing information on the source and location of income is given. (3) Information for decisions is provided about each segment individually. For a decision concerning the expansion of one segment alone, the contribution figures are relevant, since this segment would have to purchase (or sell) milk on the market. For a decision concerning reducing production in a segment, and especially for a liquidation decision, the gains of integration should be considered as well. Thus, if ice cream is liquidated, the milk will have to be sold on the market, and the total reduction in contribution will be: $1,000 + $5,000 = $6,000.

The gains of integration should be recorded and reported in special accounts. These will always show positive income, which indicates the economic rent of integration. It should be noted, however, that the gains from integration may be more than offset by losses in one of the segments; hence integration may not always be desirable.

To summarize, when there is a large difference between buying and selling prices, there is merit in using different prices for customer and supplier segments, respectively. An account for gains of integration should then be established. When a unit is engaged in actual selling or buying, the realized price (net sale price or gross purchasing price) should be used.[13]

5. Pseudo Market Prices

Whenever a market price exists for an intermediate good, there is an objective basis for partitioning the involved segments into contribution centers. When there is no market for these goods, and it is still desirable to partition the segments from one another, a determined value must be used for this purpose. A determined value is an analyst's estimate of the value of an intermediate good, an estimate that is based on market considerations.

In a spatial framework, the determined value enables the analyst to partition the firm's operations to a larger extent than he can do with market prices alone. This is of importance if the source of income generation is to be discovered. The contribution center established by means of determined values might be viewed as an "artificial contribution center." The determined value does not represent a real external opportunity and therefore cannot be used directly as a source of data for allocation decisions. The contribution of this center should be used mainly for evaluation and analysis (control) purposes. The use of determined values enables the analyst to check the efficiency of every segment and thus to provide important attention-directing information,

[13] In Gould's two first cases, outlined in note 12, the transfer price is determined by the real opportunity. For example, if ice cream buys extra milk from the market at $0.13 per unit, this is the price credited to cows. Note that implicitly the gains of integration are assigned here to cows—to the segment that operates at the lower level of the two.

which in turn may suggest taking some decisions. It does not introduce error into the estimate of total contribution or income of the firm.

Assigning market price to intermediate goods means that income is recognized whenever a marketable intermediate good is produced. This is compatible with the assumption that income is generated concurrently with the production process. The same assumption should guide the determination of transfer prices for intermediate goods that are not traded on the market.

The determined values may be used to value the intermediate goods transferred between segments (spatial transfers) and should be used to value respective transfers among periods (temporal transfer). While spatial partitioning is a matter of desirability (to enable the measurement of income of each individual segment), it should be emphasized that temporal partitioning is a must if the income of a firm or part thereof for a given period is to be evaluated. In other words, for measuring the income generated in a period, values must be assigned to the temporal intermediate goods (assets) transferred to and from the period. Except when a market price for these goods exists, determined values must be assigned. The subject of determining these values for spatial transfers is discussed below; for temporal transfers the discussion is delayed until the next chapter.

The purpose of this section is to discuss one type of determined value, the "pseudo market price." A pseudo market price is the price an analyst believes would prevail if a market existed for the good. In other words, it is a calculated or estimated price which would clear the market, if a market existed.[14]

There are many ways to calculate or establish a price for a product, even if it is not actually traded in a market. For example, market prices for similar items or for the same item in a remote market, price of substitutes, quotations of outside vendors, or solicitation of bids may be used. In business there are many means for determining prices for similar purposes, as, for example, in forward selling, in contracts associated with vertical integration, and so forth. As a matter of fact, deter-

[14] A similar term, "hypothetical sale price," is used by Bonbright (1937, pp. 59–61) in a legal context.

mining prices for intermediate goods which are not traded on the market is a common procedure in decentralized firms.[15]

Let us illustrate the use of pseudo market prices by means of extending the example provided in Table 1. Cows are aggregated with the heifers in the first OAAS analysis. Suppose the analyst can assign a pseudo market price of $30 per head to the female calves by reference to the market price for bull calves and $300 per head to the heifers by reference to a remote market. As a result, cows and heifers can be partitioned into two artificial contribution centers in the analysis framework. This is illustrated in Table 3.

Table 3. Artificial contribution centers in firm A (in U.S. dollars)

Item in analysis	Cows and heifers	Artificial contribution centers: Cows	Artificial contribution centers: Heifers
Revenue			
Milk	60,000	60,000	
Culled cows and heifers	5,000	2,000	3,000
Bull calves	2,500	2,500	
Female calves		1,500	
Heifers			9,000
Total revenue	67,500	66,000	12,000
Cost			
Variable inputs	40,000	30,000	10,000
Intermediate goods:			
Female calves			1,500
Heifers		9,000	
Total cost	40,000	39,000	11,500
Contribution	27,500	27,000	500

[15] Many articles report on such procedures (for example, National Association of Accountants 1956, Dearden 1960, and Menge 1961). Notable is a list of criteria indicated by Whinston (1964*a*, p. 412).

The example in Table 3 indicates that the "heifer" activity produces a low contribution ($500; see the final analysis in Table 12, Chapter VI). This is an important piece of information, although the results come from the use of pseudo market prices. With this information, the manager might investigate the reasons for the low economic efficiency of raising heifers. He may search for a market for heifers or may sign a contract with another farmer to supply heifers.

Determining the transfer price when there is no reference price is more complicated. In this case, the analyst should consider the two production processes involved in the transfer of the intermediate good, as hypothetical supplier and customer, respectively.[16] This procedure is discussed in Chapter IV, Section 9.

As long as the intermediate good is transferred between only two segments, determining an acceptable transfer price may be possible. The problem becomes more complicated when there are several stages in the production process.

One can view the procedure of arriving at a pseudo market price as a "negotiated price" in a decentralized firm. But since the present analysis is relevant to a centralized firm, there is no place for real negotiation. Hence, this price should be viewed as a "formula price" set by an analyst. In agriculture, where governmental or quasi-governmental advisory services exist, it is recommended that these formula prices be computed and disseminated by such services. The use of such prices in analyzing the business operations of individual farms may be helpful in carrying out interfarm comparison studies.

The use of such prices, especially when computed by a central agency, might induce the development of a real market for the good in question (for instance, the calves and heifers in the former example). Notable is Menge's report (1961, p. 218) on the result of introducing transfer prices in a decentralized firm. The volume of intermediate goods, priced by

[16] This resembles a "profit-sharing" procedure used by firms (Ophir 1960, pp. 133–139). A procedure resembling the one outlined, with the difference that the customer unit "demand price" is based on substitution price, is used by the electric power industry in the U.S. for pricing two-party interchange transactions of energy (Hughes 1962, p. 601).

means of some formula price, decreased considerably. Real market prices resulted from the search for alternative opportunities.[17]

6. Service Departments as Contribution Centers

Service activities differ from regular activities in that they render services to other segments rather than sell their services or products on the market. In the OAAS this difference is ignored and, instead, the service departments are considered as contribution centers like any productive segment.[18] The assumption that income is generated concurrently with the process of production implies that the service activity, just as any other activity, should earn income, since it is a part of the entire production process.

Economically and practically speaking, refraining from spending affects the firm's income just as does additional revenue. Thus, saving $10,000 (net of cost) in producing in-plant electricity is equivalent to a gain of $10,000 (revenue minus cost) from an increase in sale volume of some other product. A steel mill producing electricity instead of buying it can be considered as an integrated firm incorporating two kinds of business—steel and electricity; or a farm producing cotton can be considered as integrating cotton production and tractor services. The same argument holds for most other productive services. As a matter of fact, it is easy to find many independent business concerns which sell only "services," as for example, electricity, accounting, transportation, cleaning, or research.

Traditionally, services that a service department renders to other departments are priced on the basis of cost. That is, total cost of providing the service is forwarded to the departments that use the service. Total costs are used as the transfer price for the service. In addition to the regular objections to conventional full-cost procedures that might lead to misallocation of resources (for example, charging fixed cost),

[17] Ophir (1960, p. 149) reports on a firm that uses standard manufacturing cost plus the markup obtained on the most nearly similar output in the firm until the good is finally sold in the market.

[18] See Gross (1964, pp. 590–602) on this subject. For a contrary argument, see Dean (1955).

other points can be criticized. First, not charging cost of capital on the capital invested in the service department gives a subsidy to the user of the service. Second, even in a centralized firm, the service department often has an independent manager. It is generally agreed that cost-plus contracts in industry (for example, sales of military goods) lead to inefficient production. A similar tendency might and, indeed, does appear in a service department that "sells" its services at cost.[19] Third, when part of the service is sold to outsiders, a conventional practice is to deduct the revenue from the costs of the service department. Thus, the price to the customer departments is reduced, although there may be no change in the unit cost of production.[20]

In decentralized firms a distinction is often made between a profit center and a service center. While the former is evaluated on the profits it makes, the latter is evaluated on its cost level—how well it succeeds in keeping down the cost. The service department "sells" its services at a predetermined standard price. This procedure implies that if costs are kept down, "profits" will emerge. Under conventional, standard cost accounting, the "profits" are termed favorable variance. When the standard price is based on market price, or even on a pseudo market price, there is no material difference between the two centers.

When there is a market for the service, there is no problem in assigning transfer prices and considering the service activity as a contribution center. When a regular market does not exist, management can search for a market and a market price. For example, a firm known to the author is quite successful in arriving at market prices for its service centers by soliciting bids. To make the bids real rather than fictitious, management accepts some of them to substitute for those jobs which the firm might conduct inefficiently (or substitute former contractors). Suppose that a cleaning job costs $11,500 per period. As a result of soliciting bids for this job, an outside firm offers to contract the job for $12,000 per period. The contribution of this segment is therefore $500.

[19] See Menge (1961, p. 220).

[20] Carrying this procedure to an extreme, suppose the revenue of a service department exceeds total cost; then each user of the service, according to this practice, should be credited rather than debited for his use of the service.

When there is no market for the service, a pseudo market price might be used. One of the important applications of the pseudo market price is to price nonmarketable services. In this case, the service segment is only an artificial contribution center, and the reported results should be used mainly for evaluation purposes.

As indicated in the former sections, one aim of the OAAS is to provide reports that can be analyzed to discover the locations where income is generated. Consider, for example, a profitable mining concern which uses trucks to a large extent for hauling ore. In the OAAS, the trucks are considered as a contribution center rather than a service center. Suppose the report indicates that the mining activity has a loss and the truck activity has profits. This is important information as to whether there is a readily available opportunity to render trucking services outside the firm or not. This information should initiate an analysis of the reasons for the inefficient mining operations and a search for a market for the efficient trucking operations—for either substituting for the ore hauling or expanding the trucking operations.

It is necessary to indicate and elaborate on some of the conceivable difficulties that may exist in setting a price for a service (on the basis of market prices). Consider a maintenance job or repairs made by a workshop. A practical procedure used in business by independent concerns is to compute the price for such a service on the base of cost plus a profit margin. Following this procedure may involve some serious difficulties. There is no incentive for efficiency. Still worse, when the department faces underemployment in "profitable" jobs, the more inefficiently the repair job is done, the more it costs and, in turn, the more "profits" are earned from the job. On the other hand, if "profitable" jobs are at hand, they will get priority over the maintenance and repair jobs, and thus "profits" will be high, even if the loss to another segment from the postponed repair is larger.

Like service departments, self-owned resources (such as land and capital) can be viewed as segments that render services to other segments. The market price of the services of the resource should be used as a transfer price. As such, the resource, like a service or production activity, can be considered as a contribution center, a subject to be discussed in later chapters. Capital assets may be viewed in a manner similar to self-owned resources, a subject to be discussed in the next chapter.

7. Summary and Conclusions

The centralized firm is viewed, in the analytical framework, as a conglomerate of contribution centers. Transfer prices are assigned to the intermediate goods that are "traded" among the contribution centers. When a market for the intermediate good exists, the market price serves as a transfer price. In this way the income of each segment can be measured (or estimated)—an important factor in decision making and control.

The management of a firm occasionally estimates the market prices of intermediate goods and services. Why not make these estimates periodically and more formally? It is recommended that market prices be incorporated as transfer prices into the OAAS.

When the difference between the selling and the buying price is large, both prices might be used in the analysis. In a producing firm, where usually the selling price is lower than the buying price, the use of both prices (selling price for the supplying segment, buying price for the customer segment) will require establishment of a special account. This account will indicate the gains of integration. In a trading firm, where usually the buying price is lower than the selling price, the use of both prices stand for cost and revenue items respectively.[21]

When market does not exist for the intermediate good, the correct procedure is to transfer it, in a decision-making framework, at avoidable (marginal) cost. Or, if resources are limited, the intermediate good is transferred at its shadow price. In a decision-making framework, both supplier and customer segments must be considered simultaneously—that is, as one integrated segment.

Sometimes it is desirable to decompose a segment that is used as a unit in a decision-making framework into artificial contribution centers. For this purpose a determined value must be used as a transfer

[21] It should be noted that the use of both prices in the accounting report of a producing firm might suggest that the firm should include trading business in its operations as well.

price for that intermediate good that is not marketable. Both shadow prices and pseudo market prices can be used in this case as transfer prices. The contribution of an artificial contribution center, however, cannot be used for decision purposes, but only for evaluation purposes. This contribution, as well as the determined value, can be used, nevertheless, as a basis for further investigation. Thus, a market for the involved intermediate good can be searched for. The very existence of pseudo market prices may stimulate the development of a market for the corresponding good.

An important implication of the suggested procedure is that service activities such as trucking or cleaning are considered similarly to production activities.

IV
VALUING CAPITAL ASSETS AND COSTING THEIR SERVICES[1]

If all capital assets were bought at the beginning of a production cycle or an accounting period and salvaged or sold at the end of the cycle or period, the problems of valuing capital assets and in turn determining their periodic service cost would not exist. In practice, however, assets serve for several production cycles or accounting periods. This is a source of conceptual and practical problems in both ex ante investment analysis and ex post reporting. How then should an existing asset be valued each period, or how, in turn, should its service be priced?

In this chapter two special aspects of valuing capital assets and costing their services are suggested: the use of current market prices as a basis for valuation and the practice of charging interest for the use of capital. The discussion is aimed at answering two questions: why current market prices should be used for valuation (when the objective of the OAAS is to provide data inputs for decision making), and how these prices can be used as a basis for asset valuation. Although the discussion integrates these points, the emphasis in the early and the later sections is on the answer to the "why" and "how" questions, respectively.

[1] With few modifications, Sections 1–6 and 10 are reproduced from Goldschmidt and Smidt (1969) and are used by permission of *Accounting Review*.

There is not one best solution to the problem of how to value assets.[2] The attitude taken here is that the method of valuation that should be chosen depends on the purposes to be served by the information system. In this chapter a method of valuation is explored that is appropriate for managerial purposes—that is, for decisions and control. The cost of services from an asset are based on the asset's value during the period under consideration and on holding costs associated with it. Holding costs are the explicit and implicit costs incurred as a result of holding an asset. An important item is interest. In the OAAS, interest is charged to the various segments according to the amount of capital in use. The conventional practice of measuring the rate of return on invested capital, on the other hand, is not used.

The value of inventories that are used in production and the decline in value of durable assets are included in the period costs. The value of goods that are produced during the period and an increase (if any) in value of durable assets are included in the period revenue. The subject of recording the effects of price level change on income is beyond the scope of this study.[3]

Durables are classified into liquid and nonliquid assets (Sections 5, 6, and 7). Inventories are classified into raw materials and finished goods, which often are liquid (Section 8), and goods in process, which often are not liquid (Section 9). A summary of the OAAS rules for valuing capital assets and costing their services is as follows:

Type of asset	*Valuing temporal transfers*	*Costing of service*
Inventories		
Liquid:		
Raw materials	Replacement cost (market price)	Value + holding cost including interest
Finished goods	Avoidable cost or realizable price	Credit (value − holding cost including interest)

[2] For a list and a round table discussion on various methods of valuing durable assets, see Sprouse (1964).

[3] Edwards and Bell (1961), for example, partition the period income into holding gains and operational profits.

Type of asset	*Valuing temporal transfers*	*Costing of service*
Inventories		
Nonliquid:		
Goods in process	Pseudo market price	None
Durables		
Liquid (e.g., trucks)	Market price	Change in value during period + interest on value at beginning of period
Nonliquid (e.g., buildings)	Appraisal based on market value	Change in value during period + interest on value at beginning of period

1. The Basis for Asset Valuation: Three Approaches

Three basic approaches to the valuation of individual assets are available.[4] They are: past transactions, future earning power, and present market price. These approaches can be stated in terms of the costs that are used as a basis for valuing the assets: original cost, internal opportunity cost, and external opportunity cost. External opportunity cost is defined as the market price of an asset that is used in production rather than being bought or sold. Internal opportunity cost is the present value of the incremental cash flow an asset (or a set of assets) can earn in its best feasible use within the firm.

The values arrived at by each approach have some specific uses, but also have some severe limitations. This study deals with the third approach, namely the use of current market prices as a basis for valuing assets.

Conventional accounting tries to solve the problem of valuing durable assets by using past transactions to establish a cost basis, and by periodically charging a depreciation expense "which aims to distribute the [original] cost . . . over the estimated useful life of the [asset]." (American Institute of Certified Public Accountants 1953*b*, p. 25). The asset is valued in terms of original cost adjusted for that part of

[4] The sum of the values of the individual assets, arrived at by any of the three approaches, do not provide for the value of the firm. The problem of valuing the firm is beyond the scope of this study; for discussions of this problem, see Bodenhorn (1961) and Edwards and Bell (1961), for example.

original cost already charged as depreciation to past operations. The portion to be charged to current operations is determined by means of a "discretionary procedure"—that is, a decision on a depreciation method (straight line, decreasing charges) and on the life span of the asset. This approach provides a precise and operational figure, based on objective historical information.

The valuation procedures based on the first approach have some severe shortcomings from the point of view of managerial decision making. The value shown for the asset does not necessarily reflect the asset's condition and serviceability. For example, a serviceable asset may be valued at zero (or close to zero) when it continues to render services beyond its original estimated life span. The historical acquisition cost figure is distorted when the price level changes.[5] Also, it may not represent a normal market price; for example, an asset might have been acquired at an unusually low or high price. It should be noted that even if adjustments are made for price level changes by means of a price level index, the costs are still historical and thereby retain some of the limitations of such figures.

The second approach is the economist's convention. The economist values the asset in terms of the value to the firm of the expected cash flow that the asset will generate throughout its productive life. This value, although estimated, represents the real value of the asset to the firm.[6] This valuation procedure requires estimating the associated future cash flows which are uncertain and also interdependent with

[5] Conventional accounting practices provide information in terms of historical cost and ignore the change in the purchasing power of the dollar. Boulding (1962, p. 54) notes: "A hundred feet plus ten centimeters is certainly not a hundred and ten anythings, and the accountant's balance sheet total is not much better" since it "is reckoned in dollars of different ages." In an opinion survey on the need for price-level adjustment of depreciation, 69% of the business executives and 94% of the educators replied in the affirmative (*Journal of Accountancy,* April 1958, pp. 36–43). For examples of the use of price-level adjustments in practice, see American Institute of Certified Public Accountants (1963, pp. 167–218).

[6] Smidt (1965) indicates that as a basis for accounting valuation and depreciation, the present-value method has two special advantages in that it provides for an equal rate of return on investment for all future periods (except for period 1) and no change in the assets' value when income tax is considered.

other assets' cash flows and deciding on a discount rate.[7] Therefore, this kind of valuation is a subjective procedure. Moreover, since the cash flow is often jointly generated by more than one asset, the cash flow can only be attributed to the group of assets in aggregate.[8]

In the case of an asset to be acquired, the acquisition is profitable only if the economic value exceeds the acquisition cost. In the case of an existing asset, the asset is profitable when its economic value exceeds its liquidation value. Therefore, the liquidation value of an existing asset is an important piece of information for decisions.

Assuming that the main task of management is to make decisions, the data supplied to management should be compatible with the decision rules. Because decisions are concerned with opportunities, the current market price of an asset (its external opportunity cost) is the relevant basis for valuing it in the context of internal accounting.[9] The general use of current prices is usually considered to violate the traditional accounting principle of objectivity. Edwards and Bell (1961, p. 284), however, note on this subject: "Current costs are in most cases as objectively verifiable as the historic costs. . . . The historic costs which may be so accurately known are simply not events of the current period."

This opinion is supported by the striking results of a study by McDonald (1968),[10] who concludes: "The empirical data reported for automobiles provided evidence that direct reference to available market

[7] With uncertainty, either the discount rate must allow for the subjective disutility that arises from the fact that the expected cash flows are uncertain, or an estimate of the dollar equivalent of this disutility must be made separately.

[8] For an attempt to surmount this problem, see Thomas (1966, ch. 9).

[9] Many authors suggest using this procedure for external financial statements: for example, Edwards and Bell (1961), Moonitz (1961), Sprouse and Moonitz (1962), Mattessich (1964), Chambers (1966), and Thomas (1966), to mention only books and booklets. M. Cannon (in Sprouse and Moonitz 1962, p. 66) summarizes this idea: "We are about to make the great stride from cost-based to current-valued assets and net worth in financial statements." For elaboration on the subject of market value and its use in a legal context, see Bonbright (1937, ch. 3).

[10] Since dispersion is a measure of objectivity, where objectivity is defined as verifiability (see discussion in Ijiri and Jaedicke 1966, p. 476), one might infer from these results that the use of market prices for valuing durable liquid assets in general, not only automobiles, is at least as objective as other valuation methods.

price indicators results in less disperse measures than those now obtained under 'generally accepted accounting principles'" (p. 49).

Although the analyst or accountant has to search for the market prices of the assets, such prices can be treated as exogenous to the analytical framework. That is, the market prices are "given" data and as such can be used as an input to the decision-making information system. On the other hand, the value sought through the economist's convention, as described above, is the result of using data from various sources, including the accounting system. This economic value can be considered as the internal opportunity cost of the asset, whereas the current market price is an external opportunity cost. In summary, current market prices are inputs to the information system; economic (present) values are outputs of the system.

The current-market-price approach, compared to the present-value approach, is often also more objective, since it is based on prices that usually are available from market sources, and simpler, because the analyst is less dependent on estimates pertaining to the uncertain future. The economic value of assets should be evaluated periodically, recorded in an auxiliary report, and compared to the established value, based on market prices, if the grouping of assets warrants such a comparison.

There are three distinct complications that must be overcome if market prices are to be used to evaluate systematically all durable assets. These problems arise because: there may be a significant difference between the acquisition cost of an asset and its liquidation value; a direct market estimate of the current acquisition cost of an asset may be unavailable or irrelevant because of technological change that has occurred since the asset was acquired; and even when a technological change did not occur, the existing assets very often do not provide the same service as an equivalent new asset because of wear and tear. Methods that partially overcome these complications are discussed in later sections.

2. Decomposition of Operations into Quasi-independent Periods

The continuous operations of a going concern are usually decomposed in the analytical framework into individual periods. Each period is conceived of as a distinct entity of finite duration. Each "buys" assets (durables and inventories, which may be termed temporal intermediate goods) from the former period, "sells" assets to the next period, and buys and sells commodities (inputs, products, and sometimes assets) on the market. In other words, the period "trades" commodities on the external market and "trades" assets internally.

If an accurate and unique market price could be determined at the end of every period for every asset transferred from that period to the next, then these prices would provide an objective valuation of such assets. In turn, these asset valuations could be used to provide objective measurements of the income earned during the period. Unfortunately, for the reasons indicated at the end of the previous section, such precise market prices do not exist for many assets.

In principle, management always has the alternative of buying new assets for period $t+1$ rather than "buying" them from period t. If there were no significant difference between the acquisition cost and liquidation value of any asset, this alternative would be available in practice, as well as in principle. Under such conditions, the periods would be fully independent, and it would be a reasonable goal for management to attempt to maximize the income of each period.

In practice, for many assets, the differences between current acquisition costs and current liquidation values are significant. It is usually more economic for period $t+1$ to "buy" the assets needed from period t, rather than to buy new assets on the market. The periods cannot be considered as strictly independent because of the differences between current acquisition and liquidation values. Rather the periods must be considered as quasi-independent. Managers should seek to maximize the income of each quasi-independent period subject to certain constraints. Without these constraints, actions that increase the income of a particular quasi-independent period might result in uneconomic decreases in the income earned in some later quasi-independent period. For example, deferring normal maintenance on a long-lived asset may increase the income of the current quasi-independent period at the expense of a larger decrease in the (present value of the) income of later periods.

In terms of the accounting framework, the methods used to value assets transferred from one quasi-independent period to the next should take account of these constraints and should discourage unwise short-term income maximization that violates the constraints necessary for long-run maximization.

The implication of this temporal model is that the ceiling for an asset's value is its acquisition cost—that is, replacement cost; the floor is its liquidation price.[11] Either of these values, or some amount in between them, should be used for valuing the firm's assets.

3. A Measure of Asset Liquidity

An asset's liquidity is one of its most important characteristics. Because the asset's value is determined by its market price, the more liquid an asset, the easier it is to arrive at a value for it. If the acquisition cost (value) is close to the liquidation value of an asset (for example, the common stock of a corporation), there is one figure for its value. But if these values diverge (for example, an individual building on a farm), there are two values for the asset—acquisition and liquidation values. A measure of the relative liquidity of an asset is the ratio of its liquidation value to its acquisition value. When the acquisition value equals the liquidation value, the asset is perfectly liquid. The measure of liquidity is 1.00 in this case. If the liquidation value of an asset is zero, its liquidity measure is also zero. (If there are costs associated with liquidating an asset, its liquidity measure will be negative). This scale takes into account the various relations of the firm to the market such as the type and location of the market or the type of asset.[12]

Also, the liquidity of the asset determines the length of the corresponding planning horizon that may need to be used in considering whether to acquire the asset. The less liquid the asset is, the longer the planning horizon for that asset should be.

On the other hand, managers are likely to classify an asset as "liquid"

[11] Both acquisition and liquidation prices can be used, employing the notion of "gains of integration" discussed in Chapter III. Thus, period t "sells" the asset at selling price and period $t + 1$ "buys" the asset at acquisition price. The difference can be seen as "gains of the firm" rather than the gains of period $t + 1$.

[12] In some cases an asset may be liquid per se, but for the firm it is not liquid, since liquidation of the asset implies liquidation of the firm. This is contrary to the going-concern assumption used in this book.

if the appropriate planning horizon for the asset is shorter than the planning horizon of the production process in which the asset is employed. Thus a manufacturing firm that planned its production on an annual basis might classify a five-year government bond as a liquid asset. A bank managing its cash position on a day-to-day basis might consider the same five-year government bond to be relatively illiquid.

Since one does not know in advance of an analysis of a firm whether the most relevant alternative is to buy another unit of an existing asset or to reduce the existing stock owned by the firm, a comprehensive accounting system should report both acquisition and liquidation values of assets.[13] The relevant value depends on management plans. If management intends to expand the scale of operations or wants to estimate whether entry by other firms would be profitable, the acquisition value should serve as a basis for valuation; if a judgment is needed as to whether a firm should stop a production line or liquidate a segment, the liquidation value should be used. In making replacement decisions, both the acquisition value of an asset (adjusted for its age and obsolescence if acquisition values must be based on the price of comparable new assets) and its liquidation value are relevant.[14] One signal that an asset should be replaced is that its acquisition value (based on the prices of comparable new assets) is less than its liquidation value. Finally, but by no means least important, the loss in liquidity to which a firm is subjecting itself by acquiring a new durable asset is an important consideration in estimating the risk the firm will bear if it acquires the asset and therefore the return it must expect to earn to compensate for that risk.[15]

[13] Usually authors suggest the use of only one type of value. Commonly it is the replacement value (for example, in Edwards and Bell 1961), but Chambers (1966) suggests using the liquidation value. For a review of Chambers, see Baxter (1967).

[14] Both the acquisition price and the liquidation value of assets should be stated on an after-tax basis. Normally the price that must be paid to acquire the asset is also the relevant after-tax acquisition price. The after-tax liquidation value of an asset, however, may differ significantly from the cash received, depending on the tax basis of the asset (see Goldschmidt and Smidt 1969).

[15] When liquidation values are used, the difference between an asset's acquisition value and its liquidation value must be charged to expense in the period during which the asset is acquired. This expense item measures the decline in

Deciding whether acquisition values or liquidation values are relevant is part of the decision-making process; and an accounting system based on market values is mainly useful as an input to the decision-making process. The above logic suggests that an accounting system should systematically record asset values at both their acquisition value and their liquidation value.

For practical purposes, we suggest selecting an arbitrary point on the liquidity scale to use in classifying durable assets as either liquid assets or nonliquid assets. This distinction is based on the availability of a market or a second-hand market for the assets and the relative ease of selling the assets on the market. For existing liquid assets, there is a (second-hand) market by definition; thus both acquisition and liquidation values are close. The use of only one value may therefore save analyst's time and costs without causing a large bias in the accounting reports.[16] For nonliquid assets, on the other hand, there is no effective second-hand market, hence the liquidation value is close to zero. The adjusted acquisition value of a nonliquid asset should take into consideration the asset's condition.

To summarize, for practical purposes it is suggested to report the following values: for liquid assets, sale price (the equivalent for nonliquid assets is zero); for nonliquid assets, replacement costs adjusted for estimates of the serviceability of the existing asset.

4. Decisions Requiring Asset Valuation on the Basis of Current Prices

For management decisions and control, the period income of the various segments of the firm must be estimated. An important item in

---

liquidity that the firm suffers by using cash to acquire the asset. Automobile depreciation provides a good illustration. The value of a new car, after it has been driven for a week, drops considerably. One reason is that there is not a real second-hand market for cars that have been used for one week. If a market does not exist, determined values might be used for valuation purposes (see Sections 6 and 9). There may also be an expense associated with acquiring liquidity; a firm that borrows money typically promises to pay more in present values than the amount of cash it receives (see Bierman and Smidt 1967).

[16] It should be noted that the actual conditions of a particular liquid asset are represented by its sale price. In practice it might be difficult to estimate the purchasing price of a similar asset. If so, the liquidation value might be used.

calculating income is the costs related to capital assets. The value of inventories is included directly in the cost of production (raw materials and goods in process) or in the revenue (goods in process and finished goods). On the other hand, the level of some of the costs (mainly depreciation and interest) is determined by the value of the durable assets. Thus, these durable assets must be valued if the related costs are to be estimated.

In order to determine whether the costs related to durable assets should be included in calculating income and to define these costs if they are included, the ultimate use of the income figures must first be specified. The period income of each segment of the firm is required for two purposes.

First, there are decisions regarding the product mix and the scale of each production process in the next production planning period. These decisions are carried out within the framework of the existing fixed resources and (durable nonliquid) assets. New investment alternatives are not directly relevant to these decisions because the planning horizon is too short.

The costs (mainly depreciation and interest) related to holding nonliquid assets are of no relevance for estimating the income figure that is required for this purpose—that is, the attainable contribution, because these costs exist irrespective of the production alternative chosen. But the costs related to the liquid assets are relevant and should be included in calculating the attainable contribution. The reason is that changes in the quantities of liquid assets owned are a direct and immediate result of decisions to expand or contract the scale of the process using the liquid asset. In other words, the costs related to liquid assets can be considered as avoidable costs, whereas the costs related to holding nonliquid assets are nonavoidable.

The attainable contribution of a segment can serve as a basis for estimating the present value of the segment, assuming that this income will continue at this level in the future. Thus, it serves for estimating the economic value of the segment's durable nonliquid assets.

The second purpose for period income measurement is to call management's attention to segments of the business whose operating results are unusually good or unusually bad by making comparisons. Comparisons of income measures may lead to further investigation and corresponding decisions in regard to such aspects as improving performance, expanding operations, or even setting price policies (if prices are set by the firm).

As indicated in Chapter II, the contribution to overhead is designed to serve for comparison purposes. This contribution is figured after the costs related to all the assets (liquid and nonliquid) that take part in the production process are included in the calculations, since different amounts of capital are used by various segments and during various time periods. Suppose the cost composition is changed over the years through investment in nonliquid assets that substitute for labor. If income over the years is to be compared, the costs related to these assets should be included.

The income figures of various segments whose assets are at different ages may be compared. Suppose one segment uses old assets that were acquired at low costs, and some assets are already written off the conventional accounting books. How can the income of this segment be compared to income of a segment that uses recently acquired assets? The value of the assets and, in turn, the income should be made comparable regardless of the age of the assets. The asset's ability to render service compared to a new asset should determine its value.

Income figures derived using current market prices for valuing all assets will presumably provide meaningful information pertaining to the profitability of individual production lines. If product prices are set by the market, a high income suggests one might want to consider expansion possibilities. If prices are set by the firm, a high income may indicate that expansion is desirable or that the entrance of a rival into production is possible. In both cases the decisions pertain to new investments that naturally are priced at current market prices. It makes sense therefore to use the same prices for calculating the income.

Although it appears reasonable to use current market prices for valuation, it is difficult to provide a workable method for carrying out this objective. The rest of the chapter is devoted to the subject of how assets can be valued for the purposes just indicated.

5. Durable Liquid Assets

Durable liquid assets are those assets that can be sold with relative ease on an active (second-hand) market. A share of a corporation is an example of this kind of asset. In many respects, valuation and costing procedures are most easily illustrated when applied to common stocks. The value of a share of stock is its market price at the point of time under consideration. If the owner believes he will profit more from keeping it than selling it, he will hold it. If the owner sells his share, he expects to earn interest on these funds invested elsewhere. In the same manner, interest should be charged on capital invested in terms of the share's market value. The change in value during the accounting period should be recorded and credited to the share's account. The same holds for any durable liquid asset such as livestock, trucks, land, and equipment.

The value of these assets is determined by their net liquidation value, if the relevant alternative is to sell some units of the asset, or by the acquisition price, if the relevant alternative is to acquire additional units. As indicated earlier, because of practical considerations it is suggested to report in the OAAS only one value—the liquidation value.[17]

The difference in the market values of the assets between the beginning and the end of the period should be debited (credited) to the user of the assets, as "depreciation" (appreciation). Note that the market price at the end of the period takes into account any increase in maintenance or obsolescence of the asset, during the accounting period, and also the price level change.[18]

The liquidation value at the beginning of a period is crucial, since it serves as a base for computing interest charges and figuring "depreciation"—the change in value during the period. Consider firm A's

[17] The use of a net liquidation price for valuation assumes that the scale of an operation is constant. This price is suitable for performance evaluation, as well as for analyzing the alternatives of contracting or even discontinuing the operation. For expansion decisions, however, gross acquisition price rather than net liquidation price should be used.

[18] It should be noted that in this case the period's income includes both profits from operation and holding gains (losses).

assets. The only liquid assets of this firm are the herds of livestock. The market value of the cows declines during the year because they are older or because market prices fall. The sale value of the cow herd is estimated to be $30,000 at the beginning of the year and $25,000 at the end. The change in value of $5,000 is considered as depreciation. The sum of $30,000 at the beginning of the year has an opportunity to earn interest at the rate of 10 per cent per annum.[19] Thus, the foregone interest is $3,000. The total annual capital charges for the asset "cows" are: $5,000 depreciation plus $3,000 interest = $8,000.

The market value of a steer, on the other hand, increases during the year. Because the number of bull calves and steers that enter and exit from the herd is constant, however, the herd's value does not change during that time. Thus, only interest is charged on the asset "steers." The same argument holds for the asset "heifers." The respective figures are summed up in Table 4.

Table 4. Values and capital charges for firm A's durable liquid assets (in U.S. dollars)

Values and charges	Ice cream	Steers	Cows	Heifers	Total of segments
Sale values					
Beginning of year	None	9,000	30,000	6,000	45,000
End of year	None	9,000	25,000	6,000	40,000
Annual charges					
Interest, 10%		900	3,000	600	4,500
Change in value			5,000		5,000
Total charges		900	8,000	600	9,500

It is conventional to consider the capital charges of the assets—depreciation—as a fixed cost. Here, on the other hand, the capital charges

[19] This is true if the alternative of selling the asset exists only at the beginning of a period (year) when plans are set. If there is an alternative to sell the asset during the year, interest should be charged on the average value of the asset.

of liquid assets—depreciation and interest—are avoidable costs in the sense that the asset could have been sold at the beginning of the period. In addition to the capital charges, there are other explicit cost items, such as maintenance and insurance, that are related to the assets, but ignored here for simplicity.

6. Durable Nonliquid Assets

Some or, occasionally, most of the individual assets are not liquid. This is because an active market for the used, specialized facilities does not exist. Before the investment takes place, the capital required may be considered as an avoidable cost. After investment has been undertaken, however, the historical costs of acquisition are sunk and nonavoidable; they are of no relevance for further decisions. The historical acquisition costs are of interest only to provide information on how good the estimates made in advance were, by comparing the actual costs to the estimated ones.

The requirements for the valuation of these assets should be kept in mind. The valuation is required mainly for comparison purposes, which in turn may lead to further decisions, only after the problem is further studied. This procedure can best be illustrated by example.

Suppose that at the beginning of the period the assets employed by a segment are valued close to their replacement cost and that at the end of the period the reported income of the segment is high. The high level of income is a signal for management to investigate the source of the high income and to consider whether any actions are appropriate. Since the income is calculated after the current market values of the assets have been considered, it provides a signal for investigating expansion of the operations. Such expansion naturally requires investment in new assets. Investment decisions are made only after an analysis is carried out.

Alternatively, the trend of income of a segment over several periods may provide a factor in evaluating the segment's performance. This trend is estimated by comparing the income in various periods. Since many factors that affect income are unstable, such a trend can provide only a rough measure of performance.

For the purpose mentioned, accuracy is of secondary importance.

What is important here is that the figure, even a rough one, represents the actual situation. Thus, if an old asset provides a service that is comparable to a new asset's service (or vice versa), the charges for the service should be comparable as well. The value of the assets should be determined or appraised accordingly.

Appraised Value. "Appraise" means to determine the value of a durable nonliquid asset by a systematic procedure that includes technical examination (by an engineer and a manager) and an economic estimate (by an accountant and a manager) of the asset's potential to render service compared to a new asset.[20] The details and accuracy with which such appraisals are carried out in a business concern depend on economic considerations—the cost and benefits associated with the additional information. It is reasonable to expect management to carry out rough valuation except for cases where detailed and accurate analysis is required.

The method suggested below is based on estimates and appraisals which are influenced by the subjective judgment of the analyst. If a value is to be assigned to an asset and service costs calculated, the procedure should be carried out by following economic concepts applied by qualified people, rather than by following accepted, "cut and dried" rules. It can be argued that management should make such estimates. Moreover, such estimates and appraisals are made by management, implicitly and often explicitly. So why should they not be made explicitly on a regular basis?

In a temporal framework, management "sells" an asset from period t to period $t+1$. The ceiling price in period $t+1$ is the price of a new asset. The floor price in period t for the nonliquid asset, on the other hand, is zero.[21] Suppose the asset is a multipurpose facility, potentially used for many activities in the firm. The various activities may

[20] Some authors indicate the possibility of using the conventional appraisal procedure (for example, Edwards and Bell 1961, pp. 186–187, and Sprouse 1964). This is not the method suggested here. The procedure here is more in line with Davidson's recommendation (1962, p. 11): "Attempt an appraisal of the assets in terms of their economic significance" as a base for "charging depreciation in a decentralized operation."

[21] There is a large leeway here that could be exploited if period $t+1$ were considered as a monopsonist.

"compete" for the facility and the price will approach the current market acquisition cost, given that the old facility provides a service similar to that provided by the new one. Suppose further that a new facility is to be installed. In this case the value of the existing facility becomes an external opportunity cost, since there is an opportunity not to install the new facility.

The implication of the argument above is that if the existing facility provides more or less the same type of service as a new facility, the values of the old and new facilities are both equal. An example may be helpful.

An Example. Consider a warehouse in a firm, providing storing services. If constructing a new warehouse costs $100,000, and if the old one can provide the same service, then the appraised value of the old one is $100,000 also. Note that because of the fact that an old asset provides the same service as the new one, there is no depreciation on the asset. But interest should be charged because implicit interest is considered as a cost item. If the cost of capital is 5 per cent per annum, the annual interest charge on the warehouse is $5,000. The treatment of such assets is similar to the treatment of land, which is conventionally considered as a nondepreciable asset. When the price level changes, the change in replacement costs for a comparable facility during the accounting period will be considered as "appreciation" or "depreciation."

Now suppose that the old warehouse requires a higher level of maintenance than the new one, say $2,000 per year. The old and new assets provide the same service, except for the maintenance cost. Rendering equal services, both assets' annual cost should be equal. This means that the residual for interest charges is: $5,000 interest on new asset — $2,000 = $3,000. The equivalent value for $3,000 of annual interest charges at 5 per cent is $60,000. The value of the old warehouse may be calculated to be $60,000. Management in the temporal framework would be indifferent about choosing between buying a new warehouse for $100,000, paying $5,000 as interest charges, and "selling" it after a year for $100,000 to the next time period, or "buying" an old warehouse for $60,000 from the former time period, paying $3,000 as interest and $2,000 for maintenance, and "selling" it for $60,000 after a year.

It should be noted that the annual costs related to an asset are constant along the years and equal to the annual costs of a replaceable new asset. In some cases this situation is due to the fact that the asset is kept for a considerably longer period of time by repairing it. Repairs and maintenance may be thought of as substitutes for replacement.[22] The same ideas can be extended to short-lived assets and to cases where the asset's serviceability is reduced.

When the asset's life is short relative to the planning horizon, the yearly valuation should be based on technical knowledge, as for example, engineering estimates of changes in productivity, or inferences from other assets which are liquid. For example, if tractors are not liquid, the value of a used tractor may be inferred from the value of a used truck for which a second-hand market exists. This procedure resembles the choice of a depreciation method. However, the main difference is that the potential service of the asset is appraised, rather than valued by applying a standard depreciation formula to the historical acquisition cost and date.

If the change in value cannot be estimated, an appropriate depreciation method (straight line, decreasing charge) might be used. In addition to the depreciation charges, however, interest on the non-depreciated value should be charged as well. When the quality of a service rendered by a short-lived durable asset throughout its life does not change, a fixed periodical charge (for both depreciation and interest) should be used. This can be done by using a capital recovery factor.[23] For example, the replacement value of the equipment in the ice cream department of firm A is estimated to be $4,000. The estimated productive life of new equipment is six years. At a 5 per cent interest rate per annum, the capital recovery factor is 0.197 (rounded to 0.2), and the annual charges are $800 (see Table 5).

The annual charges for the asset's service consist of the difference in the values of the asset at the beginning and the end of the period, interest on the value at the beginning of the period, and explicit hold-

22 See Lowe (1963) and Ross (1960, p. 424).

23 "Capital recovery factor" means a factor for establishing a uniform series of end-of-period payments that are equivalent to an initial sum. It is equal to the reciprocal of the factor for the present value of a uniform series.

Table 5. Values and capital charges for firm A's durable nonliquid assets (in U.S. dollars)

Values and charges	Ice cream	Steers	Cows	Heifers	Total of segments
Values					
Buildings (appraised value):					
Beginning of year	3,000	6,000	15,000	5,000	29,000
End of year	3,000	6,000	12,000	5,000	26,000
Equipment (replacement value)	4,000	None	5,000	None	9,000
Annual charges					
Buildings:					
Interest (5%)	150	300	750	250	1,450
Change in value	None	None	3,000	None	3,000
Equipment:					
Capital recovery (5%, 6 yrs. factor = 0.2)	800		1,000		1,800
(Interest)*					(300)
(Depreciation)					(1,500)
Total charges	950	300	4,750	250	6,250

* The arbitrary separation of the figures into interest and depreciation is done in order to simplify a later analysis. The basis is as follows: $9,000 value of equipment divided by 6 years provides $1,500 for depreciation. Interest equals the residual: $1,800 − $1,500 = $300.

ing costs such as maintenance, taxes, and insurance. A set of computations for the nonliquid assets of firm A are illustrated in Table 5. The explicit holding costs are ignored for simplicity.

Obsolescence. To incorporate obsolescence into the appraisal procedure consider first a gradual process of obsolescence that emerges because of the appearance of minor innovations. This process means that if one started the construction of a facility today the design would be somewhat different from that of the existing facility. The very existence of a facility eliminates the opportunity of introducing these changes, which certainly would improve the quality of the service rendered by the facility. This fact in turn implies that the old facility's economic value is less than that of the new. The asset's value declines because another, more efficient asset is available, even though the future earnings of the existing asset are unchanged.[24] These considerations should be considered when appraising the value of the facility.[25]

A major innovation may cause a complete change in the production process, which in turn may require disposing of an old facility or setting it aside as a standby facility. In other words, the facility may become obsolete instantaneously and its value drop from almost new to scrap during the accounting period. Such a valuation procedure may at first appear to have shortcomings; actually, it is an advantage of the suggested method. The objective of the OAAS is to indicate and report actual events, especially when the situation is turbulent, rather than to conceal them. If one wants to eliminate a major accounting loss in one period because of obsolescence, he may insure against it—a subject to be discussed in the next section.

Merits and Shortcomings. The value of a nonliquid asset is appraised on the basis of the asset's potential to render service compared to that of a new asset. That is, the replacement costs are adjusted for such items as increased maintenance, reduced serviceability, and obso-

[24] See Green and Sorter (1959). Bodenhorn (1961, n. 10) argues against it.

[25] There is here the difficulty of comparing the services rendered by the old asset and by a new one (see Wright 1965, p. 177, and Chambers 1966, pp. 249–250). Suppose a firm has a relatively new warehouse storing perishables. Replacement costs of this asset are $100,000. However, a more modern warehouse costs $120,000. Assuming very long life, the annual interest charges (at 5% per annum) are $6,000. The products stored in the modern warehouse are sold for a premium of $2,000 per year. The annual cash flow of the potential modern warehouse, relative to the existing one, is: $2,000 premium — $6,000 interest = —$4,000. This means that the very existence of the warehouse substitutes for annual charges of $4,000. The equivalent value for $4,000 of annual interest charges at 5% is $80,000. This is the appraised value of the existing warehouse.

There is another kind of obsolescence which arises from changes in the market's evaluation of the products (see Chambers 1966, p. 208). If the demand for the firm's product declines, the asset producing it is partially obsolete, even if it is in good physical condition. In other words, the economic value of the asset declines. Still, the replacement cost (less adjustments for increased maintenance) should provide the basis for the asset's valuation.

lescence of the existing asset. By using appraised or determined values for valuing nonliquid assets, an attempt is made to refrain from the use of the historical acquisition cost and from the use of a discretionary depreciation method, which does affect the asset's value as recorded in the books. Not only is the historical acquisition cost figure distorted when the price level changes, but also it may not represent a normal market price. For example, an asset acquired at an unusually low price will have low annual depreciation charges compared to a similar asset acquired at a normal price. Moreover, the book value does not reflect the asset's condition. For example, a serviceable asset may be valued at zero (or close to zero) because of the use of an accounting rule to determine the asset's life span.[26]

While in conventional accounting the value of an asset is based on estimates developed by means of "discretionary procedures" chosen by the accountant, in the OAAS the valuation is based on subjective estimates of the value itself made by the analyst. Both procedures involve judgment. The real difference hinges on their relevance for management decisions.

There is a distinct complication in appraising assets in addition to the problem of estimating the market price. For appraisal of future service potential, future cash flows must be estimated and discounted. Thus we find the same problems in appraisal as in the economist's present-value approach. Nevertheless, there are some merits in the suggested procedure:

1. There are boundaries to the appraised value—the acquisition cost and liquidation value. This makes the valuation procedure simpler. Thus, although the suggested procedure is subjective, it can be carried out in a similar way to procedures that are suggested in the literature for estimating subjective probability.[27]

[26] Paton's story (1947, p. 200) is relevant: "A young lady in the accounting department . . . was moving a bookkeeping machine. . . . As she came alongside an open stairway she . . . let the machine get away from her. . . . Hearing the crash, the office manager came rushing out. . . . 'Someone tell me quickly,' he yelled, 'if that is one of our fully amortized units.' A check of the equipment cards showed that the smashed machine was, indeed, one of those which had been written off. 'Thank God!' said the manager."

[27] In order to appraise some nonliquid facilities of a firm, the author posed the following question to the two managers independently: "Suppose someone wants

2. The valuation procedure is based on a comparison of the incremental cash flows (costs) for an individual existing asset compared to its potential replacement. Often it is possible to estimate incremental cash flows for an asset, but not the absolute cash flows. As a result, this procedure assigns a value to the individual assets of a segment. By contrast the conventional economic value (present value) can be calculated only for a set of assets (a segment) for which the absolute cash flows can be measured.

7. Durable Assets: Some Comments

There are some characteristics common to both durable liquid and nonliquid assets.

Groups of Assets. In some cases, a service is rendered by a group of assets of the same kind of various ages, as, for example, lathes in a workshop.[28] Every so often some individual units in the group are replaced by new ones. There may be a large number of items, each of which has relatively small value, which make up the group of assets. An example is used as a frame of reference.

Consider a firm having ten lathes, and assume that a secondhand market does not exist for lathes. Each year one lathe is replaced by a new one costing $2,000. Thus, the group of lathes in aggregate has an annual cost of $2,000. This is an explicit cost which stands for all the avoidable costs of these assets. This procedure might produce the same results as conventional depreciation practices, if depreciation were based on a value based on replacement costs. Thus, if the life of the lathes is considered to be ten years, the yearly depreciation for a $2,000 lathe, based on the straight line method, is $200. For the ten lathes in the group, the yearly depreciation is $2,000.

It is possible to avoid the acquisition of the new lathe and, in turn, the related costs. There are here two kinds of costs: one is related to the new lathe and can be considered as avoidable costs; the other

---

to buy this facility. How much would you sell it for, if replacing it would cost you $——?" With some trial-and-error questioning and answering, an appraised value was determined.

[28] This case fits a "mature" enterprise that is neither expanding nor contracting but is constantly replacing its assets. This situation implies that the enterprise will normally have a collection of assets of varying ages (Solomons 1965, p. 89).

is related to the existing lathes and can be considered as nonavoidable costs. The latter cost item is composed of implicit interest charges. Suppose the price level is constant. The average value of the ten lathes at the beginning of the year (after a new one is acquired) is:

$$\frac{(2000 + 200)}{2} \times 10 = \$11,000.$$

With a 5 per cent rate of interest, the total annual interest charges are \$550.

There is a strong resemblance between the latter type of assets and inventories of raw material. The difference is in the rate of turnover and in the liquidity of the assets. While inventories may be considered as liquid and the interest on them avoidable, for the latter type of assets interest is nonavoidable.

Assets as Contribution Centers. An asset or a group of similar assets (whether liquid or nonliquid) can be considered as a contribution center. Suppose the service of an asset can be sold or acquired on the market. For example, warehouse space or equipment can be rented. The corresponding market price provides the revenue figures for the corresponding segment. Since this price is an external opportunity cost, it should be considered as an avoidable cost for the purchasing segment.

Depreciation and Income. In the OAAS, depreciation is a result of the measurement of income. Recall that the revenue of a quasi-independent period, t, is composed of the sales outside the firm and the goods transferred to period $t + 1$. The costs are composed of purchases of inputs from the market and the goods transferred from period $t - 1$. The assets are included in the transferred goods; thus, the difference in the assets' transfer price at the end of period $t - 1$ and at the end of period t is the depreciation charged to period t. In conventional accounting, on the other hand, depreciation represents the amortization of the acquisition costs, and depreciation is thus a factor in measuring income.

Self-insurance. In the preceding section, insurance is suggested as a possible means for reducing the impact of unexpected obsolescence leading to an accounting loss. Conventionally, the capital invested in durable assets is amortized over several years, in an accounting framework. The annual amortization sum (depreciation) is charged to the users of the assets' service. When an asset is obsolete before the initial outlay has been amortized, however, a loss is recorded. Under the OAAS, on the other hand, the initial outlay is not amortized, but rather the change in the asset's value is charged to the users of the asset's service.

Suppose the market or the appraised value of an asset is stable over several years. This implies low annual charges for depreciation and high loss when the asset becomes obsolete, compared to conventional accounting practices. This gap can be reconciled in an accounting sense (not in terms of real cash flow) by a self-insurance procedure. Self-insurance can be established by retaining a portion of earnings set aside as a reserve for contingencies. Thus, any segment using an asset's service will be charged an annual insurance premium based on the asset's value (market or appraised). When obsolescence occurs, the loss will be offset on the revenue side by using the reserve set up for this purpose. This procedure conceals the actual events, however, and thus reduces one of the advantages of the OAAS.

Two procedures can be followed: (1) Annual charges as premium for self-insurance will be charged for the use of durable nonliquid assets. (These charges substitute for the conventional depreciation charges. The difference between the charges lies in the basis for computation and the required expertise.) This procedure may be used in calculating income for comparison purposes and for dividend decisions. (2) Obsolescence will be calculated and considered as an annual loss. It may be carried out as an auxiliary record.

Rate of Interest. The rate of interest to be used in business analysis is a subject of controversy in the literature. The subject will not be discussed here. The borrowing or lending rate, plus or minus relevant items, can be considered as an external opportunity cost. Hence, it is plausible to use this rate for charging interest on liquid assets. It is questionable whether this rate is the appropriate rate for nonliquid assets because of the ultimate use of the data. Recall that the costs for nonliquid assets are used mainly for comparisons. One solution is to use the firm's cost of capital, where the cost of capital can be considered as the weighted average of the cost of each type of capital employed by the firm. Another solution is to use the rate of interest (the internal opportunity cost of the capital or the shadow price of the capital constraint) which has been used in the ex ante investment analysis for the asset.[29] This procedure, which is an evaluation device, is not suggested for the OAAS. There are inherent difficulties in charging and reporting shadow prices in an accounting system (see Chapters II and XIV).

Controlling Investments. The procedure of excluding capital charges for the services of nonliquid assets when calculating costs of production is in controversy in the literature (the controversy over direct costing). Unfortunately, the conventional procedure of full costing does not solve the problem either, since interest is not charged and the depreciation charges are determined by means of "discretionary procedures." Even when all the capital charges are included in the costs (nonavoidable cost), the cost figure cannot be used as an evaluation device concerning investment itself.

Investment decisions are of major importance. Actual decisions cannot be evaluated as such but rather the expectations that provide the assumptions and the reasons for the decisions must be evaluated. There are two kinds of expectations to be evaluated: the estimates (costs and timing) regarding the installation of the facility, and the expectations regarding cash flow.[30] The evaluation of the latter is important because the results of investment decisions occur over a long period of time, long enough to forget the initial expectations regarding cash flows. An auxiliary record must be kept in order to control the expectations pertaining to investments (this record is called "diary of expectations" in Chapter XIII). Two types of records must be carried out: records of the assumptions and the capital budgets for accepted and discarded alternatives, and records of actual events. The deviations of the actual events from the expected events should be used for evaluation purposes. At the start of every period (year) new expectations and accordingly

[29] Bierman (1966) suggests basing depreciation charges on the ex ante cash flows used in investment analysis.

[30] See Heebink (1964), Kemp (1966), and Horngren (1967, p. 255). When the price level changes over the years, both expectations and measurements might be made for the holding gains and income from operations.

new decisions regarding existing assets are made. The evaluation at the end of the period should be with regard to the most recent set of expectations. Still, the variance between initial expectations and actual events related to durable assets should be analyzed for several years.

Data Requirements. There is no accounting method without shortcomings, especially when capital charges are estimated. The methods suggested have a practical limitation. Data on every asset are required, especially external information on market prices for new and used assets. If the firm is interested in periodic investigations of existing and newly available assets, these data are necessary anyway. If these procedures are used by small firms, such as farms, a central institution (such as the agricultural advisory service) should supply a list of quoted market prices for new and used assets. This would simplify the process of the annual appraisal.

8. Inventories of Raw Materials and Finished Goods

Inventories are classified in this study into: raw materials, finished goods,[31] and goods in process. The first two inventories are usually traded on the market and hence a market price can be used for their valuation. If a good in process can be traded on the market, it should be considered as an intermediate good, valued on the basis of its market price, and treated as either raw material or finished good. When a market for a good in process does not exist, a determined value must be used—a subject to be discussed in the next section.

Raw Materials. Inventories of raw materials must be replenished constantly. The replacement costs are relevant and thus should be used to value the inventories.[32] Even if the scale of operation of the segment using the inventory is to be changed, the replacement costs

[31] Accounts receivable can be considered as loaned capital or, like finished goods, as liquid assets.

[32] Conventionally, inventories are valued and priced at historical costs. A similar procedure is used by Stigler's lazy shop owner: "Occasionally one walks into the shop of a lazy man and observes identical goods with two prices, and is told that the lower priced items were in an earlier shipment that cost less. This is foolish merchandising unless the cost of remarking the price is more than the rise in price" (Stigler 1966, p. 104). Interestingly enough, in the Netherlands the replacement cost concept is regarded as a generally accepted practice (Mueller 1964, p. 153).

are relevant. This is because either more or less of the material must be acquired. For a decision regarding discontinuing a process, however, the liquidation price is relevant.

Where inventory prices or volume is not stable, or where a slow turnover exists, or where holding the inventory requires high-cost services, it is suggested that inventory be considered as a contribution center. As such, the segment "inventory" would be charged the historic purchasing price plus holding costs and credited with the current replacement price. In a period of rising prices, this segment would produce profits; that is, "holding profits" will be reported when the increase in price exceeds the holding costs.

When an inventory is held for speculative purposes, it is natural to consider it as a separate segment, the revenue of which is the sale price of the inventory. Similarly, if an inventory is held for both production and speculation, it should be considered as a separate segment. Many firms speculate by holding larger stocks of raw material (for in-plant use) when they expect a (seasonal or other) price rise, and smaller stocks when they expect a decline. This activity is hard to control and to evaluate unless the inventory is considered as a separate segment.

The costs to be charged to the segment inventory are: gross acquisition costs; regular operating costs such as labor, electricity, warehouse space (if the space has an alternative use), and spoilage; and interest on the average acquisition cost.[33] If this stock were not held, the capital released would have an alternative use; for example, it could be loaned or, alternatively, it need not be borrowed. The interest charges are an important cost item that conventionally is not recorded. Thus, the conventional practice leads toward underestimation of the cost of holding inventory.

The revenue to be credited to the segment inventory, on the other hand, is based on the (internal) "sale price" of the material to the consumer of the inventory. The "sale price" includes replacement cost and holding costs, where "holding costs" mean costs which are incurred as a result of holding the inventory. In this way the costs of

[33] The inventory of cash should be charged only for interest, since no other holding costs occur.

holding the inventory are passed to the consumer of the inventory. On the other hand, the holding profits or losses will be recorded in the inventory account. When an inventory is kept for speculation purposes, however, the holding costs for the extra amount should be matched to holding profits and not forwarded to the internal customers.

Finished Goods. The net realizable value of finished goods should serve as a basis for valuation—that is, as a temporal transfer price. This is an objective yardstick provided that the price is ascertainable and that the product is marketable. An intermediate good, transferred among segments (spatial transfer), is considered here (in the temporal transfer framework) as a finished good.

The periods involved are viewed as quasi-independent. Period t "sells" finished goods to period $t+1$ at the net realizable price. However, if the marketability of a certain product is questionable, its transfer price is lower than its sale price. In case of excess capacity, transfer of, say, 100 units of finished goods would only substitute for production of 100 units in period $t+1$. Thus, for period $t+1$ the inventory is worth the cost avoided by not producing the 100 units. These avoidable costs should be used as the transfer price.

The various situations and the corresponding pricing rules for inventories of finished goods are as follows:

Situation no.	*Inventory situation*	*Production-capacity situation*	*Temporal transfer price*
1	Marketable	No excess	Net realizable price
2	Marketable	Excess	Avoidable cost
3	Marketability in question	Excess, no excess	Between zero and net realizable price

Let us elaborate briefly on these pricing rules.[34] The net realizable price (corresponding to situation 1) is net of holding cost that will be accrued until sale takes place. The net realizable price should be either the selling price less holding costs (including interest) or the present value of the selling price and holding costs (not including interest).

[34] See also Horngren and Sorter (1961) and Bierman (1967) on this subject.

Actually only the latter is operational, since in the former the interest should include interest on the net realizable value, which is the variable to be determined. The avoidable cost here is a surrogate for marginal cost. The third price is a typical case of a determined value.

When no excess capacity exists (situation 1), the suggested procedure means, in accounting language, that profits are included in the inventories. One may argue that this procedure will motivate lower-level managers to produce for inventories.[35] But note that the very fact of no excess capacity reduces or eliminates the possibility of producing for inventory. Interest is charged on the transfer value. This procedure and the valuing procedures under other situations (2 and 3) will hopefully eliminate this possible motive to produce for inventories when accumulation is not desirable.

When the inventory requires special services such as warehousing or transportation, or it is kept for a long period of time, or when there is the possibility of large fluctuation in the volume and/or prices of inventory held, it might be helpful to consider it as a contribution center.

9. Valuing Nonmarketable Goods in Process

The valuation of goods in process—that is, partly finished products—is important, since their value is included in the avoidable costs (or in variable costs in conventional accounting), on the one hand, and is considered as revenue, on the other. As long as the level of production and the level of inventories of goods in process in each period are stable, the method of valuing these inventories will not affect the reported income in a given period, because the value of these inventories is included in both cost and revenue categories of a period. But when production lasts for more than one accounting period and when the level of the inventory fluctuates between accounting periods, the valuing method may greatly affect the reported income in a period.

[35] The same problem exists when conventional costing is used, by charging off to the inventory account a proportion of fixed overhead. Davidson (1963*b*, p. 124) tells the story of a manufacturer who "bolstered [his] profits substantially by adding to inventories for several successive periods. In fact, the firm was reporting profits all the way to bankruptcy." For a numerical example, see Sorter and Horngren (1962).

In conventional accounting the costs of production provide the basis for valuing goods in process. In some analyses the liquidation value is used as a basis for valuation. Of course, when a developed market exists for the good in process, the market price should be used for valuation. But this is a rare situation.

The assumption that the income is generated concurrently with the production process implies that goods in process are worth more than the raw materials and other production costs accrued during production.[36] The problem is how to value these goods that are transferred in the analytical framework from one period to another.

To arrive at a value for these goods, the analyst should imitate the marketplace by considering a hypothetical seller and buyer for the good. The seller is analoged to the former period; the buyer, to the next period. One can conceive of a price floor for a hypothetical supply—the avoidable costs of the seller—and a price ceiling for a hypothetical demand—the realizable income (realizable revenue at the end of the process minus avoidable costs) to the buyer. These figures differ considerably from conventional supply-and-demand figures, since they are derived from factual figures—avoidable costs and realizable income, respectively.

As a second step the analyst should select a price that lies between these two figures. In other words, the hypothetical demand-and-supply figures provide boundaries, and the analyst must set a price, based on his judgment, in between them. This price is called determined value.

A good in process may be transferred at any stage of the production process. This implies that an array of prices is required—one for each possible stage. An example of this, used as a frame of reference and illustrating an actual problem of valuing a good in process, is the production of a steer under standard conditions in Israel. The example is somewhat cumbersome, but it illustrates the use of the method and its applicability.[37]

[36] The liquidation value may be lower than the cost of production, or of the raw material used in production. For example, "plain paper is worth more than printed pages, unless the process can be completed by assembling the printed pages into a book" (Moonitz 1961, p. 40).

[37] For an application of a similar procedure to finance firms, see Comiskey and Mlynarczyk (1968).

Consider a bull calf purchased at the age of two weeks for I£300 and sold at the age of fourteen months for I£1,350. Variable costs of production are presented in Table 6, column 3. Interest at the rate of 1 per cent per month is charged on variable costs (column 4). The accumulated variable cost and interest charges for each month of the steer's life provide the hypothetical supply figures, as presented in column 5.

The hypothetical demand projected for the steer originates from the fact that it will be sold for I£1,350 and that total costs will be lower than I£1,350. At the end of the fourteenth month the price ceiling is I£1,350. At the end of the thirteenth month the corresponding figure is equal to the present value of the future cash flow, specifically I£1,350, minus I£85. The present value (at 1 per cent per month) is:

$$(1{,}350 - 85) \times 0.9901 = \text{I£}1{,}252.5.$$

The corresponding present value for the twelfth month is:

$$[(1{,}350 - 85) \times 0.9803] - (83 \times 0.9901) = \text{I£}1{,}157.9.$$

These computations are repeated for every month (column 7).[38] In other words, the ceiling for the "demand" figure is the present value of the cash flow starting at the month under consideration throughout.

Accumulated costs—that is, compounded costs—provides for the "supply" figures in column 5 of Table 6. Discounted income provides for the "demand" figures in column 7. The entries of both columns are charted in Figure 2. The determined value can now be set in a subjective manner by picking a figure in the margin between the two curves.

Because of risk and the nature of entrepreneurship, it is assumed that a longer production process requires a larger profit margin or discount rate. This assumption means that a hypothetical buyer of a young calf would require a relatively high income for raising this calf. The price will be close to the costs of production—that is, to the hypothetical supply figure. When he buys the steer at greater age, the buyer would be satisfied with a relatively low income. On the other

[38] For simplifying the computations, income as realizable at the end of the process can be discounted each month (Table 6, column 6). By adding the latter to the accumulated cost figure (column 5), one arrives at the entries in column 7.

Table 6. Computations of the values of a steer at various production levels*

(1)	(2)	(3)	(4)	(5)	(6) Present value of	(7)	(8)
Age	Market price†	Variable cost†	Interest charges (1% mo.)‡	Accumulated costs ("supply")§	Income‖	Future cash flow ("demand")#	Determined values
2 weeks	−300	300		300	122.4	422.4	300
1 month		26	1.5	327.5	123.0	450.5	330
2 months		53	3.3	383.8	124.2	508.0	390
3 months		53	3.8	440.6	125.4	566.0	455
4 months		36	4.4	481.0	126.7	607.7	500
5 months		36	4.8	521.8	128.0	659.8	550
6 months		52	5.2	579.0	129.3	708.3	620
7 months		54	5.8	638.8	130.6	769.4	690
8 months		59	6.4	704.2	131.9	836.1	760
9 months		62	7.0	773.2	133.2	906.4	840
10 months		70	7.7	850.9	134.5	985.4	930
11 months		72	8.5	931.4	135.9	1,067.3	1,025
12 months		80	9.3	1,020.7	137.2	1,157.9	1,130
13 months		83	10.2	1,113.9	138.6	1,252.5	1,240
14 months	+1,350	85	11.1	1,210.0	140	1,350	1,350
Total		1,121	89				

* All figures are in I£ (I£1 = $0.33), assumed to hold for the end of the period (month).
† Based on standard norms as existed in Israel in 1965.
‡ Calculated on the former month's entry in column 5.
§ Sum of entries in columns 3 and 4 and former month's entry in same column.
‖ Income as realizable at the 14th month, viz. I£140.
Cash flow starting at the specific month up to the end, as given in columns 2 and 3.

Figure 2. Hypothetical supply and demand curves used in valuing steers at various production levels

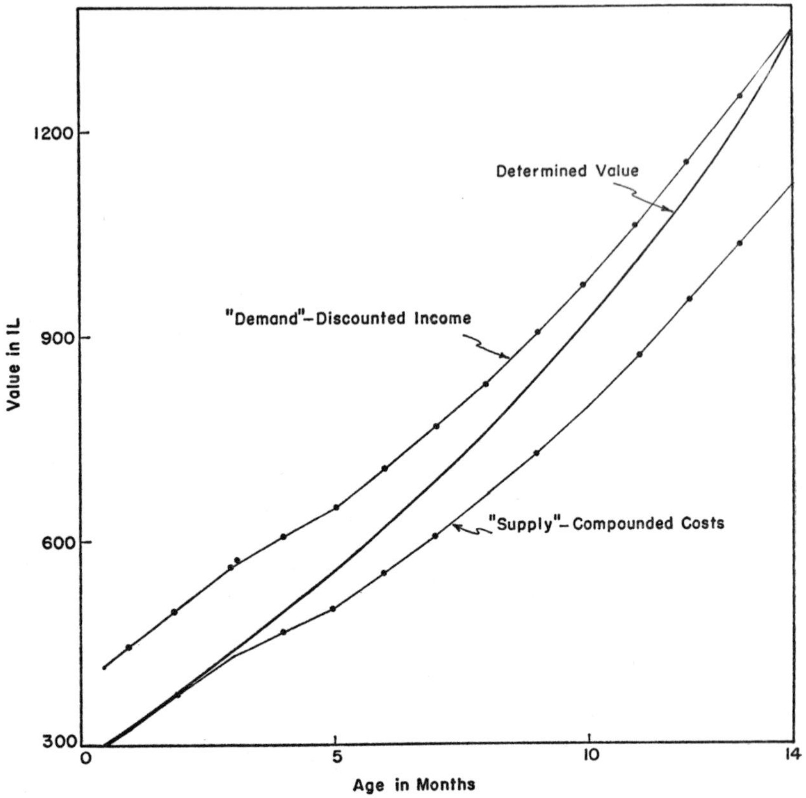

hand, the hypothetical seller would be ready to sell the calf at an early age almost at cost. He would be reluctant to sell it at a greater age except at a price close to the present value of the income realizable at the sale of the "finished" steer.

The assumption as outlined above is taken into consideration in the example, and a freehand line is drawn in Figure 2 along the margin between the two curves. This line, starting at the "supply" (that is, the compounded costs) curve and ending at the "demand" (that is, the discounted income) curve, provides a schedule for the determined values. The entries in column 8 of Table 6 are based on this line.

A set of determined values is needed for each production process, and these sets can be used as long as technology and prices do not change. In any case, the accountant prepares a set of values for goods in process, but he bases the values on costs of production. In agriculture, where central advisory services exist, sets of values for some standard processes, mainly for livestock enterprises, can be prepared and disseminated to individual farms. Such prices may be helpful to the farm in valuing casual transactions of products like young livestock.

As mentioned earlier, the use of determined values for evaluating goods in process is essential when production lasts for more than one accounting period and when the level of the inventory fluctuates between accounting periods. Consider a farm buying 100 bull calves early in January 1965 and selling 100 steers (assuming no deaths) in March 1966. The accounting period covers one calendar year. The steers are transferred at the age of twelve months from 1965 to 1966. The income statement for this batch under both conventional accounting and the OAAS procedures, assuming no other cost, is given in Table 7. It should be noted that under the proposed procedure, interest is charged

Table 7. An income statement for a batch of 100 steers

Procedures	Temporal transfer price per unit	Profits or income			Interest charges
		1965	1966	Total	
Conventional accounting	953*	0	22,900†	22,900	0
OAAS	1,130‡	10,930§	3,070‖	14,000	8,900

Source: Table 6 (all figures in I£).

* Total costs up to the end of the 12th month (column 3).

† 100 steers × (1,350 − 1,121) (see columns 2 and 3).

‡ Entry for the 12th month (column 8).

§ Determined value (1,130) minus accumulated costs (1,020.7) for the 12th month (column 5) times 100 steers.

‖ 100 × (1,350 minus sum of determined value and entries for the 13th and 14th months) (see columns 3 and 4).

as cost. This charge reduces the total reported income by I£89 per steer. This production process, just like any other production process, ties up funds, which are committed to the production process until it ends. For the interim, interest is charged (see Chapter X).

10. Summary and Conclusions

Three approaches are available for asset valuation. Each has some severe shortcomings, but is nevertheless required for some purpose.

1. Past transactions are used as a basis for valuation in conventional accounting. Although this valuation is based on objective data, it is also based on what can be described as essentially a "discretionary procedure" of choosing a depreciation method and the asset's life span. This valuation is required for external reporting.

2. Future earning power in terms of present value provides for the economic value of an asset. This valuation is based on a judgment regarding the future cash flows associated with a segment (a production process), on the time value of money and on an appropriate allowance for risk. When a set of assets, rather than a single piece of asset, is employed by a segment, this approach provides a value for the set of assets, but not for each individual asset separately. This procedure is required for long-range decisions.

3. Present market prices are recommended here for use as a basis for valuation in internal accounting. Since the assessment of the market price requires assertion of some judgment, this type of valuation is to some extent subjective.

The costs associated with liquid assets (external opportunity costs) are used for calculating the income measure that is needed in making short-range decisions on resource allocation and in estimating the economic value of an asset (the internal opportunity cost). In both uses, management must exercise its judgment in interpreting the data and in arriving at a decision. Thus, the use of some judgment in valuing liquid assets is compatible with the ultimate use of these values. The appraisal of existing nonliquid assets, which is meant to provide a measure of the asset's serviceability, is also based on judgment. This valuation suffices for those internal purposes which it should serve (for comparisons of performance, for indicating weak and strong points in production, and in some cases for pricing, as will be indicated in Chapter VII).

The amount of judgment used in valuing assets differs among assets. For both liquid and nonliquid assets the market prices (acquisition and liquidation) must be assessed; for nonliquid assets the serviceability must be appraised as well. The appraisal also provides the basis for determining the economic value of the individual nonliquid assets.

Assertion of judgment is an indispensable part of asset valuation in either of the three approaches. Faced with a choice between making subjective estimates of values (approach 3) and making subjective choices of methods to arrive at values (approach 1), the former seems more useful for internal reporting. In other words, it is suggested that the current market prices be used as a basis for valuing assets for the OAAS, which is designed to provide data for internal decisions and control. Comparisons of the values derived by means of approaches 2 and 3 may provide important information to management.

All the approaches should be used in a firm's information system. Approach 1 is required for external ex post reporting; approach 2 for ex ante decision making; and approach 3 for internal ex-post reporting. The data derived from approaches 1 and 3 provide inputs into the system, whereas approach 2 provides data that are an output of the system.

Some additional facts have been discussed in this chapter. It has been suggested that the continuous operations of an integrated firm should be decomposed in the analytical framework into periods and segments. Assets have been classified into durables and inventories. One of the important characteristics of assets, especially durables, is their liquidity; therefore, a measure or scale of assets' liquidity has been suggested. For practical purposes, durables have been classified as liquid or nonliquid assets. The valuation procedure of each as well as for inventories (raw materials, finished goods, and goods in process) has been discussed. Auxiliary procedures, such as self-insurance against a high loss caused by the obsolescence of assets or control of investment decisions, have been suggested.

V
AVOIDABLE COSTING

The concepts of marginal cost and opportunity cost are crucial for economic decision making. The problem is how to make these concepts operational, or how to estimate these costs in practice. This chapter suggests a cost concept, termed "avoidable cost," that is designed to provide an operational figure that surrogates for the theoretical concept of marginal cost. This concept is also related to, and provides for, an estimate of the opportunity cost.

The chapter also indicates how costs should be analyzed, given the needs of decision makers. There is no simple answer to this question, but the issues involved can be clarified by examining various methods of analysis under different assumptions about the uses decision makers have for cost data.

In the OAAS a distinction is made between two types of costs—avoidable and nonavoidable.[1] An avoidable cost is any cost that can be or could have been eliminated by an appropriate managerial decision. Avoidable costs include costs of variable inputs (items purchased directly, raw materials from inventory, and goods in process), of

[1] The term "avoidable cost" has been chosen deliberately to emphasize the most important aspect of cost in relation to decisions. Some other costing concepts suggested in the literature as substitutes for the traditional variable (direct) cost concept are: incremental costs; differential costs (Clark 1923, p. 49); user costs (Lutz and Lutz 1951, ch. 4); relevant costs (Sorter and Horngren 1962); and attributable costs (Shillinglaw 1963).

intermediate goods, and of durable liquid assets. Nonavoidable costs are cost items that can be traced to a segment but that are not avoidable. They include costs of durable nonliquid assets (when the services are marketable, these are avoidable) and common costs (in liquidation analysis, for example, these are also avoidable). This distinction differs considerably from the conventional distinction between variable and fixed costs (see Chapter VII, Section 2).

The objective of the OAAS is to serve the decision maker by providing data for decisions and motivation. By and large, the most important data for this purpose are avoidable costs. In the literature and in practice, variable costs are used to fulfill this function. The accounting literature is filled with articles on costing methods that estimate variable costs (variable costing, direct costing, marginal costing).[2] Some of these methods are applied in business, and even in external reporting.[3]

The avoidable cost in a particular situation is measured by the variable costs plus the external opportunity cost, both at the margin. There are two special facets in the avoidable cost concept: external opportunity cost and costs on the margin. Because avoidable costs include some implicit costs as well as costs on the margin, calculating this cost figure may cause some accounting complications. In order to overcome such complications, special accounts, termed "rent centers," are designed to absorb the difference between the incurred costs and the costs that are charged in the OAAS.

Costs that are not traceable to a segment, mainly the firm's admin-

[2] Gillespie (1962) provides a list of 56 articles on this subject. The subject is also discussed in many textbooks—for example, Shillinglaw (1961), Bierman (1963), and Horngren (1962*a*). Marple (1965) provides a short history of the development of direct costing; Earley (1955), an overview; Fremgen (1964), a review. Langholm (1965) makes a distinction between variable costing and direct costing.

[3] A number of surveys indicating some use of direct costing by business concerns have been published—for example, the National Association of Accountants (1953*a*, p. 1081), Fog (1960, pp. 11, 13, 84), Early (1956, p. 50), Sack (1958), Howe (1962, pp. 81, 86), Langholm (1965), Solomons (1965, p. 101), and the National Association of Accountants (1961). Wright (1962, pp. 213–216) and Marple (1965, pp. 11–12) provide examples of the use of these costing procedures in external reporting.

istrative costs, are termed "overhead costs." These are not distributed to the segments, but rather are kept in aggregate to comprise another, special segment. This segment, just as any other segment in the firm, incurs both avoidable and nonavoidable costs.

Some cost items can be seen as overhead costs of the segment. They may be avoidable if the segment is liquidated, but nonavoidable if the scale of operation is considered. These costs are termed "common costs" and considered as nonavoidable. Just as overhead costs are not distributed to segments, common costs of a segment are not distributed to units of products.

1. External Opportunity Cost

One of the basic concepts underlying decision making is the principle of opportunity cost. While for an economist the foregone alternative is the cost, for an accountant cost is typically the outlay actually incurred, or historical cost. In developing a cost concept that is related to decision making, the opportunity cost should not be ignored. Only the relations between avoidable costs and opportunity costs are discussed below.

A distinction is made here between external and internal opportunity costs. External opportunity cost is defined as the market price of a commodity (good or service) that is used in production rather than sold or bought. This price is due to the existence of a market outside the firm, competing for the use of the input with the activity that now uses this input. Internal opportunity cost (shadow price), on the other hand, is defined as the contribution (revenue minus avoidable costs) that a limited and versatile resource or facility could earn in its best feasible use within the firm. In other words, it equals the contribution of the relevant activity, imputed to the limited resource. This opportunity cost results from internal competition for the use of the limited resource by productive activities.

The avoidable-cost figure is closely related to the concept and figures of opportunity cost. By definition, avoidable costs include external opportunity costs. On the other hand, the internal opportunity cost is derived after avoidable costs are considered as a factor in the computations. The sequence of determining these cost figures is: external opportunity cost, avoitable cost, internal opportunity cost.

Costs of purchased inputs can be viewed as external opportunity costs since the foregone alternative is not to purchase these inputs. This opportunity is available also in the future, when the same production processes will be repeated.

When the firm has an opportunity to sell or buy an intermediate good or service on the market, the market price of this good or service is considered as an external opportunity cost for the process using it. Conceptually there is no difference between an input bought on the market and an input "bought" from another process.[4] Both are considered to be avoidable costs.

The same holds when the service is rendered by an asset. For example, suppose a firm owns a warehouse. There is an alternative to lease the warehouse for $0.50 per square foot per period. Given that this alternative is a real opportunity for the firm, this rate should be used in the OAAS as the period cost of the warehouse service. The same holds for any other self-owned resource or facility (see application in Chapter VIII).

By far the most significant resource for which external opportunity costs are assigned is capital. The borrowing or lending rate plus or minus relevant items, is an external opportunity cost. When inventories are kept for a going production process, the firm has an alternative not to purchase or produce these inventories. The inventories in turn tie up capital that has an external opportunity cost. Hence interest should be charged to inventories. This charge as well as the costs associated with liquid assets (interest, change in value) are included in the avoidable costs. Although this subject is discussed in Chapter IV, another example may help to illustrate the point.

Consider a firm that has three trucks. The sale value of these trucks on the secondhand market is $20,000 at the beginning of the period and $15,000 at the end. Assume for simplicity that all the firm's capital consists of equity funds and that the firm has an alternative to lend money at 6 per cent per period. The firm could sell the trucks at the

[4] Assuming that the supply function has infinite elasticity.

beginning of the period and thus save $5,000 of decline in value and earn $1,200 in interest by lending the released funds. The $6,200 is considered as avoidable cost of the trucking activity.[5] A special account must be established to absorb the extra charges of interest. Thus, a capital account should be established to which $1,200 is credited (see Section 3).

The figures for each external opportunity cost have to be searched for. They are not provided automatically by the internal information system, and often they have to be estimated rather than recorded from actual transactions. Nevertheless, these figures are needed for decision and evaluation purposes. Since the external opportunity cost figures are required, and hence are estimated, why not include them in the OAAS? [6]

2. Variable Costs on the Margin

Marginal cost is a crucial factor both in the theory of the firm and in actual management decisions. In practice, the exact shape of the production function of the firm or of a single process is often not known over the full range of production. Hence, there is no direct way to determine the marginal cost curve. In business, however, the marginal costs are usually estimated by means of average variable or direct costs. Only when the total variable cost curve is linear do average variable costs equal marginal costs.[7] An example is used as a frame of reference in the analysis.

Consider a farm pumping water for irrigation from two sources. The water is used by three segments, each large enough to require a manager. Data pertaining to the water are presented in Table 8, and

[5] It should be noted that these costs are avoidable in the context of a liquidation analysis pertaining to liquidation of trucks. They are not avoidable in the context of estimating unit costs for an additional hauling job.

[6] The procedure of including external opportunity costs in the system as avoidable costs complies with standard linear-programing formulation. The marketing of an input is considered as a separate activity with which production activities using the input must compete.

[7] For a discussion of the shape of the cost function in business, see, for example, Heflebower (1955, pp. 369–373), Alchian (1959), Johnston (1960, ch. 2), and Hirshleifer (1962).

Table 8. Data on water for irrigation

Source	Quantity available (units)	Variable costs (U.S. $/unit)	Usage (units)	Total costs (U.S. $)	Average costs (U.S. $/unit)
A	1,000,000	0.30	1,000,000	300,000	
B	Unlimited	0.45	500,000	225,000	
Total			1,500,000	525,000	0.35

the corresponding cost curves are charted in Figure 3. Only variable costs are considered—assuming, for the sake of simplicity, that external opportunity costs either do not exist or are included in the variable-cost figure. The example pertains to a cost function rising in steps, assuming that such a function is quite common in actual business.

Figure 3. Cost curves for water

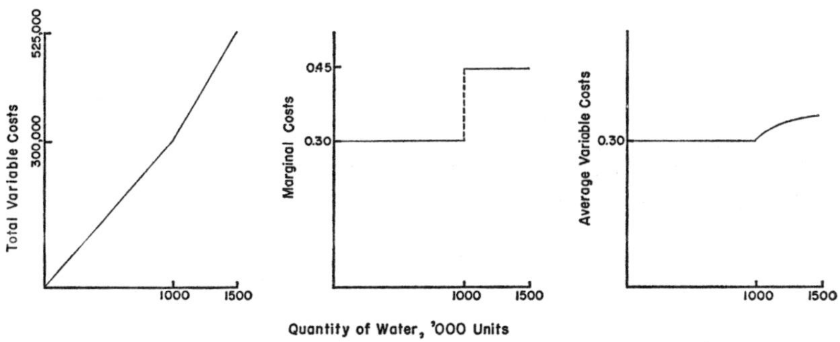

The cost of water on the margin is $0.45 when 1,500,000 units are used, since any increase (or any decrease up to 500,000 units) in the use of water affects only source B. For decision purposes, the cost of $0.45 per unit is appropriate. Suppose each of the segments using water is charged the average cost of $0.35. If a manager of a segment has to decide on the amount of water to be applied, he will use water inefficiently from an economic point of view because the marginal costs are $0.45 and he is informed that they are $0.35. Even if the manager knows the marginal costs, conventional accounting practices will lead him to consider the fictitious figure of $0.35, since his performance is measured and evaluated by this figure.[8]

Economically speaking, each price category (water from each source) is considered as a separate input, although physically they are perfect substitutes. The problem is how to match (in the analytical framework) the various types of inputs with production activities. In conventional accounting no distinction is made among the various types of inputs, and an average price is debited as a cost to the users of the homogeneous input, as illustrated in the example above.

Another procedure that induces misallocation of resources is to allocate the various types of inputs according to the paying ability of the activities using the input. Thus, the cheap input (source A) is allocated to the low-income activity, the more expensive one (source B) to the high-income activity. In a decision context, the decision maker, following or simulating the linear-programing iteration procedure, will first introduce into the program the high-income activity and the low-priced input, up to their capacities (constraints). In later iterations, low-income activities and high-cost inputs are introduced. These enter the program only if the low-income activity can "pay" for the high-priced input.[9]

The crucial test in resource allocation is at the margin: does it pay to produce the low-income product with the high-priced input? The fact that these two are included in the optimum program for the firm provides an affirmative answer. In the ex post analysis the same price at the margin should be used to test the decisions and their execution. Therefore the costs that hold at the margin are considered as avoidable costs and as such should be charged to the segments using the input.

[8] The procedure of reporting average variable costs may mislead managers in another direction. Managers certainly learn by means of trial-and-error experience. Suppose the volume of water use changes from one period to another. The periodical accounting reports, which show the costs corresponding to various levels of water use, will indicate that the average variable costs (surrogating marginal cost) increase when the usage increases (see the third curve in Figure 3). But the fact is that marginal costs do not change over a wide range of water use.

[9] These observations have also some implications for national resource allocation.

Under this procedure the total charges to the users are higher than the actual expenses for the input, a subject to be discussed in Section 3.

This analysis assumes a cost function rising in steps. However, the same analysis is applicable to a decreasing cost function. Such a situation exists where there are economies of scale. For example, the input (electricity) is purchased by special contract, the first quantity at a high price and extra units at a lower price.

Reporting costs of variable inputs as suggested above is appropriate only for decisions associated with the same marginal step of the cost function. Since most decisions concern the margins, this procedure of reporting is helpful. For decisions regarding expansion or contraction of operations beyond the marginal step, additional information is required. For decisions regarding liquidation of segment, total costs of variable inputs used by the segment should be provided. Average cost figures for variable inputs, together with costs on the margin, will indicate the general shape of the marginal cost curve—whether it is horizontal, increasing, or decreasing.

The discussion above implies that avoidable costs should be estimated in two contexts: analysis of the scale of operations (costs on the margin) and liquidation analysis (total avoidable costs). This requires a more elaborated and expensive reporting system. If only one cost item is to be reported, the first one (that is, avoidable costs on the margin) should be reported, since most decisions concern the margin.

Let us relax the assumption that the supply function for the firm's variable inputs is horizontal. It is quite reasonable to assume a function rising in steps, as charted in Figure 4. The volume of production determines the price of the input to be paid for all the purchased units. The firm purchases q units and pays p per unit. Note that p is paid for all the units. Therefore, this price, which is an ex post average price, is a reasonable cost figure to be used in the accounting reports. Of course, when the accounting data are used for decisions, the fact that price is determined by the scale of the operation should not be forgotten. In an ex ante context the price (p) holds for a certain range of activity because of the step nature of the function. Therefore, the reported price for the input can be used for decisions, as long as the

Figure 4. A supply curve

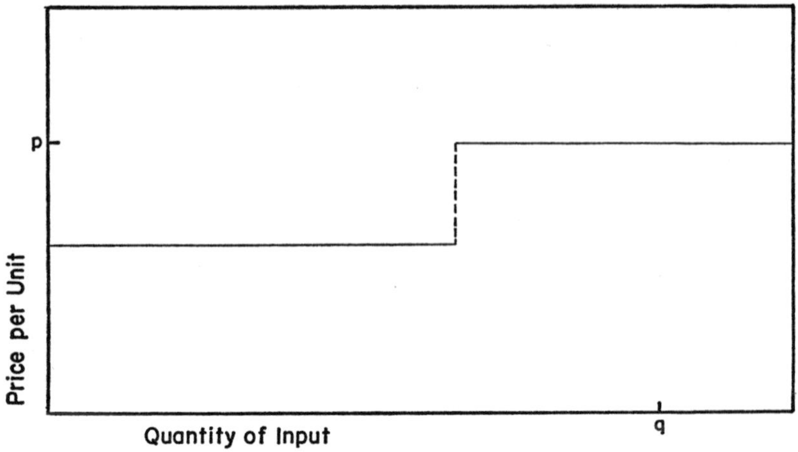

decision does not cause a change in volume beyond the marginal step.

The discussion in this chapter is related mainly to costs and inputs. But to obtain an income figure, revenue must be considered as well. The same kind of analysis made for input-supply function holds for the product-demand function, when the assumption of infinite elasticity is relaxed. Assuming that the demand function for the firm's output decreases, the price on the margin should be used for computing revenue. This holds also when a physically homogeneous output is sold at various price levels. For example, when a product is sold at a high price in the domestic market and at lower prices in foreign markets, or when different marketing expenses exist for the same product in various markets, the firm sells the same product for different levels of net revenue.

3. Rent Centers

In the first two sections we have suggested charging external opportunity costs which are implicit costs, not accrued cost items, and variable costs on the margin rather than using average costs. Adhering to these procedures may cause some complications in accounting. Special accounts must be established to meet these needs. These accounts are termed "rent centers."

Consider the earlier example, where a firm owns a warehouse of 50,000 square feet which can be rented for $0.50 per square foot per period. Each segment using the warehouse is charged $0.50 per square foot. Debiting the segments is balanced by crediting the warehouse account. Assume that there are no costs involved in holding the warehouse. The warehouse account will show income of $25,000. This income is the warehouse's implicit rent. It is suggested that in the OAAS such an account will be called a rent center and will stand side by side with contribution centers. Similarly, rent centers should be created for every self-owned resource that has a market price—that is, an external opportunity cost for its service.

Suppose that there is no market and hence no market price for warehouse services. Suppose further that the "internal demand" for warehouse space exceeds its size. Warehouse space has an internal opportunity cost—a shadow price. This price can be used as a determined value for the intermediate good, "warehouse service." In this case, however, the warehouse and each of the segments using its service will become artificial contribution centers. Recall that the contribution of an artificial contribution center can be used for evaluation purposes but not for allocation decisions. By charging the shadow price of the limited facility, the regular contribution centers are converted into artificial ones. The most important aspect of the OAAS—to provide data for decisions—will then be destroyed. Hence, shadow prices of the limited resources should not be included in the OAAS. The warehouse in this case is not considered as a segment.

Since the most important self-owned resource is capital, a rent center for capital should be created. This center has some special characteristics. It has two types of revenues. First, there is "realizable revenue," which is equal to the interest charged to the users of liquid assets. There is also "nonrealizable revenue," which is equal to the interest charged to the users of nonliquid assets. This distinction is made because interest charges in the first case are considered as avoidable costs, whereas in the second case they are nonavoidable costs. An example may be helpful.

Recall from Table 4 (Chapter IV) that firm A owns at the beginning of the year $45,000 worth of liquid assets, for which interest charges of

$4,500 are debited to the users. These charges are balanced by crediting the liquid-assets account as illustrated in Table 9. The firm owes

Table 9. An income statement for firm A's rent centers (capital accounts) (in U.S. dollars)

Item in analysis	Liquid assets	Nonliquid assets	Total
Revenue*	4,500	1,750	6,250
Avoidable costs	1,200		
Attained contribution	3,300		
Contribution to overhead†	3,300	1,750	5,050

* Computed from Tables 4 and 5.
† For simplicity, nonavoidable costs are not included.

$10,000 and $5,000 on short-term loans for which it is paying interest at 7 per cent and 10 per cent per year, respectively. The total interest payments are $1,200, to be debited to the liquid-assets account. If liquid assets are sold, the loans can be repaid.

There are two other situations where rent centers can or should be created, situations where costs are not incurred. First, consider the case of a rationed input—the example in Table 8. The total charges to the users are determined by the price at the margin: 1,500,000 × $0.45 = $675,000; whereas, the total costs are $525,000. Extra charges of $150,000 are recorded. This is due to the fact that water from source A costs $0.30 per unit, but the amount is limited to 1,000,000 units and extra water costs $0.45 per unit. Thus the $150,000 represents the economic rent to source A, and it will appear in the OAAS as the contribution of the rent center "water from source A."

Suppose the three segments using water consume 1,000,000, 400,000, and 100,000 units of water, respectively. Charging $0.45 per unit (marginal costs) rather than $0.35 (average costs) means a reduction in the contribution of each segment by the quantity of water used times $0.10 (0.45 — 0.35). The respective amounts are: $100,000, $40,000, and $10,000. The reduction in the contribution of the three segments totaling $150,000 is balanced by the contribution figure of the rent center.

Similarly, for any input characterized by an increasing (or decreasing) marginal-cost function, a rent center should be created. Under a case of decreasing marginal costs (economies of scale), the special account will show a loss. This loss indicates the required "subsidy" for marginal cost pricing.

Secondly, any account standing for gains of integration (see Chapter III) can be considered as a rent center, showing the rent to the factor "integration."

To summarize, rent centers should be established for special situations and to stand for special accounts. These centers should be treated like any other center in the OAAS. In the final analysis or in the income statement, the contribution of the rent centers may be added to the contribution of other segments or canceled while totals are figured. For the sake of simplicity in further discussion, only capital accounts will be considered as rent centers (Table 9).

4. Common Costs and Joint Products

The subject of common costs and joint products is a troublesome area in accounting. In conventional cost accounting, common costs are unitized and distributed to the users of the involved inputs or services. Since distribution of such costs must be discretionary by nature, this distorts the data for decision purposes and such action is eliminated in the OAAS.

When an analyst breaks down accounting data to determine the profitability of a segment, the question to be asked is: What would the income have been if the scale of this segment had been contracted or the segment had been dropped. To answer this question information on the attainable contribution (that is, revenue minus avoidable costs) is required.

Two cases are considered: where common costs serve several segments, and where common inputs are split among several products. The avoidable costs that are relevant to the two kinds of analyses differ somewhat. The various costs of production that are related to a segment or a group of segments must be established. The relevance of these to both scale and liquidation analyses is indicated and illustrated. For simplicity, the external opportunity cost is ignored in the analysis.

Variable Costs. Some inputs and their costs vary in direct proportion to the volume of production. These are variable costs. Some inputs such as equipment are used in a lump sum, leading to a discontinuous step function. The costs of these inputs are considered semivariable, since the volume of production can be changed over a given range without changing these costs. Whether these costs are approximated by a smooth function or considered as a step function, they are a function of the scale of the operation, and thus are avoidable.

Common Costs for a Segment. Some cost items (such as management) that are incurred by a segment are not affected by the scale of production. These costs may be avoidable if the segment is liquidated. In other words, these cost items have a dual meaning. For one analysis (scale) they are considered as nonavoidable and ignored; for another analysis (liquidation) they may be considered as avoidable. Therefore these costs are considered and reported separately.

Common Costs for a Group of Segments. Some cost items may be avoidable if liquidation of a whole group of segments is considered. These costs are ignored in analyzing each segment. However, these costs, being avoidable in some cases, should not be ignored in a subsequent analysis of the group as a whole. Thus, overhead for a department can be considered as avoidable when the department is liquidated (Table 10, last column). In other words, the more lines of production included in a segment, the larger the portion of common costs that can be identified with the segment. Some common costs are determined by the formation of a group of segments. There are different costs for each different combination. The more possible combinations there are, the less chance there is of recording and reporting these costs as avoidable. Overhead for the whole firm never is considered as avoidable to a segment, because of the going concern assumption which eliminates the alternative of liquidating the whole firm.

An example of this costing procedure may help to illustrate the application of these concepts. A simplified example of reporting the various kinds of costs and in turn the resulting contribution is presented in Table 10. Some comments should be made with respect to this table: (1) Only the direct avoidable costs such as variable inputs or inventories (row 1) can be unitized; that is, be figured per unit of

Table 10. Two kinds of avoidable costs and the resulting contribution (in U.S. dollars)

Item in analysis	Segment A	Segment B	Total
1. Avoidable costs (direct costs)	15,000	17,000	32,000
2. Common cost for each segment	2,000	3,000	5,000
3. (Subtotal: Avoidable cost for segment)	(17,000)	(20,000)	(37,000)
4. Common cost for both segments			7,000
5. Total			44,000
6. Revenue	22,000	21,000	43,000
7. Contribution for scale analysis	7,000	4,000	
8. Contribution for liquidation analysis	5,000	1,000	−1,000

product. These are the figures to be considered when the scale of a segment is under analysis. (2) All the avoidable costs should be considered, including the common costs which are avoidable, if a liquidation analysis is carried out. In row 8, each segment has a positive contribution (for liquidation analysis), but both segments together have a negative contribution. The firm would be better off if both segments are liquidated. (3) Suppose the common costs for both segments (row 4) are distributed to the two segments, as is practiced in conventional cost accounting. The distribution could be made proportional to direct costs (row 1). Thus, out of the $7,000, $3,300 and $3,700 are distributed to segments A and B, respectively. In this case the income of segment A is $5,000 — $3,300 = $1,700; the income of segment B is $1,000 — $3,700 = —$2,700. It is easy to see how the results of such a practice may be misleading. (4) Nonavoidable costs, such as the cost of nonliquid assets, and the firm's overhead costs are not included in the analysis.

The subject of scale and liquidation analysis may be extended to another situation, in which the firm uses a multipriced, physically homogeneous input (section 2). An example is used as a frame of reference. Consider firm A, which holds the following liquid assets: cows and heifers valued at $36,000 and steers valued at $9,000. The firm owes \$10,000 and \$5,000 on short-term loans for which it is paying interest at 7 per cent and 10 per cent per year, respectively. The appropriate rate of interest to be considered as avoidable cost for scale analysis is the 10 per cent rate. If the scale of any of the herds is reduced, short-term debt with an interest rate of 10 per cent can be repaid. Thus the corresponding avoidable costs for the steers are \$900. But this argument holds only for \$5,000; that is, it holds for only the marginal step on the supply function for capital. If the steers are liquidated, short-term debt of \$9,000 will be repaid: \$5,000 at 10 per cent and \$4,000 at 7 per cent. In this case, the avoidable costs for the liquidation analysis are: $5{,}000 \times 0.10 + 4{,}000 \times 0.07 = \$780$. This illustrates again the need for two sets of data for different decisions concerning the same subject. To make the reports simpler, it is suggested that only avoidable costs on the margin be reported. The avoidable costs needed for liquidation analysis, whether common costs or a multipriced input, should not be ignored. For the same reason, common costs are considered as nonavoidable costs.

Joint Products. Costing joint products requires separate consideration. When a production process yields more than one output, usually in some constant ratio, the outputs are defined as joint products—for example, refining crude oil, packing meat, and production of sugar beets yielding beets (for sugar) and tops (for fodder). Milk, meat, calves, and manure are all produced jointly by a cow. However, in this case some of the products (milk, calves) can be considered as intermediate goods which may be transferred at their market price to another segment (see Table 1, Chapter III).

The conventional practice is to distribute the cost of the common inputs to the various products produced simultaneously from it or, in some cases, to subtract the sale value of the by-product from the cost of the inputs. A procedure for handling joint products is suggested by using the practice of a linear-programing formulation of the problem as an analogy. Each of the joint products is considered as a separate activity, conditioned or constrained by the activity for the common input. Consider an example.

Suppose two products, A and B, are produced from a given raw material. The raw material and both products require some processing.

Hence, each is considered as a separate activity (in a linear-programing sense). The processing activities, standing for both products A and B, are conditioned by the raw material activity.

The various joint products, whether they are considered "co-products" or "by-products," can be defined as subactivities. The avoidable costs and the revenue for each subactivity on the one hand, and the avoidable cost of the common input (activity), on the other hand, should be reported separately and jointly. This costing procedure is illustrated in Table 11.

Table 11. The avoidable costs and contributions of joint products (in U.S. dollars)

Item in analysis	Raw material	Product A	Product B	Total
Avoidable cost	10,000	4,000	3,000	17,000
Revenue		22,500	2,500	25,000
Contribution	−10,000	18,500	−500	8,000

The kind of reporting illustrated in the table provides directly the information required for decisions and for analysis using a linear-programing formulation. The contribution measured for each subactivity provides a surrogate for allocation decisions and motivation. An important aspect here is that the costs of the common input ($10,000) should not be unitized and distributed to the final products. In the final OAAS report the figures pertaining to the individual subactivities should be grouped as one contribution center, represented by the last column.

Distribution of common costs may be meaningless or even misleading. This has been shown to hold when the common cost serves several segments (Table 10) or when there is a common input from which joint products are produced (Table 11). Vatter (1954, p. 1704) summarizes these ideas well: "The real problem of cost accounting . . . is not so much the working out of 'bases for distribution' joint costs but of establishing when and how much cost is relevant to a given question."

5. The Firm's Overhead as a Cost Center

A distinction is made between two types of overhead or common costs: those that accrue to a segment or a group of segments together, termed "common costs," and those that accrue to the firm at large and are not traceable to individual or groups of segments, termed "firm's overhead" or "overhead." Neither of these types of cost is distributed: the common costs are not distributed to the units of production (unitized); the overhead costs are not distributed to the segments.

Conventionally, overhead costs, or true fixed costs, are distributed to the segments or the individual production processes. In the OAAS these costs, after the traceable items are charged to the responsible segments, are kept in the aggregate in a cost center. "Cost center" means a segment for which only costs are measured. These costs can be evaluated, analyzed, and thus controlled best in the aggregate.

Under the OAAS there are two kinds of centers: contribution centers and cost centers. The first includes both production and service activities and rent centers. A multiproduct or integrated firm should be decomposed into several contribution centers, even if some of them are artificial contribution centers. A cost center deals mainly with administrative activities. Again, in a large firm, there might be several cost centers of this kind.

There are two types of costs that are traceable and therefore charged to the individual segments—avoidable and nonavoidable costs. An administrative department has avoidable costs and nonavoidable costs, which in total make up overhead costs.

Distributing and charging overhead costs to the various segments of a firm may provide misleading information.[10] For example, it may cause a paper loss for a segment even though this segment is economically efficient (provides a contribution) and is useful to the firm. Thus, it may lead to bad decisions. It also undermines the motivations of lower-level managers (see Chapter XV).

The act of charging overhead costs to the firm's segments can be compared to the action of levying taxes by a government. There is one

[10] Walters (1960) claims that under certain conditions it is rational to distribute these costs.

crucial difference, however, which is relevant to the discussion. The government has to levy taxes on autonomous economic units in order to meet its commitments. The firm and its segments, on the other hand, are one economic unit. As a result, there is no need to charge each segment some share of overhead costs. The act of charging overhead, just as levying a tax, creates a reaction and resentment from the "taxed" units. Any distribution is necessarily discretionary or arbitrary. A manager at a lower level whose performance is measured by total cost or by profits calculated in this manner would naturally resist such an "arbitrary tax" or argue about its calculation and incidence. Everyone who is familiar with practical accounting problems in business can quote cases of dispute concerning this point. What is it needed for? Dean (1958, p. 9) says: "After all, the president knows what his own salary is and how it is determined. Of what help is it to him to see how somebody thinks it ought to be spread over the various divisions?"

Unfortunately, the problem of distributing overhead and common costs is quite an issue in textbooks of cost accounting and in practical application.[11] It is of interest to quote a statement by an authority like Paton (1949, p. 522): "In general, it is better to deal with common or joint costs in total, without allocation, than it is to distribute such charges artificially, thus obscuring departmental data which have considerable significance and suggesting conclusions of very doubtful validity."

A common presentation made by proponents of the distribution of common and overhead costs is of this kind: If these costs were not distributed to the segments, who would pay them? Of course, top management would like the earnings of its segments to cover all the overhead (it would like to earn much more). However, this desirability would not be improved by distributing them. The distribution procedure may also encourage the political skills of the managers instead of stressing economic incentives. The author recalls a department manager stating proudly, "Yesterday I earned the highest income in a long time—I convinced the accountant to deduct $20,000 of unjust overhead charges to my department."

[11] Schrader (1959, pp. 70–74) provides a short review of the evolution of the distribution of common costs.

To summarize, economic analysis indicates that overhead costs should be kept in the aggregate, after charging the traceable parts to segments. These costs can be analyzed best in an aggregate form. If overheads "must" be distributed, as for example, in a decentralized firm,[12] the distribution should be based on an intrafirm arrangement well recognized as essentially noneconomic in character. It should pass one test: not to lead toward misallocation of resources. One possible method for such distribution is suggested by Shubik (1964). According to his formula, as long as the whole firm has profits and all segments make positive contributions, the distribution of overhead would always leave a positive income for each segment.[13]

6. Summary and Conclusions

Costs are classified according to their traceability to the segments of the firm. Overhead costs that are not traceable are not distributed to the segments. The traceable costs are classified into avoidable and nonavoidable costs. The latter type is composed mainly of the costs related to nonliquid assets and common costs.

The terms "avoidable costs" and "nonavoidable costs" are not a substitute for the conventional terms "variable costs" and "fixed costs." The terms "avoidable costs" and "variable costs" convey similar connotations, unlike the terms "fixed costs" and "nonavoidable costs." While fixed costs are composed mainly of depreciation on assets, common costs, and overhead costs, nonavoidable costs include depreciation and interest on nonliquid assets and common costs. Overhead costs are not included in the nonavoidable costs.

The main cost concept in the OAAS is avoidable cost. This cost figure surrogates for the more theoretical concept of marginal cost, but it surrogates marginal costs only for a given volume of production. Avoidable costs include both the costs of variable inputs and external opportunity costs. Since this cost concept stands for all the controllable costs, it suits for both decision and motivation purposes. Subtracting this cost

[12] Notable is the practice of the National Tea Co. not to distribute overheads to individual stores (National Commission on Food Marketing 1966, p. 491).

[13] This method has the character of an "income tax," while the traditional distribution methods (usually based on one of the direct inputs) have the character of a "direct tax."

figure from the revenue provides for the attainable contribution (see Chapter II).

When average variable costs equal variable cost on the margin and when external opportunity costs do not exist (marketable intermediate goods, liquid assets, and other inventories do not take part in production), variable costs equal avoidable costs. If these conditions do not hold, both cost figures differ.

The avoidable-cost figure includes external opportunity costs, on the one hand, and is a factor in determining the internal opportunity cost, on the other. This provides additional weight to the avoidable-cost concept in a decision-making framework.

It should be noted that external opportunity costs are implicit not explicit costs. Including these costs in the OAAS is contrary to accepted (conventional) accounting principles. The figures for the external opportunity cost must be searched for. Often they are not the result of actual transactions made by the firm. Sometimes judgment must be exercised in estimating these figures. But both the search activity and assertion of judgment are required for management decisions. Including these figures in the OAAS will provide the required data for decisions in a more systematic procedure.

The fact that there is no single cost figure that suits all kinds of decisions (for example, scale or liquidation decisions) should be kept in mind. The particular cost required differs from one problem to another.

Common costs, whether they are common to a segment or a group of segments or originate in a common input from which joint products are produced, should not be distributed to the production units.

Overhead costs should not be distributed to segments. By not distributing overhead costs, management of a firm must recognize that it is impossible to evaluate the final net contribution (profit) of any segment of the firm.

VI
THE INCOME STATEMENT: AN EXAMPLE AND AN EMPIRICAL TEST

The discussion in Chapter II suggested that one unequivocal, objective income figure that is best in all circumstances cannot be determined. It is suggested here that four types of contribution margins be used: for a segment—attainable contribution and contribution to overhead; for a firm as a whole—net contribution from operations and net contribution to owners. Contribution margin is defined as revenue minus some set of appropriate costs, where revenue is the sum of realized and realizable revenue and appropriate costs are made up of several explicit and implicit cost items. Among the costs are implicit interest charges (except for the last type of contribution).

The contribution margin includes the gains or losses resulting from a price-level change. The effect of price-level change might be singled out as Edwards and Bell (1961) suggest, by differentiating between holding gains (or losses) resulting from a rise (or decline) in values of assets, and operating profits, resulting from the use of the assets per se. For the sake of simplicity, this procedure is not incorporated in the present analysis. Nevertheless, when there are significant price-level changes this differentiation should be carried out.[1]

[1] This differentiation has some shortcomings, since management decides on both factors simultaneously. For example, a process with relatively low income

The uses of each of the contribution margins in regard to a segment or contribution center and the firm at large are discussed below. An income statement for firm A is presented at the end of each section (Tables 12 and 13) to illustrate the application of these contribution margins.

1. Income Measures for a Segment

Attainable contribution, the first type of contribution margin listed above, has been defined in Chapter II as the difference between revenue and avoidable cost. The second type, contribution to overhead, is calculated by subtracting from the segment's revenue all the traceable costs (avoidable costs and nonavoidable costs) or by subtracting the nonavoidable costs from the attainable contribution.

The attainable contribution is evaluated in terms of a change in the scale of operations (contraction), assuming for the sake of simplicity an avoidable cost curve that is linear per unit. If income that would be lost if a segment were liquidated is to be evaluated, further analysis might be required. Some of the common-cost items might be considered in this case as "liquidation avoidable costs."

The attainable contribution is the result of charging only avoidable costs that are, in fact, also controllable by management. Therefore, this figure is used for allocation decisions and for motivation of lower-level managers. The contribution to overhead, on the other hand, since it is the result of charging all costs incurred by the segment, is the figure to be used for comparisons.

The difference between these two types of contribution is nonavoidable costs. Perhaps the main item of nonavoidable costs is represented by the capital charges for the services of durable nonliquid assets. These charges effect the two contribution figures in two ways.

First, while computing the attainable contribution, the liquidation values of all assets are considered. (The liquidation values of nonliquid assets are considered to be zero; see Chapter IV). While com-

---

from operations may be retained because management expects some holding gains from keeping the assets used for this process. The sum of income from operations and holding gains makes this process "efficient" enough to be continued. See Drake and Dopuch (1965) on this subject.

puting the contribution to overhead, the replacement costs of the nonliquid assets are considered. (The replacement costs of the liquid assets are close to the liquidation value, therefore only one—the latter—is considered). As a result, the attainable-contribution figure fits for decisions pertaining to contraction of the scale of a segment or even its liquidation. The contribution to overhead, on the other hand, provides some crude information for expansion decisions.

Second, the capital charges for the services of durable nonliquid assets are based on the "appraised value" of the assets—a subjective estimate made by the analyst and therefore judgmental in nature. The avoidable costs, on the other hand, are not a result of an analyst's judgment (except for the value of goods in process). Both types of contribution have some deficiencies as measures of a segment's performance. The contribution to overhead includes all the traceable costs, but some of the cost items are based on estimates or on judgment. The attainable contribution does not include all the cost items, but it is not based on estimates.

In Chapter III, two types of contribution centers were distinguished: regular and artificial. For each, both contribution figures are computed. A regular contribution center can often be decomposed into several artificial contribution centers. The income measures of the artificial contribution centers are used for evaluation purposes. For allocation decisions, the contributions from a group of related artificial contribution centers should be consolidated. A simplified income statement for both types of contribution center pertaining to firm A is presented in Table 12.

In Chapter V the notion of two additional centers was introduced, namely the rent center and the cost center. The income measures for a rent center, like those for any other contribution center, should be used for both allocation decisions and evaluation purposes. The cost measures for a cost center replaces the income measure of a contribution center in evaluating performance. Some of the arguments pertaining to the income measures, as indicated in Chapter II, apply to cost centers as well. The concepts of attainable contribution and contribution to overhead used in considering contribution centers are respec-

Table 12. A simplified income statement for the segments of firm A (in U.S. dollars)

	Regular contribution centers*				Artificial contribution centers	
Item in analysis	Total	Ice cream	Steers	Cows (and heifers)	Cows	Heifers
Revenue	152,500	70,000	15,000	67,500	66,000	12,000
Avoidable costs:						
Variable inputs	55,000	4,000	11,000	40,000	30,000	10,000
Intermediate goods	62,500	60,000	2,500		9,000	1,500
Liquid assets	9,500		900	8,600	8,000	600
(Total)	(127,000)	(64,000)	(14,400)	(48,600)	(47,000)	(12,100)
Attainable contribution	25,500	6,000	600	18,900	19,000	−100
(Nonavoidable costs, total)	(6,250)	(950)	(300)	(5,000)	(4,750)	(250)
Contribution to overhead	19,250	5,050	300	13,900	14,250	−350

* Data from Tables 1, 3, 4, and 5.

tively comparable to the concepts of avoidable costs and avoidable and nonavoidable costs used in considering cost centers.

2. Income Measures for the Whole Firm

The discussion in the previous chapters involved only the individual segments of the firm. Aggregating the costs and income figures of the individual segments would not always provide the relevant figures for the whole firm, mainly because individual assets rather than the whole firm are valued. Discussing the problems of the valuation of and income measurement for the whole firm is beyond the scope of this study. In order to provide a better presentation, however, the relevance of the former discussion to the whole firm is briefly pursued here.

It is suggested that two types of contribution figures be used for the whole firm: net contribution from operations and net contribution to owners. The difference between the two types of net contribution results from including or omitting implicit interest charges (or the contribution of the rent centers) from the contribution figure. The net contribution from operations includes these implicit costs and is the smaller figure. Net contribution to owners, on the other hand, does not include these costs. The rules for calculating the net contribution figures for the whole firm and the contribution margins for various types of segments are as follows

Single center:

- Regular contribution center: attainable contribution − nonavoidable costs = contribution to overhead
- Artificial contribution center: attainable contribution − nonavoidable costs = contribution to overhead
- Rent center (mainly capital accounts): revenue − avoidable and non-avoidable costs = "rent"
- Cost center: avoidable costs + nonavoidable costs = overhead

Centers in aggregate:

- Regular contribution centers: contribution to overhead − overhead = net contribution from operations; net contribution from operations + rent = net contribution to owners
- Whole firm: revenue − total costs = net contribution to owners

The net contribution from operations is the residual after charging all costs, including the implicit costs for the "services" of the variables that are included in the rent centers, mainly interest on capital. As such, it is now appropriate for measuring performance and making comparisons. This is because all the costs (explicit and implicit) are charged to operations. The debits and credits for the intersegment transfers within the regular contribution centers cancel each other when total costs are deducted from total revenue.

The net contribution to owners is the residual after charging only the explicit costs and the change in value of assets (depreciation charges).[2] The debits and credits for the transfers between the rent centers and the regular contribution centers cancel each other when total costs are deducted from total revenue. Hence the implicit costs for the "services" rendered by the rent centers (mainly interest on capital) are recorded for internal analysis but do not affect the contribution figures for the firm as a whole—the net contribution to owners.

The net contribution to owners is comparable to the conventional profit figure. The difference lies in the pricing methods used for temporal transfers (of assets); that is, the pricing of inventories and depreciation of durables. While the net contribution is based on current values, profit is based on historical values.[3] The net contribution to owners can be considered as a return on self-owned capital, or economic rent. Thus this contribution margin should be used in establishing dividend policy.

Attainable contribution is not measured for the whole firm. Such a measure, which assumes liquidation of the firm by definition, is in conflict with the going-concern assumption.[4]

[2] The depreciation charges are based on the change in value of the individual assets. The change in value of the whole firm might differ from the summation of the changes in values of the individual assets. A major innovation during an accounting period causes the value of some assets to drop considerably. If one wants to eliminate such an outcome to keep the income stream flowing more smoothly for dividend policy purposes, an internal insurance system can be implemented (see Chapter IV, Section 7).

[3] Holding gains (or losses) due to price level changes, which are included in this contribution figure, might be singled out in the report.

[4] Summing up the avoidable costs for all the segments does not provide the avoidable cost figure for the firm at large, since some of the common-cost items

Table 13. An income statement for firm A (in U.S. dollars)

Item in analysis	Firm at large	Cost centers (total)	Rent centers (total)*	Regular contribution centers (total)
Revenue	158,750		6,250	152,500
Avoidable costs:				
Variable inputs				55,000
Intermediate goods				62,500
Liquid assets				9,500
(Total)	(130,200)†	(2,000)	(1,200)	(127,000)
Attainable contribution				25,500
(Nonavoidable costs, total)‡	(9,250)†	(3,000)		(6,250)
Contribution to overhead			5,050§	19,250
(Overhead, total)		(5,000)		(5,000)
Net contribution from operations				14,250
Net contribution to owners	19,300‖			

Source: Tables 9 and 12.

* A full treatment of these accounts requires details that are ignored here for simplicity.

† This figure sums up the entries in the other columns.

‡ Only charges for nonliquid assets are included. Common costs are ignored for simplicity.

§ This figure has been termed "rent" in the text.

‖ Depreciation (change in durables' values) at the level of $9,500 is included in the costs (Tables 4 and 5).

An income statement for firm A, as illustrated in Table 13, provides

that are considered as nonavoidable costs are avoidable for the firm at large, nonliquid assets might be liquid in this case, the value of the whole firm differs from the values assigned to the individual assets, and some of the overhead costs are avoidable.

an example of the computations required to obtain the four contribution margins.

3. An Empirical Test: Conventional and OAAS Income Statements for a Firm

The OAAS can perhaps be illustrated most succinctly by a brief description of the final results (in terms of an income statement) of its application to a large, diversified farm in New York State. Although the empirical test pertains to a farm, inference can be drawn from this application to firms in other industries, since the farm resembles a manufacturing firm in some respects; some of the farm's activities—trucking, warehousing, construction—are typically nonagricultural.

The objective of the test was to assess the applicability of the OAAS and to gain more insights into the use of the system. In particular the objective was to get answers to the following questions: How can the OAAS be applied in practice? Does the information it provides differ from that provided by conventional cost-accounting systems? How valuable is the OAAS information to the management of the firm?

The second question is answered in this section and the third in the next. Because of space limitations, a full answer to the first question is beyond the scope of this discussion, but it may be said here that this test indicated that the OAAS procedures are applicable in practice and that the OAAS can be installed without difficulty as a subsystem of the conventional accounting system.

The test farm cultivates 3,500 acres of cropland. It has a fleet of tractors and a fleet of trucks, buildings for storing the machinery and keeping the livestock, and a large warehouse for storing some of the finished products. The analysis covered operations in the year 1967. The farm's receipts that year were approximately $800,000. The retained earning declared by the financial income statement was approximately $78,000. The end-of-the-year value of the land, buildings, equipment, and livestock, as recorded in the financial balance sheet, was approximately $500,000, but the valuation for the OAAS was close to $1,000,000.

The farm had a good set of accounts that were used as a basis for establishing the accounts that are reported here. To save labor, the

Table 14. Summary of an income statement for a New York State farm, 1967, conventional accounting and OAAS (in U.S. dollars)

Account items	Conventional accounting, profit	OAAS, attainable contribution	Difference
Cash crops:			
1. Crop A	97,837	132,872	35,035
2. Crop B	36,473	47,068	10,595
3. Crop C	21,336	40,138	18,802
4. Crop D	23,088	22,320	− 768
5. Crop E	5,965	11,547	5,582
6. Crop F	2,575	3,072	497
7. Crop G	− 1,558	− 1,571	− 13
8. Crop H	−17,574	− 7,561	10,013
9. Experimental crops	− 1,875	82	1,957
Total	166,267	247,967	81,700
Livestock:			
10. Cows		22,630	
11. Heifers		− 3,772	
12. Fodder		− 3,312	
Total	− 4,480	15,546	20,026
Services:*			
13. Trucks		2,368	
14. Warehouse		− 2,087	
15. Construction		5,449	
16. Land, own		2,406	
17. Houses, own		1,038	
18. Land, rented		2,588	
19. Farm B, rented		2,595	
Total		14,357	14,357
Capital account		36,361	36,361
Overhead		−83,310	−83,310
Miscellaneous	1,179	274	− 905

Table 14 (continued)

Account items	Conventional accounting, profit	OAAS, attainable contribution	Difference
Adjustments:			
Investment†		−15,177	−15,177
Depreciation‡		− 6,252	− 6,252
Realizable revenue§		−46,800	−46,800
Total‖	162,966	162,966	0

* See note 6.

† Expense items that are charged as costs for 1967 in conventional accounting, but are considered as investment in the OAAS.

‡ Depreciation charges for buildings under conventional accounting. In calculating the attainable contribution, the costs associated with nonliquid assets are not charged.

§ See note 5.

‖ Special expenses, such as bonuses and advanced purchase of inventories, exceeded special revenues, such as certificates, by about $49,000. Income tax was approximately $36,000. The residual for retained earning amounts to about $78,000, as is declared by the financial income statement.

existing system was used as a framework for two other systems: the OAAS—by discarding some of the data, introducing additional data, and making some necessary adjustments in the accounts—and a conventional accounting system based on accepted accounting principles. The latter, required for comparison with the OAAS, had to be prepared afresh since the existing system violated some of the accepted principles. The use of the existing set of books helped to prove that the OAAS can be carried out as a part of the general accounting system.

All the OAAS procedures were not applied to the farm's data because there were time limitations, the types of operation did not require it, and the data did not warrant it. Moreover, only the attainable contribution figures, those required for allocation decisions, are reported and discussed here.

Two income statements for the analyzed farm are presented and compared in Table 14. It should be noted that, in general, the level of income of the individual segments as reported by the OAAS is higher than the corresponding conventional accounting figures. Overhead costs and costs associated with nonliquid assets are not included in the OAAS costs. On the other hand, external opportunity costs (interest charges, intermediate goods at market price) are included.

On the revenue side, most of the revenue figures are equal in both systems. For three crops, however, the OAAS revenue figures are higher. The present value of future revenue that is not recorded as accounts receivable (cooperative certificates) is considered in the OAAS as a realizable revenue, and thus included in the revenue figure.[5]

4. Some Implications for Management Decisions

Some of the significant differences between the income figures of both accounting systems should be indicated. These differences have important implications for, and some (conceivable or real) effects on, management decisions.

The firm's operations are grouped in the OAAS income statement (Table 14) into three types of segments: cash crops—regular production activities, the product of which is sold on the market; the livestock enterprise—including both a regular production activity (cows that produce milk for sale) and two activities (heifers and fodder) that produce intermediate goods; and services—contribution centers that are established for those activities that produce services that can be traded on the market. Implications pertaining to each type of segment are discussed below. For the sake of simplicity, the figures as reported for 1967 are considered as "normal"; that is, the management expects future conditions and thus the results of the operations to resemble those in 1967.

[5] Realizable revenue in a form of certificates given by a processing cooperative, to be redeemed in the future, is credited to crops A, B, and C ($31,500, $2,300, and $13,000, respectively). These certificates are not considered as accounts receivable, since they are granted only after the accounting books are closed. Hence this revenue is not credited to the respective crops under conventional accounting. The face value of the certificates is $78,000; the computed present value that is credited to the crops is $46,800.

Intermediate Goods and Services. An important difference between the two accounting systems can be seen in the contribution centers established for the activities that produce intermediate goods and services, namely segments 11 to 19 in Table 14.[6] The OAAS income statement provides an important insight into these segments of the firm. Specifically, it indicates the profitability of the service activities. The income figures provide the best criterion for evaluating these activities, despite the fact that the contribution figures are a result of an estimate of market prices. (The market prices are used to value the intermediate goods and services that are produced or rendered by these activities, and in turn these values provide the revenues for the corresponding segments).

The low income or loss that some of these segments show would certainly initiate some further investigation. Management should, for example, check the reasons for the reported level of income, examine its policy concerning some of these activities, or recheck the level of market prices used in the analysis and simultaneously examine the possibility of buying rather than producing some intermediate goods and services. Thus it is quite reasonable to examine the possibility of purchasing heifers and fodder—the intermediate goods that are produced internally—and liquidating these activities (segments 11 and 12), which create a considerable loss. In fact, the management of the farm considered the new type of information—that is, the income statements for the special segments—as valuable. The chief executive indicated several uses and decisions that this information might generate.

Cash Crops. The differences in both accounting systems' reported income for most of the cash crops is not of major significance. A profitable production process will show income under any accounting system. But this fact is known to management without the accounting report. The same holds for a process that is losing. The crucial test of

[6] These segments can be divided into five groups: heifers and fodder (segments 11 and 12) that produce intermediate goods for one segment—cows; trucks and warehouse (segments 13 and 14) that render services to various cash crops; construction of buildings for farm use (segment 15); own land and houses that are "rented" internally; and contracts for rented land (several contracts) and for rented farm, including land, houses, and barns.

the accounting report concerns those segments whose income is marginal, or those segments whose scale of operations is examined. Let us check one case.

Suppose that management considers liquidating one of the two marginal crops E and F (segments 5 and 6). Suppose further that either of these crops substitutes for the other, acre for acre. If one of these crops is liquidated, the other is planted instead. The following income figures are relevant for a decision on these crops: crop E (214 acres)—per acre income under conventional accounting, $27.9, under the OAAS, $54; crop F (66 acres)—per acre income under conventional accounting, $39, under the OAAS, $46.5. Note that the two systems provide conflicting recommendations. While crop E generates a higher per acre contribution, conventional accounting figures suggest liquidating this crop. The reason for the conflicting recommendations is the conventional practice of charging the segments with fixed costs.

Livestock. Here is another example of conventional accounting's income figures supplying misleading information. While under conventional accounting this enterprise has a loss, it shows a considerable contribution under the OAAS despite the losses accrued by the heifers and fodder (segments 11 and 12) serving this enterprise. In other words, the OAAS report shows that without the livestock enterprise, the firm's income in 1967 would have been lower by approximately $15,000. This is true, assuming that the heifers and fodder (segments 11 and 12) cannot be liquidated without liquidating the cows (segment 10) and that there is no alternative profitable use for the resources employed by this enterprise. The OAAS report, nevertheless, provides information for checking these assumptions as well.

To summarize, the OAAS income statement provides more and better information for management decisions than the conventional accounting income statement. In some cases the two systems provide figures that suggest conflicting conclusions about the profitability of segments. As a result, the conventional accounting figures may lead toward a wrong decision.

Part Two
Extensions

VII
COST INFORMATION FOR PRICE SETTING AND MICROECONOMIC AND MACROECONOMIC IMPLICATIONS

The main objective of the OAAS outlined in this book is to provide information for decisions on resource allocation, assuming that the prices for the firm's product are given. The system can also provide correctly specified cost data for pricing decisions when such decisions are partly under the control of management. To understand the role of cost calculations in pricing decisions as related to the OAAS, we must examine the special features of the OAAS compared with the conventional accounting system in providing cost data and the conceivable effects caused by the use of either accounting system in pricing decisions.

The special aspect of the OAAS is that it is based on such economic concepts as marginal analysis and opportunity cost—concepts that are not used in accepted accounting principles and procedures. Specifically, the OAAS provides an operational procedure for estimating marginal costs (at a given level of production) from the firm's accounts.

The use of the OAAS for internal decisions should improve a firm's resource allocation. It might also improve resource allocation in the economy if it is used for pricing decisions. This chapter, however, concentrates on the conceivable effect of using cost information from the OAAS on price flexibility in the economy, especially when many firms do so.[1]

1. The Role of Cost Information in Business Pricing Decisions

Many business firms exercise some control in setting prices for their products; that is, the management has enough market power to set the selling price of its product. A price is set when the firm produces a completely new product, a variant of an old product, or a product that exists on the market but is new to the firm. Whenever a product can be differentiated clearly, its price is partly under the control of management. The decision maker is regularly concerned with whether to change the price and by how much.

Anyone who makes decisions on prices presumably needs at least expectations about the demand curve for the product of the firm, the actions of rivals and the government, and costs of production for different levels of output. While the information concerning the first two points is vague and the expectations are based often on experience and judgment, information concerning ex post costs for a given production level is tangible and can be procured relatively easily. This ex post information is considered as a surrogate for ex ante costs and, after adjustments, is used for decisions.

Heflebower (1955, p. 392) concludes his study and review of pricing decisions by stating the following hypothesis on the full-cost pricing doctrine: "[Under conditions of] uncertainty both about rivals' reactions to price moves and future development impinging on the group . . . firms may place more faith in cost guides than in considerations ordinarily viewed as reflecting demand." Whether or not Heflebower's hypothesis is correct and still holds at present, the pricing decision maker needs information on costs.

Economic theory teaches that marginal costs are required for these decisions. Many studies assert, however, that in practice businessmen use full-cost data for their pricing decisions (see Appendix A). It is beyond the scope of this chapter to discuss the problem of which costs are really in use. It is assumed that a sound accounting system should

[1] There is a place for further study of welfare and taxation effects induced by the use of the OAAS procedures by many firms.

provide the cost figures or surrogates for both marginal and total costs. Unfortunately, conventional accounting methods fail to provide correct estimates for these cost figures.[2] Hence the use of the OAAS is suggested to surmount some of the limitations of the conventional method.

2. Cost Specifications for Pricing: Conventional Accounting and OAAS Procedures

The pricing decision maker would like to obtain from the accounting system cost figures that can be used as surrogates for marginal costs and total costs. The surrogate for marginal cost also usually provides the figure that suggests the floor below which prices should not be set.[3]

The various items included in the figures surrogating both marginal and total costs in either conventional accounting or the OAAS can be summarized as follows. A multiproduct, monopolistic firm, for which the prices of the intermediate goods are given, is assumed.

This summary illustrates the differences between the main cost figures included in either of the accounting systems. Almost all the cost items in the OAAS are based on current market prices, whereas in conventional accounting most of the costs reflect historical acquisition costs. This difference is of major importance in an economy in

[2] For a presentation and criticism of the traditional cost and pricing methods, see Tucker (1966).

[3] Some clarification is required regarding the establishment of a floor below which price will not be allowed to go. Management has to get information about appropriate costs which will prevent sustaining losses. Usually the surrogate for marginal costs (variable costs) provides this figure. The marginal cost figure should be used as long as there is excess capacity;—that is, as long as the fixed amount of resources and facilities do not restrict production. When the latter restricts production, however, the opportunity cost of the restriction should be consulted as well. The OAAS provides appropriate cost data for this purpose.

Consider a firm selling product A in a perfectly competitive market. Suppose a new product—B—is introduced, for which the firm is a monopolist. Suppose further that B competes with A for the use of a limited machine. The income productivity (see Chapter XIV, Section 4) of the machine in producing A is $5 per hour. A unit of B requires two hours of the machine, hence the opportunity cost of the machine for B is $10 per unit. The price floor of a unit of B is the marginal cost per unit plus $10. Of course, management may set a price below this floor or even below avoidable costs under some conditions (see Devine 1950, p. 386).

Concepts and methods of calculation	*Conventional accounting*	*OAAS*
General concepts		
Marginal costs	1. Average variable costs	1. Avoidable costs on the margin
Other costs	2. Average fixed costs	2. Average nonavoidable costs
		3. Overhead costs as a markup
Total costs	Full costs = (1) + (2)	Total costs = (1) + (2) + (3)
Methods of calculation		
Marginal costs:	Variable costs:	Avoidable costs:
Variable inputs, purchased directly	Actual costs	Actual costs
Inventories of raw materials	Acquisition costs	Replacement costs
Intermediate goods	Cost of production	Market prices
Goods in process	Cost of production	Market based values
Durable liquid assets	None	Change in market value, interest charges
Other costs:	Fixed costs:	Nonavoidable costs:
All durable assets	Depreciation on acquisition costs	None
Durable nonliquid assets	None	Change in market based value, interest charges
Common costs	Actual costs	Actual costs
Overhead costs	Distributed	None

which the price level is not stable, a subject discussed later. But first assume an economy with a stable price level.

Implicit interest is charged in the OAAS, whereas only explicit interest is charged in conventional accounting. This means that in the OAAS, costs are higher than in conventional accounting when a large amount of capital is used and when the equity ratio is high.

Variable costs differ from avoidable costs. Avoidable costs stand for costs on the margin. When the per unit cost curve for the variable input is increasing, avoidable costs exceed variable costs. Avoidable costs also include costs associated with durable liquid assets. This point, as well as the procedure of including market prices in determining costs, causes the avoidable costs to exceed conventional variable costs.

Fixed costs differ from nonavoidable costs. While implicit interest charges are included and overhead costs are not included in nonavoidable costs, the reverse holds for fixed costs. In conventional accounting, depreciation charges for durable nonliquid assets are based on acquisition costs and some depreciation method. In the OAAS, on the other hand, the change in the market-based value of the assets during the accounting period is considered as the charge for depreciation and obsolescence. When an asset serves beyond its expected life span (that is, is written off the conventional accounting books), the OAAS costs will exceed the conventional accounting figures.

Overhead costs, considered as fixed costs, are distributed to the products in conventional accounting. These costs, because they are not traceable to the products, are usually not distributed in the OAAS. Nevertheless, to determine a per unit total-cost figure, overhead costs should be calculated as markup and added to the sum of the avoidable and nonavoidable costs.

To summarize, the surrogates for both marginal costs and total costs are nearly always higher in the OAAS than in conventional accounting. This difference depends directly on the level of the capital use, the level of equity, the number of cost items for which the unit variable cost curve is increasing, the amount of assets that are liquid, the number of assets that are written off the books but that still render services, and the level of integration existing in the firm. The first and last points are significant. Some implications are drawn below from these differences in cost calculations.

If price setting is based on, or strongly influenced by costs, conventional costing may tend toward underpricing of products whose production required a relatively high amount of capital. This may lead to misallocation of resources in the economy. This implication does not hold when price setting is based on costs plus a target rate of return to capital. For example, if the rate of implicit interest charged in the OAAS is set as the target rate of return, the OAAS provides directly the cost data required by the decision maker.

The OAAS procedure that considers market prices of the intermediate goods as costs may inflate the surrogates for both marginal and total costs of the final product. If price setting is based on conventional accounting costs, gains of integration are forwarded to the consumer, whereas under the OAAS costing procedures they are not forwarded. Although this makes the OAAS procedure inferior from a consumer-welfare point of view, it is nevertheless superior from several aspects when the price level is not stable.

Suppose that prices are really based on total costs. The higher OAAS total-cost figure does not necessarily imply higher average prices but rather a lower average markup as compared to that used with conventional accounting full-cost figures.[4] It only implies different prices for the same product under the two accounting systems. Some products' prices will be higher under the OAAS pricing procedures; others lower.

3. Downward Price Rigidity and Price Flexibility Induced by the OAAS

The phenomenon of downward price rigidity in Western economies can be partly explained by the extensive use of conventional accounting in business. A plausible explanation for this phenomenon that may contradict economists' expectations follows. The discussion indicates how the use of the OAAS might induce greater price flexibility under imperfect market conditions.

There are a number of reasons for changing prices to correspond

[4] The markup figure is often based on a judgment by the pricing decision maker of "what the traffic can bear," rather than on a fixed percentage over costs.

with a change in demand or costs. A depression in the economy can lead to an increase in the price elasticity of demand.[5] This is because a decrease in income increases the income elasticity of demand, which in turn increases the price elasticity of demand because of the homogeneity condition.[6] This point is confirmed by Breimyer (1961) in his empirical study of the demand and prices for meat.[7] An increase in the price elasticity of demand should lead the rational businessman to reduce prices and thus increase sales and profits, assuming that demand elasticity has increased above unity and that he has excess capacity. During a depression the costs of some inputs decline. This means a downward shift in the marginal cost curve. Equating marginal revenue to marginal cost will lead to price reduction.

It may be argued that the change in the elasticity of demand and the shift in the marginal cost curve is not large enough to induce businessmen to change prices. This might indeed be true, especially if the barriers to price change are taken into consideration. The argument that marginal costs vary slightly is discarded later.

The author believes that an important reason for price rigidity in the economy (not only in the noncollusive oligopoly sector) is the kind of information available to businessmen. The decision maker on prices gets the traditional full-cost data as his main source of information (see Appendix A). Under this accounting method, when demand for a product decreases and the volume of production drops, its cost per unit rises, since the fixed costs are divided by a smaller number of units. This kind of information is not much of an inducement to reduce prices.

This argument implies nonrational behavior on the part of the businessman in his reactions to the business cycle. Let us show first how the use of conventional accounting information induces nonrational

[5] For an intuitive argument see Harrod (1936, pp. 86–87). Galbraith (1936, p. 463) and Stigler (1952, pp. 237–239) claim the contrary.

[6] The sums of the own and cross-price elasticities and the income elasticity for a particular commodity is, taking account of signs, zero. Thus, an increase in the (positive) income elasticity will increase (the negative) price elasticity (Wold and Jureen 1953, ch. 6).

[7] Breimyer's findings (1961) are: in 1921–1929 the coefficient of flexibility was −0.88 for beef and −1.29 for pork; in 1930–1941, 0.55 for beef and −1.03 for pork; and in 1948–1960, −1.50 for beef and −1.22 for pork.

behavior, and then how OAAS information may induce more rational behavior. Lutz and Lutz (1951, pp. 70–75) show that over the business cycle prices are more stable and output less stable, under full-cost pricing than under marginal-cost pricing. Adhering to full-cost pricing also means disregarding the effect of the level of price that is set on volume and then in turn on unit cost. Businessmen generally use standard volume and standard cost in establishing full-cost prices to meet the problem of fluctuations in volume.

The cost figures provided by conventional accounting are based on historical acquisition costs. This means that part of the current changes in prices, especially of assets, are not reflected in production costs. Thus during inflation conventional accounting practices underestimate the values of assets and their costs. If prices are based on full cost, they in turn are biased downward. This effect is intensified when the FIFO (first in, first out) rule is used for pricing inventories[8] and when the rule of thumb is followed that during inflation one should build up inventories.

This discussion indicates that under the traditional full-cost accounting and pricing practices both costs and prices are relatively stable and unresponsive to changes in the level of demand. But, if the costs are specified correctly, the level of demand may be reflected more effectively in the cost figures, as happens when the OAAS is used to provide cost information.

While full-cost figures (surrogates for total costs) constitute the main cost data provided by conventional accounting, emphasis is given to avoidable costs (surrogates for marginal costs) in the OAAS. The OAAS total-cost figure has limitations similar to those of the conventional accounting full-cost figure. But two cost items—liquid assets and overhead costs—are treated differently in the OAAS, and thus the size of the economic error is reduced.

Consider a recession in the economy. The demand for some products

[8] Relevant here is Husband's story (1954) of a Chinese merchant in Singapore who was sent to prison because he could not pay the income tax due on his accounting profits. But these profits were fictitious, since the accountant used the FIFO method in a period of sharp inflation. Husband concludes: "Poor Sin Tu Bad suffered for his accountant's inflexibility; he was a victim of accounting tradition" (p. 12).

and the prices of some inputs, especially of investment goods, drop. Since the OAAS calculates almost all the costs from current market prices, any drop in input prices will lower costs, both avoidable and total. An important change in costs is associated with liquid assets. When the demand for a product drops, the secondhand market price or sale value of the facilities used in producing the product will drop sharply. Thus the cost associated with these facilities will drop and with it avoidable costs, which serves as a surrogate for marginal costs.[9]

Now suppose demand rises and the firm approaches production at full capacity. Management plans to increase the capacity by means of new investment. The new investment is avoidable, and therefore its costs are considered as avoidable. The related cost items previously classified as nonavoidable now become avoidable costs. The surrogate for marginal costs is raised and will be considered as such as long as demand is projected to remain high. This implies that during prosperity most of the cost items can be considered as avoidable. In this case the avoidable-cost figure is close to total costs, and conceivably it may be higher than the full-cost figure in conventional accounting. Note further that under this kind of analysis the marginal cost (surrogated by the avoidable cost) is a function of the level of production.

To summarize, in the OAAS the figure standing for marginal cost fluctuates with the business cycle. The total-cost figure fluctuates as well, but presumably by a smaller amplitude. This implies that whether the pricing decision maker uses marginal or total costs, the information will induce greater price flexibility than will conventional accounting data, which lead toward price rigidity.

The discussion in this chapter rests on the assumption that firms do not necessarily behave as economic theory assumes. Specifically, it is argued that businessmen often use full-cost data rather than estimates of marginal costs in making decisions on prices. Alternatively, consider the assumption that the pricing decision maker approaches rational

[9] This is true only when holding losses (that is, losses in assets' values due to decline in price level) are recorded separately. If these losses are considered as costs of production, the costs associated with these assets may even increase during a period of price decline.

The price floor established may drop even more because the internal opportunity costs of the limited facilities may conceivably be eliminated.

behavior through trial and error. When he is supplied with better information (through the use of the OAAS) the costly learning period can be shortened.

In the business world there are established, standardized practices that are followed by most firms. Presumably, traditional full-cost accounting, cost-plus pricing, and price stability are among these practices.[10] The practice of maintaining stable prices is rational under conditions of noncollusive oligopoly, since it reduces uncertainty about rivals' actions. Keeping stable prices is not rational under other imperfect market conditions, such as monopoly or collusive oligopoly, because it stands against the profit-maximizing objective of the firm. There is a conflict between the objective of the firm to maximize profits and actual behavior with respect to price stability.[11] This conflict will not be obvious to most businessmen as long as traditional accounting is used as the basic supplier of cost information. The OAAS tends to eliminate this conflict (Table 15). This method, which is designed primarily for internal decision making (that is, resource allocation and control) may also affect pricing decisions in imperfect competition and further improve profit maximization and use of resources.

4. Some Macroeconomic Implications

So far the analysis has referred to a firm or an industry. The question now is: How would the pricing procedure based on the OAAS affect the economy as a whole if large numbers of firms adopted the system? Some pertinent points raised earlier can be summarized in a tabular form in Table 15.

Under the traditional full-cost pricing method the volume of production fluctuates with stable prices, while under the OAAS's cost-pricing procedure the volume is more stable and prices fluctuate.

One conclusion of the earlier discussion was that when the OAAS is used as the source of cost information for pricing decisions, prices

[10] See Kaplan, Dirlam, and Lanzillotti (1958, p. 255).

[11] This argument holds also when the firm's objective is satisficing (Simon 1959) or sales maximization (Baumol 1965, ch. 13). When demand decreases, profit will conceivably fall below the satisfactory level and management will search for improving alternatives, or the level of sales will fall and management will act for a change.

Table 15. Expected economic changes affecting a firm over the business cycle

Item in analysis	Incidence on the firm*	
	Recession	Expansion
Expected changes:		
Cost	−	+
Demand elasticity	+	−
Desired price	−	+
Conventional accounting practices:		
Full-cost per unit of product	+	−
Full-cost pricing	Relatively stable	
Conventional accounting effects:		
Firm's volume of production	−	+
OAAS practices:		
Marginal and total cost	−	+
Marginal or total cost pricing	−	+
OAAS effects:		
Firm's volume of production	Relatively stable	

* The signs + or − stand for tendency to increase or decrease, respectively.

will be flexible whether the decision maker uses marginal or total costs for his decisions. Price flexibility per se has a countercyclical effect. But the price level is connected to the volume of production. The individual firm reduces prices during a depression period only if this action will increase its sale volume and hence its profit. The problem to be analyzed is: Will there be an aggregate demand to absorb the increased volume of production?

The answer is Yes. To construct a complete macroeconomic model for answering this question is beyond the scope of this study, but a partial and brief illustration is presented.

The macroeconomic effect of the use of OAAS information in pricing can be illustrated by means of the Hicksian cross (Hicks, 1937) depicted in Figure 5. The *LM* curve reflects all combinations of the rate of interest, i, and of real income, y, bringing into equilibrium the total

Figure 5. The Hicksian cross

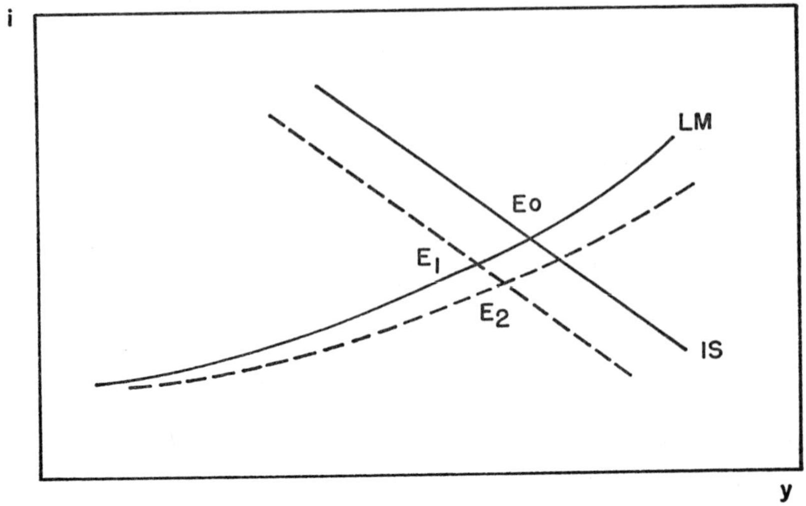

supply of and demand for money at a given level of prices. The *IS* curve reflects all levels of *i* and *y* corresponding to equilibrium in goods' markets. The point E_0 represents the equilibrium levels of *i* and *y* at a full-employment output of the economy.

Consider a recession in the economy. The *IS* curve shifts to the left, as depicted by the broken line. The under-full-employment equilibrium is reflected by point E_1. When a large number of firms use the OAAS as a source of information on pricing their products, the price level will decline, causing a shift to the right in the *LM* curve, as depicted by the broken line. The new equilibrium, as reflected by point E_2, is to the right of *point* E_1. This implies a higher level of *y* and a higher aggregate demand.

In an open economy the *IS* curve is substituted by Vanek's *ISXM* curve (Vanek 1965), where *I*, *S*, *X*, and *M* stand respectively for desired investments, savings, exports, and imports. The OAAS effect on price reduction during recession will cause this line to shift further to the right and point E_2 along with it.

Some of the micro and macro results of the use of the OAAS by many firms are presented in a condensed form in Table 16. Points 1,

Table 16. Expected changes induced by the use of data from two accounting systems in pricing decisions during a recession

Item in analysis	Incidence induced*	
	Conventional accounting	OAAS
1. Price of output	0	–
2. Real wage	0	+
3. Level of employment	—	–
4. Firm's profits, result of volume	—	–
5. Firm's profits, result of costing procedures	–	0
6. Dividend payments	—	–
7. Price of nonlabor inputs	0	–

* The signs +, 0, –, or — stand for expected tendency to increase, not to change, to decrease, or to decrease considerably, respectively, relative to a normal period.

3, and 4 are corollaries of the former discussion; point 2 is the result of the decrease in prices, where money wages are assumed to be constant; point 6 is a result of points 4 and 5. Points 5 and 7 require additional explanation.

Under the OAAS procedures, the cost level fluctuates in correspondence with market prices. Thus during a recession the OAAS total-cost figure is lower than the conventional accounting full-cost figures and, the reported total profits may be higher.[12] In other words, conventional accounting practices lead toward a report that underestimates the actual or true profits during a recession (point 5). The reverse holds during expansion.

The price of nonlabor inputs is affected by the pricing policies of the firms and industries producing these inputs. If these segments of the industrial community establish their prices on the basis of OAAS information, the prices of nonlabor inputs are expected to decline during a recession (point 7).

[12] This is true when holding gains or losses are reported and considered separately, a subject that is beyond the scope of this study.

Of course, if all industries or firms do not reduce prices during the recession the macro effect will be lessened. But the firms that do so will receive more profit by taking business away from firms with rigid prices.

To summarize, the main effect of using OAAS cost information in pricing is to introduce greater price flexibility, which should lessen the amplitude of the business cycle. Of course, under a policy that forces firms not to change prices (price regulations) these results do not hold. The analysis indicates the limitations of such a policy.

VIII
PRICING AND COSTING A SERVICE WITH SEASONAL CHARACTER: AN APPLICATION TO TRACTOR SERVICES

This chapter demonstrates how some of the operational accounting and analysis system's concepts and rules are applied to the operation of a service department. A service department is considered as a contribution center, a service is priced, avoidable costs are computed, and marginal analysis is incorporated into the analysis. The problem analyzed is the costing and pricing of services for which demand fluctuates periodically. Actual data pertaining to the services of a fleet of tractors on a large farm in Israel are used to indicate how the OAAS provides management with the basic information to solve realistic problems. Of course the method and its application have a wide range of other uses.

1. Outline of the Problem and a Plausible Solution

The demand for many kinds of service fluctuates periodically—for example, electricity, hotel accommodations, and shipping. Seasonal fluctuations are naturally common in agricultural production. Since services cannot be stored, facilities and enterprises which provide services have to be numerous enough, large enough, or have great enough capacity to meet demand at the peak season. In the slack season part or all of the facilities are idle or are employed below capacity.

In business, an attempt is usually made to differentiate the charges for service at peak and off-peak use. Telephone calls are cheaper at night and on weekends; resort hotels have off-season rates.

The two-part charging method is presumably the best procedure to use in pricing services for which demand fluctuates. The method requires the consumer to pay two charges: one for the right to use the service, commonly a charge related to fixed costs; and one for the actual use of the service, a charge which varies directly with the level of use, commonly related to variable costs. Thus, charges for electricity can be established as: a fixed charge based on the capacity required to meet needs at the station's peak output, and a variable charge based on metered consumption. This method of pricing was suggested as early as 1892 by J. Hopkinson in a paper entitled "The Cost of Electric Supply" and is discussed by Lewis (1949, ch. 2). The extent of its application in business is not known to the author. However, the method is applied by the dominant producer of electricity in France and presumably by individual producers of services.[1]

A similar problem exists when a department in a firm renders service to other departments whose demand for the service fluctuates from season to season, as is the case with the tractors in our example.

Consider a farm that has several producing segments or enterprises and a fleet of tractors that serve the various segments. There is an active secondhand market for these tractors. Assume that the genuine data is typical to the farm's situation and hence can be used for decision making.[2] Assume also, for the time being, that all the tractors are

[1] See Nelson (1963, 1964) and also Marschak (1960) and Westfield (1966). The introduction of this pricing system in France caused an appreciable reduction in the peak use of electricity and a corresponding saving in investments (Boiteux 1964, pp. 83–84) and operating costs (Westfield 1966, p. 72). An operator of several Miami Beach hotels told the author that they use two rates: in-season (winter), based on operating costs and all the fixed costs plus a small mark-up for profits, and off-season, based only on operating costs plus a large markup for profits. He added, "During the winter we pay our costs, in the summer we make our profits," because the low rates attracted many customers.

[2] The data were kindly provided by A. Atzmon. They are presented in Tables 17, 18, and 19. Some data are rounded.

in similar working condition and that their sale value is approximately equal. Data pertaining to the monthly use of the fleet of nine tractors by several segments in a large farm in Israel are charted in Table 17 and Figure 6.

The monthly fluctuations in the demand for tractors' services result from rather rigid time requirements of field operations in agricultural

Figure 6. Monthly use of tractor services, in hours (based on Table 17)

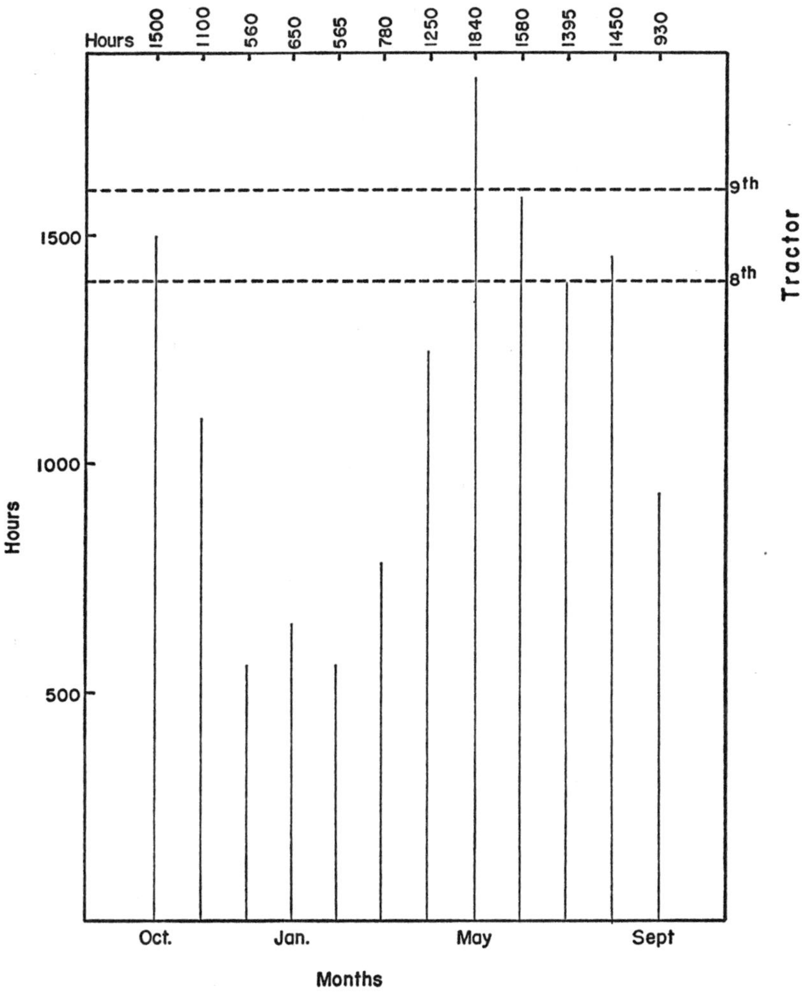

Table 17. Monthly use of tractor service, in hours, by users (Israeli farm, 1963–1964)

Month	Cotton	Sugar beets	Cereals	Vegetables	Green fodder	Orchards	Farmstead	Total
Oct.	587	406	40	22	180	47	218	1,500
Nov.	172	210	158	57	165	48	290	1,100
Dec.		100	45	27	77	113	198	560
Jan.		45	26	30	105	99	345	650
Feb.		10	76	45	94	121	214	560
Mar.	100		106	25	122	132	295	780
Apr.	370	147	228	24	54	132	295	1,250
May	200	425	425	205	15	281	289	1,840
June	100	502	270	377	15	179	137	1,580
July		400	130	366	30	205	261	1,392
Aug.		135	250	312	116	131	506	1,450
Sept.	410	104	50	37	72	127	124	924
Total	1,939	2,484	1,804	1,527	1,045	1,615	3,172	13,586

Source: Personal communication from A. Atzmon, Inter Kibbutz Economic Advisory Unit, Tel Aviv.

production. That is, tractor services must be rendered at specific dates or periods. Nevertheless it is assumed that during any given month the time requirements for tractors' services are flexible. In the example, the peak demand for tractor services is in May. This peak naturally determines the number of tractors on the farm.

In May, all the tractors are used at full capacity. Since the total amount of service in May is 1840 hours, each of the nine tractors' expected output is about 200 hours per month.[3] If peak demand could have been cut by 200 hours, by either reducing users' requirements or hiring tractor services from outside the farm, only eight tractors would have been necessary. Eight tractors will suffice to meet demand in all the other months. In other words, the marginal tractor on this farm is kept for only 200 hours of service. In practice, this fact may not be recognized because all or most of the tractors are employed during the other high-use months as well, but each is used fewer hours per month. The very act of plotting these data on a chart, as is done in Figure 6, provides information that is otherwise easy to overlook.

A distinction is made between two types of costs: operating costs, such as fuel and repairs, which are directly proportional to the amount of use, and holding costs, such as insurance, change in value (depreciation), and implicit interest, which result from the tractors being kept on the farm. The maintenance cost can be classified as both an operating and a holding cost. It is hard or impossible to trace the maintenance cost for each heading; and in the present analysis it is included under operating costs. Both types of cost are avoidable, but in different contexts of analysis. Operating costs are avoidable in the context of the level of operation of the tractors, holding costs in the context of numbers of tractors kept on the farm. The costs pertaining to the tractors are provided in Table 18.

The two-part charging method is applied in the next two sections analyzing the profitability of the marginal tractor and for charging the tractors' service costs to the various users. The discussion first assumes

[3] This figure may seem to be low. But the working schedule of tractor operators implicitly reduces the total hours of output from some larger theoretical level.

Table 18. Data pertaining to tractors and their costs*

Item in analysis	Annual costs	Units	Costs per unit
Operating costs,			
annual total	31,650	13,600 hrs.	2.33
Sale value:			
Beginning of year	40,000		
End of year	33,400		
Holding costs:			
Change in value	6,600		
Interest, 12% on value			
at beginning of year	4,800		
Insurance	1,350		
Annual total	12,750	9 tractors	1,417
Peak season (May)	12,750	1,840 hrs.	6.93
Total annual costs	44,400		

* All cost figures are in I£ (I£1 = $0.33).

that there is a market for tractor services and later that such a market does not exist.

2. Analyzing the Profitability of the Tractors

Tractors on a farm are commonly considered as a service department, but the OAAS treats service departments as contribution centers. Thus the profitability of this department should be analyzed.

Suppose that the farm can hire as many tractors as production requires at any time at a cost of I£5.00 per hour (I£1 = $0.33). During the year the farm uses 13,600 hours of tractor service, saving an outlay of: 13,600 hours × I£5 = I£68,000. This sum is considered as the tractor department's revenue. Since total annual avoidable costs are I£44,400, this department provides an annual contribution of I£23,600.

The profitability of the marginal, or ninth, tractor should be analyzed. The ninth tractor is kept only because of the demand in the peak season (May), during which it is used about 200 hours (more accurately 204 hours). This implies that the holding costs per hour in

May are: I£1,417 ÷ 204 hours = I£6.93 (Table 18). The total avoidable costs per hour in May (holding and operating costs) are: I£6.93 + I£2.33 = I£9.26. This cost should be compared to the market price for an hour of tractor service in May. Any price below this avoidable cost figure means that the ninth tractor is not profitable. The farm will profit from selling one tractor and hiring tractor services in the peak season, provided that the analyzed data accurately represent the situation that can be expected in the future and that there is tractor service to be hired in May.

The profitability of the eighth tractor should be calculated in a similar manner. Suppose there are only seven tractors on the farm, with a capacity to render 1,400 hours of service in any month. The eighth tractor is needed for service in those months when the requirements are above 1,400 hours. The marginal services that have to be rendered by the ninth and eighth tractors are illustrated by means of two horizontal broken lines in Figure 6. There are 530 hours for the year that are above 1,400 and below 1,600 hours per month (October, 100 hours; May, 200 hours; June, 180 hours; August, 50 hours). These hours are

Table 19. Data and annual cost for two groups of tractors

Item in analysis	Group 1	Group 2	Total
Number of tractors	7	2	9
Operating costs (I£)	26,450	5,200	31,650
Sale value (I£):			
Beginning of year	38,500	1,500	40,000
End of year	32,200	1,200	33,400
Holding costs (I£):			
Change in value	6,300	300	6,600
Interest (12%)	4,620	180	4,800
Insurance	1,050	300	1,350
Total	11,970	780	12,750
Hours used:			
Whole year	11,900	1,700	13,600
In May, total	1,590	250	1,840
In May, per tractor	227	125	200

assigned to the eighth tractor. The holding costs per hour are: I£1,417 ÷ 530 hours = I£2.67. Total costs per hour attributed to the eighth tractor are: I£2.67 + I£2.33 = I£5.00.

If the custom rate for tractor services is I£5.00 per hour, then there is neither profit nor loss associated with the eighth tractor. By implication, all of the other seven tractors are profitable.

Let us now assume that there are two kinds of tractors on the farm. Group 1 is composed of seven tractors in good working condition, and group 2 is composed of two older ones. The data pertaining to these groups are provided in Table 19. Up to this point, total figures (the last column in Table 19) have been used to illustrate the procedure of analysis. The data warrant a more refined analysis.[4] Assuming that the tractors in each group render the same service and are equal in value, the calculations of costs per hour are as follows:

	Group 1	*Group 2*
Operating costs per hour	$\frac{26{,}450}{11{,}900 \text{ hrs.}} = $ I£2.22	$\frac{5{,}200}{1{,}700 \text{ hrs.}} = $ I£3.06
Holding costs per tractor	$\frac{11{,}970}{7} = $ I£1,710	$\frac{780}{2} = $ I£390
Holding costs per hour in May	$\frac{11{,}970}{1{,}590 \text{ hrs.}} = $ I£7.53	$\frac{780}{250 \text{ hrs.}} = $ I£3.12
Total costs per	I£9.75	I£6.18

The figures in the last row imply that in May the tractors of group 2 provide service at lower cost. If a tractor is to be sold, it should come from group 1 rather than from group 2, provided that the two tractors of group 2 will be used only in the peak season and will be idle during the rest of the year.[5] This outcome also makes intuitive sense. Tractors with low operating costs should be employed for general use, and old ones with low holding costs retained as stand-bys.

[4] Each tractor can be analyzed in a similar way if data are available.

[5] Interestingly enough, the manager of the farm from which the data for the present analysis were drawn had contemplated selling the two old tractors because of their high operating costs.

3. Charging Tractor Services to Users

Charging tractor services to users is analyzed under two situations: when there is an external market for these services, and when no external market exists. First, when it is possible to hire tractors in any required amount and at any time, say for I£5.00 per hour, this rate should be used by the tractor service department in making charges to all users. If the marginal tractor costs more than this to operate, as indicated earlier, it creates a loss for the tractor department. Of course, when a change in the scale of a segment using tractor service is considered, a corresponding change in the expected contribution to the tractor department should be taken into account.

Second, suppose that tractors cannot be hired and that all avoidable costs are charged to the users. The conventional practice is to charge a flat rate (average total costs) for the hours of service provided to the segments during the year. Avoidable costs per hour are: I£44,000 ÷ 13,600 hours = I£3.26. This practice ignores the seasonal character of demand and does not consider extra costs caused by providing services in the peak season. A two-part charging or pricing method surmounts this limitation.

Let us return to the assumption that all the tractors are approximately equal in performance and value. Under the two-part charging method each segment is charged operating costs for all the service it used—that is, I£2.33 per hour—and holding costs for the service used in May—that is, I£6.93 per hour (Table 18). The two-part charging method implies that holding costs are paid by the users of the service during the peak season. This is because these segments determine the number of tractors on the farm. Once the number of tractors is determined, the holding costs become a "free good" in an economic sense. In other words, a particular segment's use of a tractor anytime outside the peak season does not in any way limit the availability of tractors' service to other users. Only the operating costs are avoidable and are charged to the users. A comparison of the two methods, flat-rate charging and two-part charging, is provided in Table 20. Note the difference in the charges to the various users by the two methods. The

Table 20. Tractor services and alternative charges to users (rounded figures)

User	Use of tractors*				Two-part charging method (I£)			Flat rate	Difference between totals	
	Annual		In May							
	Hrs.	%	Hrs.	%	Operating costs†	Holding costs‡	Total charges	charges (I£)§	Absolute	%
Cotton	1,940	14	200	11	4,515	1,386	5,901	6,333	−432	−7
Sugar beets	2,485	18	425	23	5,783	2,945	8,728	8,113	615	8
Cereals	1,805	13	425	23	4,201	2,945	7,146	5,893	1,253	21
Vegetables	1,530	11	205	11	3,561	1,421	4,982	4,995	−13	0
Green fodder	1,045	8	15	1	2,432	104	2,536	3,412	−876	−26
Orchards	1,615	12	280	15	3,758	1,940	5,698	5,272	426	8
Farmstead	3,180	23	290	16	7,400	2,009	9,409	10,382	−973	−9
Total	13,600		1,840				44,400	44,400		

* Data based on Table 17.

† I£ 2.3272 x annual hours.

‡ I£ 6.9293 x hours in May.

§ I£ 3.2647 x annual hours.

green fodder segment, for example, hardly uses tractors in May and pays mainly operating costs under the two-part method. Its charges are 26 per cent below those arrived at by the flat-rate method. On the other hand, the cereals segment, which requires more services in May than at other times, is charged 21 per cent more.

Let us now incorporate into the analysis more than one group of tractors. As we have seen, the operating costs of tractor service are I£2.22 per hour for group 1 and I£3.06 for group 2; holding costs in May are I£7.53 per hour for group 1 and I£3.12 for group 2. As the principles of marginal analysis suggest, the cost of the least efficient tractor should be charged to the users. In the example there is a complication because group 1 has the highest holding costs and group 2 has the highest operating costs. In this situation, tractors from group 2 should be used only in the peak season and at other times only the group 1 tractors should be used. In other words, at peak season both groups are used, off-peak only one group is used.

Charges should be made as follows. For demand at the peak (May), the operating costs of group 2 and the holding costs of group 1 should be charged. The hourly rate is: I£7.53 + I£3.06 = I£10.59. If a user can reduce its demand in May, operating costs of a tractor from group 2 will be reduced by I£3.06 per hour. On the other hand, holding costs for a tractor from group 1 will be reduced by I£7.53 per hour, assuming that the reduction in use will permit the liquidation of a tractor from group 1. During the off season only operating costs for group 1 should be charged—that is, I£2.22 per hour. In effect, a three-part charging method is put into practice.

It might well be argued that segments that use tractor services evenly during the year should be charged a flat rate per hour. In fact, the total charges are equal under both methods if the user's demand is really constant throughout the year. Still, the two-part charging method has its merits. If such a segment can reduce its demand in the peak season, it will benefit by escaping the "penalized" peak price. This may enable the farm to reduce its number of tractors. Suppose that the farmstead segment, which uses the tractors somewhat evenly, reduces its demand in May from 289 (Table 17) to 60 hours by moving some jobs to April and June.[6] This implies that one tractor of group 1 can be released, causing a saving of I£1,710 per year.

Suppose that the management found the ninth tractor to be "profitable" because the additional revenue created by its services during the peak season exceeds the high cost of holding the tractor for use in only one month. Thus, for example, the cereals segment is "ready" to pay the extra I£1,253 rather than reduce its scale of operations. Hence the ninth tractor is kept on the farm. While tractors are underemployed eleven months in a year, economically speaking they are still efficient. Any accounting system that is designed to measure performance by means of equipment utilization will fail to serve management effectively unless performance at peak production periods is measured.

There are several limitations and possible pitfalls to the outlined analysis: the nondivisibility of the tractor units; the possibility of two different peaks in demand, each with a different set of users' shares; existence of a wide plateau rather than a narrow peak, with changing users' shares along the plateau; the possibility of a shift in the peak to another period, partly because of the pricing method. Such limitations might reduce the appeal of the outlined method of analysis. Nevertheless, in principle the method is applicable and can provide useful information for internal decisions and control. This method can be applied whenever there are seasonal fluctuations in production and the firm uses inputs that are contracted for a long period of time (equipment, labor, buildings) and provide a stable service over time.

The experimental application of this method on three large farms in Israel showed that management was ready to consider reducing the demand for tractor services in the peak season and offered an inducement for increased usage in other seasons. This result can be expected, since the two-part charging method puts a "penalty" on use of the service at the peak and "subsidizes" the nonpeak user.

[6] Note a possible pitfall here—a shift of the peak to June. This might require treating the two months together or indicating some group of weeks out of the two months as the peak season.

IX
NONINCOME MEASURES OF PERFORMANCE

In principle, an income measure is the most suitable criterion for measuring performance since it incorporates the outcome of a whole series of decisions and actions. Moreover, the firm's primary objective is measured in terms of income. In practice, however, nonincome measures often are in use or should be used to supplement or substitute income measures in evaluating performance.

It has been shown in Chapter II that any income measure has some limitations as a performance criterion. It has also been mentioned that nonincome measures can be used as supplements to the income measures so as to help management in measuring performance. Thus, by using nonincome measures management can learn about the production function and the technical efficiency of operations—that is, whether improvement can be achieved and how to react to exogenous changes. For example, in order to find out whether income can be increased, the manager should check the possibility and consequences of expanding production. For this, measures of production level and input use must be available.

The purpose of this chapter is to draw the reader's attention to the difficulties arising when a nonincome measure is used for measuring performance and to some possible situations in which the measure is at odds with the primary objective of the firm. Because of these observations, it is suggested that nonincome measures be used with care. It is also suggested that several measures be used when performance is evaluated, rather than only one measure as often is done in practice. (Recall that this kind of solution has also been suggested in Chapter II in respect to the use of income measures). In particular, the objective of this chapter is to indicate some managerial uses of nonincome measures and their shortcomings. The discussion also sheds some light on the problems of how to select a performance measure and which type of measure to use in different situations; its aim is to get some insights into the problems rather than to provide a thorough analysis.[1]

In business, income cannot be measured for some activities, or computing income may be costly and reporting may be delayed. Therefore, more observable, nonincome performance measures are often developed and used, especially when management wants to control the various components of a complex production process. These nonincome criteria pertain usually to maximization of output or minimization of input (and sometimes, illogically, both). The measures are provided in physical or monetary terms and in an absolute or ratio form. Measures such as sales volume, production level, volume of an input, or cost of production are often in use. These criteria are sometimes called subgoals to distinguish them from the overall goal itself—income.

When a nonincome measure is used either for learning about the possibility of improving operations or as a direct measure of performance, it serves as a "proximate" which should reflect what is happening to income—the primary goal of the firm.[2] Thus, care must be taken that the measure is not at odds with the firm's primary objective. This is of special importance since there is evidence that managers behave so as to maximize the measure by which their performance is measured and judged (see Chapter II, Section 4).

For a performance measure (whether income or nonincome measure) to be effective it should motivate the manager to act in line with the firm's objective and allow comparisons to other measures. For the

[1] For some references on these problems, see Solomons (1965, p. 278).

[2] The term "proximate" is borrowed from Hitch and McKean (1960, p. 160). The very fact of using "proximates" rather than ultimate measures opens the door to the selection of incorrect criteria (*ibid.*, p. 161). Unfortunately, in many cases the use of a "proximate" is a must.

measure to motivate the manager, it should be compatible with decision criteria, include only (and all the) variables over which the manager has some control, and measure as much as possible the contribution of individual variables in the production process to the firm's objective.

A performance measure is meaningless unless it is compared to other measures. The comparisons might be to the plan or a budget, to performance in other segments, earlier periods, or similar activities in other firms, or to standard norms. Such comparisons enable the analyst to reconsider what should or could have been done, and thus point out weak and strong points in operations for further decisions.

1. Technical and Economic Efficiency

If the relationship between the nonincome measure and income is known and direct, then the use of the former for measuring performance is as good as measuring income itself. In this case management can translate the measure into the degree of income goal attainment. Unfortunately, in many cases it is difficult or even impossible to learn these relations—that is, to find the relationship between the nonincome measure and the firm's income objective.[3]

It is common to assume that technical efficiency is a necessary condition for economic efficiency. "For example, maximum output per head (or per man hour) seems so obviously desirable that most non-economists would never question it as a suitable criterion for oragnizing production" (Hitch and McKean 1954, pp. 181–182).

Technical performance, assessed in terms of nonincome measures, is not necessarily correlated with economic performance, measured in terms of income. Thus, a technically efficient process may provide low income, and vice versa. Improving the absolute level of performance measured in terms of a nonincome measure (for instance, sale volume), might not improve the firm's income in a case of decreasing marginal returns. In fact, the opposite may hold—that reducing the level of performance may increase income.

[3] Many statistical studies have been carried out in agriculture to reveal the effect of various factors on production or on income. But they do not provide significant information on these relations for practical use in farm management.

Often, a measure of technical efficiency is economically meaningless. Consider, for example, the fleet of tractors analyzed in Chapter VIII. Measuring the efficiency of tractor use by the number of hours of service rendered per tractor in a year is meaningless. But using the same measure pertaining to the peak season may help management in its control function. If the use of such a measure will induce change in performance—increase the number of hours of service rendered by a tractor in the peak season—the number of tractors on the farm may be reduced.

Nonincome measures often are used as measurements of efficiency when provided in a ratio form, such as cost per unit of output, or production per unit of input. There are likely to be interpretation problems with such ratios. These are similar to those pertaining to the measure of rate of return (see Chapter II). The main shortcoming is that a given ratio is related only to one variable (for instance, capital). Thus, it overlooks the contributions of the other variables in the production process (for instance, labor). Moreover, the use of a ratio assumes implicitly that the production function is linear throughout.

Let us illustrate some simplified cases where well-established nonincome measures may suggest performance to be good when in fact it does not maximize the firm's objective. Minimizing costs per unit of product is one of the better-known criteria for success and efficiency. When costs per unit of product are increasing with volume, the use of this criterion may be inappropriate. Thus, although a second shift of labor or an additional insecticide spray for cotton may be profitable (marginal revenue exceeds marginal costs), it will increase the average cost per unit. An example is used for illustration.

Consider a department producing one product which is sold on a perfectly competitive market. The level of production is determined by the number of shifts of labor employed in the plant. The estimated cost and revenue per unit of product are charted in Figure 7.

Suppose that in the second shift of labor the machines have to be laid off for maintenance. Consequently, the amount of labor hours per unit of product are increased (lowest curve in Figure 7). Machine hours per unit of product increase as well. Thus, a manager whose performance is measured by either labor or machine hours per unit of

Figure 7. Financial and technical data for a hypothetical production process

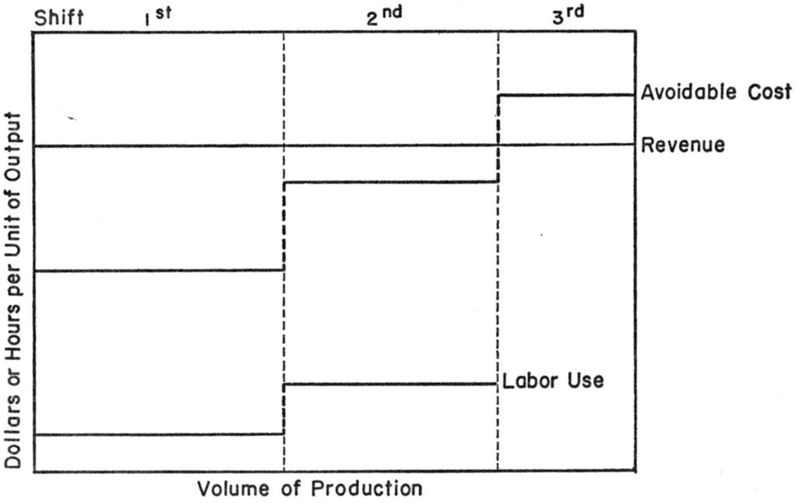

product will be reluctant to hire a second shift of labor. This is despite the fact that the second shift is profitable—revenue exceeds avoidable costs. Measuring performance by means of (avoidable) costs per unit of product would encourage the same results—that is, not hiring the second shift of labor.[4]

[4] Since managers do behave according to the performance measure that is in use (see Chapter II), irrational results may occur. Thus, for example, a business manager reported that regardless of the shape of the cost curve, he operates at the least cost point, because "his efficiency is judged by his superiors entirely on the basis of his average costs" (Eiteman and Guthrie 1952, p. 838). Similar results might occur when the "rate of return" is used as a measure of performance (see Chapter II). In order to illustrate this point, consider the example charted in Figure 7. Suppose that the volume of production is determined by the number of pieces of equipment—assets that are liquid in nature—and that each shift of labor as depicted represents a unit of equipment. No risk is involved. A manager whose performance is measured by the "rate of return" will be reluctant to operate beyond the first step in the diagram, although he should use the second piece of equipment in order to comply with the firm's objective. By moving to the second step, the denominator of the ratio is increased proportionally more than the numerator.

Let us explore another complication that a production function of the type illustrated in Figure 7 raises when the level of income is used as a performance criterion, and when the costs on the margin are charged to the segment using the equipment; that is, when the higher costs are charged for the whole volume of

Similarly, the goal of maximizing production per se or per unit of the main input is inappropriate, when production per unit of a second input is decreasing with volume of this input. Thus, the third shift of labor in the former example, although not profitable (marginal cost exceeds marginal revenue, as can be seen in Figure 7), increases the output of the department, and output per unit of invested capital. A performance measure of output per department may induce hiring a third shift.

The implication of the discussion above is that when decreasing marginal returns exist, inducement of maximization (or minimization) is at odds with the income objective of the firm. The use of one type of measure suggests operating only one shift. The use of another type of measure suggests operating three shifts. But two shifts are the optimum.[5] This optimum is suggested by the use of an income measure. It should be noted that the discussion started with the assumption that the use of income measures has some shortcomings.

There is not a simple solution to the problem of measuring performance. One solution is to use several measures. Performance then would be evaluated by means of exercising judgment, using these measures. Another solution might be to use one measure that must be maximized subject to other measures.

The former discussion illustrated some shortcomings of nonincome measures under specific situations. Despite these shortcomings, checking the technical process of production for possible improvements in performance that will also bring about improvements in income is a recommended procedure. It certainly would bring about progress in operations.

---

production (see Chapter V, Section 2). The manager in this case will be reluctant to increase volume beyond the first step in the diagram. For this reason the total contribution of the segment (that is, the contribution as represented by the shaded area) should be used for measuring performance. In other words, the contribution of the rent center, standing for the increasing cost curve of the equipment, should be added to the segment that uses the equipment (see Chapter V, Section 3).

[5] A similar problem exists when a given level of output is produced by two inputs (capital and labor) that can be substituted for one another at a decreasing marginal rate of substitution. Improving the efficiency of capital use will reduce the efficiency of labor use, and vice versa.

2. Comments on Some Uses of Nonincome Measures in Practice

Some conventional uses of nonincome measures for evaluating performance and for comparison purposes may provide misleading information to management. In principle, nonincome measures are considered as proxies for an income measure. In practice, however, the very use of a nonincome measure of performance emphasizes its importance. Sometimes the maximization of this measure becomes the goal of the manager, substituting for the real objective of income maximization.

The measure of sales volume, for example, is widely used in industry. This measure for the whole firm, like the measure of production level in a department, may be considered to be a proxy for an income measure. There are practical reasons for the use of these proxies. Moreover, the proxies can be considered to some extent as secondary goals. Thus, the department managers are proud of their production; and the corporation manager earns prestige by increasing his firm's share of the market. It seems to the author that in some cases and areas these proxies for the income goal become for a time the ultimate goal. The main goal (income) in these cases became a restriction on the secondary goal as presented by the nonincome measure.[6]

A similar situation exists in agriculture. Usually a high yield per technical unit (acre of land, head of cattle) is a sign of good management. Under certain conditions (as illustrated earlier), lower than maximum yield will produce the highest income, and good management will strive to achieve high income rather than high yield. Now, if the yardstick for performance and efficiency to which the farmer pays attention is yield, he will use all the available means to achieve this goal. Yield rather than the income becomes his goal.[7]

Comparing the firm's performance measures with those of others

[6] This is Baumol's thesis (1965, ch. 13).

[7] This situation is well known in Israel's milk industry (and in other countries as well). The Cattle Growers Association conducts monthly measurements of milk production per cow and issues a list of farms with their yields. The farmers react by striving to maximize yields. Unfortunately, the various surveys conducted by the Advisory Service of the Ministry of Agriculture (during the years 1960–1965) do not indicate any correlation between yield and income.

may be an effective way to emphasize to management that a segment (or the firm) is inefficient, and to induce improvements even if operations seem to be efficient compared to others. Since income measures for individual activities are usually confidential, nonincome measures can be used for comparisons. If technical measures are used rather than financial measures, only standard products and similar production processes can be compared, such as agricultural output, product movement in grocery stores,[8] or electricity generation.

Interfirm comparisons of performance measures are used extensively by farm advisors in many countries. Such comparisons are made also by other types of business concerns.[9] The firm's performances are compared to other firm's figures or to survey averages. Although these comparisons may help to spot inefficiencies in the production process, they have many limitations that should not be overlooked. The limitations are due to differences in physical environment, technology, and the prices of inputs and outputs. Suppose two firms have the same production function but confront different prices for their inputs and/or outputs. If the price ratios (among the inputs used, outputs produced, or inputs and outputs) are not equal in both firms, it is expected that the respective optimum points of production (input combination, output mix, or level of production) will differ.[10] This conclusion suggests that the use of interfirm comparison of performance measures, even of technical measures, may not provide any recommendation to management.

Consider two firms producing the same product. Suppose that the cost of capital for firm A is high; and for firm B, low. Assume that managements of both firms behave rationally. Recently, a new machine that is designed to substitute for labor has appeared on the market. Firm B acquired this machine, but firm A did not—because of its high

[8] For a study of grocery stores, see Gibson (1963, p. 492) and Brown and Sheehan (1966).

[9] For example, Dun and Bradstreet, Inc., publish a number of "important operating ratios" for many lines of business. These are mainly financial (not necessarily income) ratios. See also Westerdahl (1961) and Tucker (1961).

[10] For a graphic presentation, see Candler and Sargent (1962). Although they illustrate curvilinear relations, the conclusion holds also for cases of linear relations

cost of capital. A comparison will now indicate that firm B uses the labor more "efficiently"—its labor input per unit of product is lower. It is easy to conceive of a case where the new machine is not "efficient" since it does not replace the amount of labor it was supposed to replace. In an extreme case, the whole venture may be a failure and yet the comparison shows "efficient" labor use.[11]

Consider a dairy enterprise, producing a homogeneous product—milk. Most of the farms in the area use similar equipment; the process on the various farms is similar from a technological aspect. The process is not vulnerable to physical conditions as soil type or weather. Thus this enterprise seems to be suitable for interfarm comparisons. Still, the very existence of, say, other production processes on the farm will influence performance in the dairy enterprise. Suppose a farmer has a successful cash crop which results in a high shadow price for land. This farmer will not grow silage on his land but rather will feed a substitute, a factor that may reduce his yield of milk. There is an unlimited number of similar possibilities. The more firms allocate their resources according to individual economic prices, the less meaningful becomes the comparative study.

If a comparison of performance is to be made among businesses, a uniform recording and accounting system should be used by the various units that take part in the comparison study, such as farms, grocery stores, or divisions in a decentralized firm.[12]

3. Summary and Conclusions

Because of the limitations of income measures, nonincome measures can or should be used to supplement or substitute for them in evaluating performance. The use of such measures enables management to control various components of the production process for which income cannot be measured or is too costly to be measured. As a supplement to income

[11] The problem of controlling the expectations carried out before the decision took place is discussed in Chapter XIII.

[12] This procedure is now extensively carried out by various colleges of agriculture in the U.S. (Caspal and Eisgruber 1966). Solomons (1965, p. 52) claims that little importance seems to be attached to consistency in the accounting methods used in divisionalized companies. See also Moonitz (1961, pp. 43–44).

measures, nonincome measures may also help to indicate possibilities for improving on the operations and in turn, on income.

Each of the nonincome measures have limitations as a criterion of performance or efficiency, and their correlation to the firm's objective often is not known or sometimes changes as production level or input use changes. Thus, the use of several measures, when evaluating and analyzing the results of operations, may be helpful. To find out whether the performance of a segment can be improved, management should compare both income and nonincome measures to former years, to similar processes inside and outside the firm, and to norms and standards.

Naturally, it is impossible to measure, record, and report large numbers of performance measures. A sampling procedure can be utilized. A list of measures is prepared for each segment. Only a sample of the segments will be checked, imposing a latent check on the actions of the manager. This should lead each manager to learn his production function so as to be able to answer questions regarding the various performance measures—both income and nonincome measures.

The central concern in a segment should be clearly focused on the maximization of income. Therefore the crucial measure is the attainable contribution, as indicated in Chapter II.

X
ESTIMATING THE CAPITAL COSTS OF CURRENT OPERATIONS

The purpose of this chapter is twofold: first, to call the attention of the reader to a neglected area in managerial economics—the subject of the capital costs of current operations; second, to suggest some means for estimating these costs in practice. For analyzing a firm, the cost and income of each segment or production process should be estimated. The costs of funds committed to, or the cash flow generated by, the current operations of a segment should be considered or discounted, respectively.

Committed funds are defined as the cash required for operations—funds used from the initiation of production until the cash receipts from the sale of output are received. When a certain production process requires, say, $10,000 of committed funds, this sum is not used for other productive purposes. Thus, the committed funds, like any other type of capital asset, should be charged for the interest foregone. In practice, often this is not done.

The procedure of discounting cash flows may be considered almost as a conventional practice in capital budgeting. Such cash flows, which usually are generated by an investment, are considered over a period of years (interyear cash flow). It is seldom suggested, however, that cash flows which occur within a period (intrayear cash flows) be discounted in preparing data for decisions on current operations, as is suggested here.

The first reaction to this suggestion is that it is meaningless, since the interest rate is low. So why bother. Moreover, frequently financial credit is granted to finance the outlays, or advanced payments for the product are received. The repayment of the financial credit and the advanced receipts should be considered as cash flow items and discounted. Suppose receipts are received six months earlier; this sum can be used six months earlier for an alternative use and thus earn the opportunity rate of interest on this fund.

Charging interest on committed funds, or discounting the cash flow for a production process, has special merits when at least one of the following holds: the rate of interest is high, the production process is long, the outlays occur early in the production process and the receipts occur late.

The striking results of computations of income for four production processes, illustrating the second and third points above, are shown in Table 21 by means of some genuine data. Products A and B illustrate the effect of the length of the production period. Products C and D represent "favorable" and "unfavorable" cash flows, respectively. The rate of interest is 1 per cent per month in all the cases.

It is interesting to note that the data pertaining to products C and D originate from one firm. Note that the conventional income figures (column 4) indicate that the profitability (per unit of a limited resource) of both products is almost equal ($55.1 vs. $52.5). The discounted figures, however, provide completely different information on their profitability ($51.7 vs. $32.7).

The amount of capital used by the individual production process in various dates, say each month, must be figured if the cost of committed funds is to be calculated, or the intrayear cash flow is to be discounted.[1] In practice, especially in an integrated firm, this might be a laborious task. Therefore, approximations may be used from which standard figures are calculated. Two approaches are indicated below: one is a cost approach, the other a present value approach.

[1] Robichek, Teichroew, and Jones (1965) in their short-term financial decision analysis, compute the ex ante requirements for committed funds for a whole firm.

Table 21. Income figures, conventional and discounted, for four products (in U.S. dollars)*

Product	(1) Length of process (months)	(2) Total receipts (U.S.$)	(3) Total outlays (avoidable costs) (U.S.$)	(4) Income, conventional (U.S.$)	(5) Net present value (U.S.$)†	(6) (5) as % of (4)
A	5	123.5	83.7	39.8	36.7	92.4
B	21	593.3	311.5	281.8	219.3	77.8
C	22	129.7	74.6	55.1	51.7	93.8
D	18	526.3	473.8	52.5	32.7	62.3

Source: Appendix B.

* The figures are in U.S.$ per unit of limited resource (land).

† Interest rate of 1 per cent per month.

1. Cost of Committed Funds

Consider first the simplest kind of process, consisting of two payments: outlay and receipt. Two processes are illustrated in Table 22. The interest rate is 1 per cent per month.

Table 22. Cash flows, interest charges, and income (in U.S. dollars)

Process	Jan. 1	Dec. 31	Income, conventional	Interest charges	Income, corrected
A	−1,000	+1,500	500	−120	380
B	+1,500	−1,000	500	+180	680

Consider another simple process, producing more or less at a constant rate. Suppose monthly receipts and disbursements for the process are $100,000 and $90,000, respectively. The monthly income is $10,000. Thus, the yearly income may be considered to be $120,000 ($10,000 for twelve months). Each of the monthly income sums ($10,000), however, earns interest at the rate of 1 per cent per month. The compounded amount of this series at the end of the year is $126,830. Now, assume that there are inventories (raw materials, goods in process, and finished goods) along the production line, estimated at $200,000. Since the production process operates continuously, the $200,000 are tied up in the process permanently. If this process were discontinued, the firm would have $200,000 available for an alternative use. The yearly interest charge on these inventories is $24,000, or more precisely, when interest is compounded monthly, $25,370. The corrected annual income is: $126,830 — $25,370 = $101,460, compared with the conventional figure of $120,000.

In actual operations, where the cash flows of the production processes are usually not as neat as in the former examples, the computation of interest charges is more complicated. A method for approximating the costs of funds committed to a crop, which is in use in agriculture in Israel, is described next. This method suits only for production processes in which receipts precede outlay

Consider the cash flow as illustrated in Table 23. Assume that payments are at the end of the corresponding month. The relevant rate

Table 23. Computations of the costs of committed funds (in U.S. dollars)

Item in analysis	Jan.	Feb.	March	May	Income
Cash flow	−100	−10	−50	+200	40
Months that funds are committed	5	4	2		
Interest charges on outlays	5.00	0.40	1.00		(6.40)
Corrected income					33.60

of interest is 1 per cent per month. Interest is charged on the outlays for the period starting when the expenditure is made and ending when the receipts offset the outlays. Thus $100 is committed to the process for five months, from the end of January to the end of May, and interest charges are $5.

The computations as illustrated in the table can be simplified by summing up the product of dollars by months, called "dollar-months," and multiplying this summation by the monthly rate of interest. Thus the "dollar-months" summation in the example is: $(100 \times 5) + (10 \times 4) + (50 \times 2) = 640$. The total interest charges are $640 \times 0.01 = \$6.40$.

The total "dollar-month" figure is divided by 12 to convert it to a yearly base. This figure is related to the total outlay and computed as a coefficient. The corresponding coefficient for the numerical example is:

$$\frac{640}{12 \times 160} = 0.333.$$

Such coefficients are computed as standards for each of the main crops and are disseminated to cost accountants and farm managers for use in their costing and planning activities. The coefficients are applied by the farmer to his actual figures for total outlays and rate of interest.

Suppose the farmer's total outlay equals \$200 (compared to the standard of \$160), and the interest rate is 8 per cent per annum. The farmer's cost of committed funds is:

$$\underset{\text{(outlay)}}{200} \times \underset{\text{(coef.)}}{0.333} \times \underset{\text{(rate)}}{0.08} = \$5.33.$$

This is a convenient way to approximate the cost of the committed funds for each crop, assuming that all the farmer's cash-flow items differ from the standard ones by the same proportion. When this assumption does not hold, the outlined method may cause bias in the results. One way to reduce the bias is to provide standard cash-flow figures for each crop alongside the list of coefficients. When the farmer's cash flow resembles the standard one, he will use the coefficient for computing the interest charges. When he knows that his cash flow differs from the standard one, he should introduce corrections in the estimates of the interest charges. Thus, if the \$40 increase in outlay (\$200 compared to the standard of \$160) occurred in January, the interest charges should be increased by \$1.33 (\$40 × 5 months × 0.08 ÷ 12 as a monthly rate)

2. Discounting Intrayear Cash Flows

The procedure just explained is considered as a cost approach since the actual cost of the committed funds is figured. But for decisions, the present value of the cash flow generated by the production process should be computed. This is of special importance when alternative cash flows are compared.

Consider a production process having a cash flow as illustrated in Table 23, and a mutually exclusive process having the same pattern of cash flow, but starting in July rather than in January. Both have the same costs associated with committed funds. However, the present values of the two cash flows, at the time the decision has to be taken, differ.

When the interest rate is high, intrayear cash flows should be discounted, just as discounting procedures are applied to interyear cash flows. When programing the firm, the decision maker chooses those activities that provide the highest income. The income to be considered is the discounted net cash flow.

The importance of discounting intrayear cash flows can be seen when one considers the two processes as illustrated in Table 22 and reproduced in Table 24. The interest rate is 1 per cent per month.

Table 24. Cash flows and income (in U.S. dollars)

Process	Jan. 1	Dec. 31	Income, conventional	Income, corrected (discounted to Jan. 1)
A	−1,000	+1,500	500	332
B	+1,500	−1,000	500	612

Consider again the example in Table 23. The cash flow is discounted, as illustrated in Table 25, assuming that payments are at the end of

Table 25. Computations of the present value of income (in U.S. dollars)

Item in analysis	Jan.	Feb.	March	May	Income
Cash flow	−100	−10	−50	+200	$40.00
Discount factor	0.99	0.98	0.97	0.95	
Present value at Jan. 1	− 99	− 9.8	−48.5	+190	$32.70

the corresponding month. Discounting the cash flow of each production process in a firm is laborious. However, a simplified procedure for estimating the present value of standard processes can be implemented, similar to the procedure used for computing interest costs for the cost approach. Let us illustrate a possible procedure that might be applicable to agriculture.

A central institution computes the discounted income figures for the main crops, using standard cash-flow figures. The results are computed as a percentage of nondiscounted incomes, as presented in column 6 in Table 21, and disseminated as standard coefficients. The individual farm manager can use these coefficients for approximating present values for his particular production processes, assuming that all the farmer's cash flow items differ from the standard ones by the same proportion. The coefficient for the previous example (Table 25) is: $33.70 ÷ $40.00 = 0.84. Suppose the farmer's nondiscounted income is $50, compared to the standard figure of $40. His discounted income is: $50 × 0.84 = 42. Different coefficients are required for each rate of interest. Once again, the standard cash-flow figures for each crop should be provided with the list of coefficients. Having the standard cash-flow figures at his disposal, the farmer would be able to check his own figures and estimate the corresponding discounted income.

When receipts and disbursements are discounted (in either approach), inventories are included in the computations. Moreover, durable liquid assets should be included in the computations, by considering their purchase and sale values at the beginning and the end of the period, respectively, as cash flow items.

In a decision framework, the present value of the cash flow should be used. Discounting has to be carried out to the decision-programing date. On the other hand, the ex post reports, which are mainly used for evaluation purposes, are related to the end of the period. The present value figures can be easily compounded to the end of the period (year), assuming that the applied interest rate is an external opportunity cost.

Let us return to the example of steer production presented in Chapter IV, Section 9. Raising each steer implies interest charges amounting to I£89. Suppose the steer is sold at the end of the twelfth month. Suppose further, for simplicity, that every day one bull calf is bought and added to the herd, and one steer is sold. Thus, the herd is composed of 365 steers at various ages, in any point of time. The herd is a liquid asset with a market value of say I£250,000. Interest should be charged on the "inventory" of I£250,000, and the monthly income (receipts over outlays) should be discounted.

XI
EMPIRICAL USE OF LINEAR PROGRAMING IN MANAGEMENT: DATA REQUIREMENTS AND SOME IMPLICATIONS

Many of the concepts suggested in this book differ from conventional practices. Some of the concepts have proven to be operationally applicable in managing farms in Israel. In the author's research, the linear-programing technique was applied successfully in helping management make decisions for twenty large-scale cooperative farms. Organizationally, these farms have more resemblance to a regular manufacturing corporation than to a typical farm.[1] A thorough analysis was made for each farm, and a feasible and acceptable program for the product mix given certain restrictions was developed in each case.

This chapter is an amalgamation of various topics; the aspect common to all of them is their relation to the actual use of linear-programing analysis. The practical use of linear-programing, as described in the second section, provided the impetus for developing

[1] Such a cooperative farm, called a kibbutz, is a typical Israeli community which owns and operates a large diversified farm, workshops, and often a processing plant or a factory. Economically, this business resembles a regular firm in a capitalistic economy. In Israel, there are over two hundred kibbutz communities. All prepare a yearly plan or budget, and many of them keep detailed historical cost accounts. These, as well as other aspects, make the farms an excellent "laboratory" for testing management techniques.

the OAAS by illuminating the problem of what type of data is required for allocation decisions. Inferences are drawn from this experience to such practical problems as planning procedures, marginal analysis, and the applicability of the OAAS. Some assumptions taken in this book (objective of income maximization, the organization of the firm) are based on this practical experience.

The linear-programing analysis was developed on farms which made use of detailed cost accounting. The conventional full-cost accounting system failed to provide the required financial data for programing. Interestingly enough, several of the concepts and rules incorporated in the OAAS were developed while the financial figures for linear-programing formulations were being prepared. They were necessary as a preparatory step for the linear-programing analysis. If the OAAS had been available and used, the linear-programing analysis would have been simpler and cheaper.

The success of linear-programing in solving practical problems in business testifies to the willingness of businessmen to abandon existing procedures when a better alternative becomes available.[2] The problem is how to make them aware of the better alternative. One inference from this experience is that the potential acceptability of OAAS by business concerns is high.

It is well known that it is easier to introduce a new technique into an existing organization than to change an existing technique. In his consulting work in Israel, the author tried and failed several times to introduce changes in the existing full-cost accounting system used by these cooperative farms. During and after the linear-programing analysis, many farms were ready to introduce changes in their cost accounts to facilitate the use of linear-programing. It can be said that some of the OAAS concepts rode in on the back of linear-programing analysis.

The cooperative farms that served as a laboratory for this research can be considered as centralized firms. Each department is to some extent independent, however, because the department's manager has

[2] A similar experience is indicated by Dorfman (1960, p. 621) and Hitch and McKean (1961).

an option to participate in the decision-making process for his department. This aspect of decision making on these farms provided a background for the ideas about the quasi-decentralized firm (see Chapter XII).

1. Data Requirements for Linear Programing Analysis and the OAAS

Formulating a firm's operations in terms of linear-programing requires specifying and estimating in advance lots of data, both financial and technical coefficients. The empirical application of linear-programing analysis, therefore, made clear the problem of what type of data is required for decision making on resource allocation, not only by means of linear-programing analysis.

Because the validity of the results of a linear program depend on the quality of the data, special emphasis must be given to the preparation of data. In the empirical research, most of the planners' time was spent on working with the farm officers on collecting, estimating, decomposing, and reassembling the data.

The preparation of data to meet the requirements of linear-programing is an indispensable part of the programing process. The preparation pertains mainly to (1) determining the relevant coefficients of each activity and (2) adapting the ex post data (accounting) for ex ante purposes (programing). When the information system is designed to serve the linear-programing function, the amount of preparatory work hopefully would be reduced considerably,[3] since the main portion of the relevant coefficients (point 1 above) will be supplied by the system. This is partially the intent of the OAAS—in respect to the financial data.

Formulating the production process of a firm (or a part of it) in terms of a linear program—that is, in a simplex matrix—requires three types of data. The first is technical data—that is, input-output coefficients for each activity. These include the demands of each activity

[3] A common record-keeping and cost-accounting system in all the farms, or all the divisions in a decentralized firm, will simplify considerably the application of linear programing by a central office.

upon the firm's limited resources and upon intermediate goods and the amount of intermediate goods produced by an activity. The second is financial data—that is, objective function coefficients for each activity. These include the income (attainable contribution) generated by each activity whose products are sold on the market or the cost (avoidable costs) of each activity that produces intermediate goods, as well as the market value of each intermediate good, service of a limited resource, or liquid asset that can be sold or bought (external opportunity cost). The third type of data required is the amount of limited resources that is available for use and the level of other restrictions.

The bulk of the data are technical and financial. Therefore, an accounting or information system should be designed to supply these data. The rest of this section indicates some aspects pertaining to these data. A further discussion of the third type of data—the level of restrictions—is given in Section 3.

There are no conceptual problems regarding the type of technical coefficients that are required in the analysis. These coefficients are composed of such estimates as the number of machine hours used in producing a product or the space needed for storing the product in a warehouse. This type of data is required only for those versatile facilities or resources that are limited in their service capacity and for which the internal demand for their service exceeds capacity. Some of these data might be estimated relatively easily by managers and engineers. Similarly, estimating the amount of production of an intermediate good or service, and the use of this good or service by another (existing) activity in the firm, is a straightforward procedure.

Consider, for example, the fleet of tractors analyzed in Chapter VIII. Recall that there is a peak season in which tractor services are limited, assuming that the number of tractors on the farm is fixed. In off-peak seasons the tractors are employed below their capacity. If linear-programing analysis is carried out, two types of technical data are required: the amount of tractor services available in the peak season and each user's need for service in this season. Technical data pertaining to other seasons are not necessary.

The preceding discussion assumes that the restrictions are known in advance, an assumption that does not always hold in reality. One of the advantages of linear-programing analysis, as indicated below, is that it determines the binding restrictions. Another problem arises from the need to formulate the matrix in advance; hence, a large amount of data (mainly technical) is required. These problems are partly surmounted by the planning process that is described in Section 3. In this process, only the main aspects of the firm under analysis are formulated in the initial matrix. Additional data are supplied during the planning process—for those aspects which the analysis indicates are crucial to the firm and its objective.

Specification of the financial data is more elaborate. This data must be provided so as to fit linear-programing analysis, which is an economic analysis. This means that there are conceptual problems in preparing the data.

In business, the financial data are usually supplied by the cost-accounting system. Unfortunately, conventional cost-accounting systems often do not provide these data in a correctly specified manner. Thus, in the empirical research, the planners have had to estimate, decompose, and reassemble much of the financial data for analysis. And this was true despite the fact that every farm has a cost-accounting system, which is designed to provide information on product costs and department profits. This odd situation provided an impetus for developing the OAAS. The preparation of the financial data for linear-programing analysis was similar to preparing an OAAS report.

Let us mention that the OAAS is designed to provide data for allocation decisions irrespective of the technique used (linear programing, regular planning). Recall that in the OAAS the external opportunity costs (market values of intermediate goods and services and liquid assets) are included in the avoidable costs and, in turn, taken into account while computing the attainable contribution. In a linear-programing formulation, however, these values are used as the financial coefficients for the activities standing for selling or buying the respective goods, services, or liquid assets. Thus, if the segments in the OAAS correspond to the activities formulated in the linear-programing analysis, the OAAS financial data can be used for that analysis after allowances are made for the fact that external opportunity costs are included in avoidable costs[4]—and, of course, after the ex post accounting figures are adapted for ex ante analysis.

Another point requires some clarification. It is true that linear-programing results are stated with a degree of precision which the quality of data available often does not warrant. But this holds for all managerial tools, including conventional accounting. The point is that the analyst and the manager have to be aware that the results are based on inexact or estimated figures. The figures do not have to be exact, but close enough to reality to give better results than could be obtained by conventional methods without the use of linear programing.

In the empirical application, when a linear-programing solution suggested a major change in an activity or in the use of resources, the sensitivity of the suggested change to various estimates on the basic data was determined. Where there are uncertainties about the context, the problem has been solved anew on the basis of several alternative assumptions. Correspondingly, a set of solutions has been provided. Thus, management could see how the outcome varies with changes in assumptions. Two examples may illustrate this point.

On one farm the linear-programing solution suggested the introduction of a new crop at a level of forty acres. Since the farm did not have any experience with this crop, management wanted to know how much additional income could be expected. The difference in the total income for the two programs—with and without the new crop—was about $2,000. This means that an error in the estimates of up to $50 per acre ($2,000 ÷ 40 acres) is allowable, on an original estimate of $160 income (attainable contribution) per acre.

Another farm used to plant fifty-seven acres of a particular field to cotton. The linear-programing solution indicated planting ninety-nine acres. This corresponded to an estimated yield of 1,100 pounds per acre. Since cotton yield is sensitive to weather conditions and hence

[4] Allowances or adjustments must also be made for the procedure of charging avoidable costs on the margin. In a linear-programing formulation it may be reasonable to consider each step in a cost function (see Chapter V) as a separate activity.

fluctuates, management wanted to know what would be the optimum solution in case of a low yield, say 880 pounds per acre. The solution was ninety-six acres. Thus, in any case, given the other assumptions, increasing the land area for cotton should be profitable.

One of the lessons learned from the project was that the most important type of information provided by linear-programing analysis is information about the direction of changes in production that should be followed. A similar comment can be made about the OAAS. Suppose the OAAS report indicates that a tractor is not profitable. This result would be based on estimates of the market value of the tractor and the prevailing market rate for tractor services. The analyst next must check the range of custom rates over which the tractor is not profitable. The report should indicate the weak and strong spots in operations. A further analysis can and should be made to verify the results.

An interesting consequence of linear-programing analysis was that in many cases managers, who usually considered the accountant to be a burden, were convinced that there can be a good and profitable use for detailed records. On the other hand, accountants, who played an important role in preparing the data, were ready to incorporate "alien" data, such as external opportunity cost and marginal prices, as variables in their system.

2. Application of Linear Programing to Actual Programing of Twenty Large Farms in Israel [5]

A project where the linear-programing technique was applied to twenty large, diversified farms in Israel is briefly described in this section. This project was carried out by the author with five coworkers (most of them part-time) during the years 1964–1965.[6]

[5] The author is indebted to his coworkers in this project—D. Frumkin, U. Gilead, A. Levinger, M. Noy, and D. Shalem—and to the individual planners for carrying out the project. Thanks are due to the management of the farms who agreed to participate in this experimental project. Mr. Frumkin and Mr. Gilead deserve special acknowledgment for their part in developing the working procedures and solving the many problems confronted.

[6] During the period 1958–1963, several applications of the linear-programing technique to cooperative farms were made by research workers and various

Although the experience gained in linear-programing analysis pertains to agricultural firms, this experience can be generalized to other types of firms and industries.[7] Two important aspects characterize the agricultural firm: the firm usually confronts completely elastic demand and supply functions for its products and inputs, respectively; and the variability of the data is high because of the biological aspect of the agricultural production. While the first aspect makes the application to a farm easier than to a firm in another industry, the second makes it more difficult.

There is no doubt that linear-programing solutions provide programs equal to or better than those developed by means of conventional planning methods. The feasibility and profitability of using this method of planning by many business units was studied in this project. The ultimate goal of the project was to bring the art of applying linear programing to such a stage that it would be available for use by any type of farm (or even industrial firm) and by any planner. In order to facilitate this general goal, more specific objectives were set.

One objective was to test the applicability, the effectiveness, and the efficiency of the linear-programing technique in a wide range of situations. In testing applicability, it was necessary to determine whether the various, actual farm problems could be formulated into a linear-programing model and whether a feasible and acceptable program (with regard to management subjective restrictions) could be provided for each farm. In testing effectiveness, it was necessary to measure the superiority of linear-programing solutions over conventional plans and to determine if any additional advantages exist. In testing efficiency, it was necessary to determine the cost of the actual linear-programing analysis. Another objective was to provide each farm

---

planners, often using Heady and Candler (1958) as a guide. One of the applications proved to be useful and acceptable to the management of the planned farm (Regev, Levinger, and Yaron 1964), opening the door for this project.

[7] In some respects these farms resemble manufacturing firms—for example, they are integrated firms, composed of several departments and having detailed cost accounts for each department and product. The same type of linear-programing analysis discussed below has recently been applied by the Inter Kibbutz Economic Advisory Unit to some industrial firms in Israel, arriving at similar results.

that served as a "laboratory" with a feasible and acceptable program for the product mix on the farm.

The first step was to carry out the analysis on a few well-managed farms, and to prepare the working procedures, including forms, instructions to planners, connection to a computer, and technical assistance. This step can be viewed as the pilot stage.

In the second stage, the analysis was carried out for a large number of farms, by guiding, directing, and providing the required services and facilities to various farm planners and advisers. The research workers became also initiators and directors of linear-programing analysis to be carried out by others.[8]

In total, twenty farms were analyzed, and for each a program was developed and submitted. The extent of the project and its results are indicated by data provided in Appendix C.

All programs were approved by the management of the farms as feasible and acceptable. Most of the farms adopted the suggested changes in product mix. The very fact that feasible programs were obtained for twenty heterogeneous farms illustrates again that the linear-programing technique is applicable to a wide range of situations.

The application of the linear-programing technique proved to be effective by virtue of providing useful new information to management. Such information usually is not provided by conventional planning, especially in a complex firm. The effectiveness can be measured by the difference in income between solutions obtained when the two programing techniques were applied to the same farms for identical periods and restrictions (see Appendix C).[9] The project provided pro-

[8] Every planner got a set of written directions concerning each step in the planning process. A revised version was published after the project was completed (Goldschmidt *et al.* 1965*a*).

[9] The comparison is between the solutions of two programing procedures, not only the techniques per se. Although the same source of data was available in both cases, the thorough analysis and search for data carried out while applying linear programing is usually not done in the case of regular planning procedures. The realization of the ex ante data used in programing has not been examined.

A similar comparison has been made between the results of the so-called programme planning technique and linear programing. "Program planning" is "an arithmetical technique, involving an initial selection of enterprises in descending order of [contribution] margins per unit of the scarcest factor of production;

grams for twenty farms with a potential increase in aggregate income (contribution) of about $230,000 or an average of $11,500 per farm, with the lowest and highest increase of about $2,700 and $26,000, respectively. The average increase in income was 9 per cent (a range of 2 per cent to 23 per cent).

The possible profitability resulting from large-scale use of linear programing can be suggested by comparing the costs of the project with its potential benefits. The costs amounted to roughly $22,000[10] (an average of $1,100 per farm, compared with an average of $11,500 potential increase in yearly income). The cost of managers' and accountants' time is not included.

Some of the problems in applying linear programing can be learned from the amount of time required for programing work on each farm, which ranged between two and eleven months. The reason for this lies in the character of the project, where no stress was laid on dates for termination of individual programs.

The experience indicated some important "by-products" of the use of linear programing in practice. First, its application requires a thorough analysis of the existing operations. It enabled (or really forced) management to make an overall review of the firm. In some instances, such a complete analysis itself indicated a profitable change, even before linear programing had been used. Second, the very fact of

---

. . . followed by the marginal substitution of enterprises when a bottleneck is reached in the supply of another fixed factor of production e.g. labour, when land has been the initial basis for selection" (Giles 1962, p. 3). (For details see, e.g., Clarke 1962.) This method can be viewed as falling between regular application of production economics concepts and linear programing. It is in use by the European agricultural economists (McFarquhar 1962).

Twelve sets of data drawn from farms in Israel have been used as an exercise in programme planning carried out by farm managers attending a one-year course in management and by some farm advisers. The linear-programing solutions (developed by the author and M. Noy) provided in seven cases superior programs over the programme planning solutions (expressed in income figures) by 2 to 6%. In five cases, both solutions provided the same or similar results. (Details are given in Goldschmidt *et al.* 1965*b*, pp. 26–33.)

[10] Rough figures for the costs are (I£1 = $0.33): research workers, 6 (4 of them part-time) equivalent of 3.5 workers per year, I£30,000; planners, equivalent of 15 workers per month, I£10,000; computer, 500 minutes, I£15,000; technical assistance, office, etc., I£10,000; total, I£65,000.

presenting the whole firm (or a significant portion of it) in a matrix form provides an excellent picture of the firm and the interrelationships between its various components. Third, a linear-programing solution provides a set of shadow prices that convey important economic information on possible ways to increase income. This information has been used to test various possible changes in the assumptions regarding constraints, activities, and coefficients. Fourth, the number of mechanical errors, mainly in arithmetic, which are quite unavoidable in regular planning and thus cause plans to be inferior, were greatly reduced. And fifth, the application of linear-programing analysis introduced the management of these farms to the idea of using explicitly such concepts as marginal analysis and opportunity cost. On many farms these concepts became part of management's jargon.

In making the analyses, the farm's executives, officers, and department managers were encouraged to participate in the programing work. This assured getting all the required data, which existed in some cases only implicitly, and convincing the managers that the final program was their own rather than an alien suggestion provided by the analyst. The very fact that most of the farms adopted the programs and introduced the suggested changes indicates that this policy was successful.[11]

There is a danger that unrealistic programing solutions will be developed and accepted because they are wrapped in a mathematical and scientific package that makes evaluation more difficult. To avoid such dangers, individual planners were assigned to work closely with both the farm management and the research team, while planning individual farms.

The ultimate goal of this project has been achieved—to bring the art of applying linear programing to such a stage that it would be available for practical use by any manager or adviser. As a result of this project, the linear-programing technique became a conventional technique extensively used by the cooperative farms in Israel.

[11] Forms and procedures were prepared and established so that managers would comprehend the subject matter easily. Each farm got a final report at the end of the planning work. For an English translation of one report, see Frumkin and Gilead (1966).

3. Shadow Prices and Management Judgment in an Iterative Planning Process

Linear programing as a formal technique provides quantitative information about the firm—in the form of a program and a set of shadow prices. On the other hand, planning cannot be effective without management judgment on the qualitative aspects of the firm. The application of linear programing to many farms demonstrated that both judgment and a formal technique can be incorporated into a fruitful planning process.

Management judgment is important since many variables cannot be stated in the form of a discrete or exact figure, mainly because of uncertainty. In addition, some of the data are based on a crude approximation or estimate rather than on exact measurement. This is presumably the reason that decisions in business are often based on judgment and rules of thumb, and formal techniques are suspected to be nonoperable.

One way to combine management judgment with quantitative analysis is to provide management with an array of solutions, based on a sensitivity analysis (that is, one or a few variables are changed, thus showing their respective effects on the solution). This procedure has been employed while using linear-programing analysis, by supplying nine farms with several (two to seven) alternative plans (Appendix C). The manager can apply his own judgment in interpreting the results, and in choosing among the alternatives. Still, the valuable judgment of the experienced manager is not incorporated directly into the planning process itself.

In conventional planning, managers apply judgment while carrying out the planning work. Every suggested change or several conceivable changes in the program are checked for feasibility and suitability. Judgment is used in each step of testing alternatives. The planning process can be viewed as a kind of trial-and-error procedure in which computations and judgment take place alternatively until a satisfactory solution is achieved. This procedure has been simulated to some extent in applying linear programing.

Persons in three different categories take part in programing a farm with the aid of linear programing: management, which provides information and judgment; analysts, who perform the computations and provide feedback information and advice; and accountants, who provide much of the data. They enter into the planning process both sequentially and simultaneously. The planning process can be described in an abbreviated and somewhat mechanistic form of sequential steps as follows:

Step	*Job*	*Main actor*
1-A	Defining the problems of the farm	Management, analyst
1-B	Making assumptions on various factors	Management
1-C	Formulating the problems for linear-programing model	Analyst
1-D	Assembling necessary data	Accountant, analyst
2-A	Constructing the linear-programing tableau	Analyst
2-B	Running the problem through computer	Analyst
3-A	Analyzing the results	Analyst, management
3-B	Introducing changes in assumptions and formulations	Management, analyst
3-C	Assembling additional data	Accountant, analyst
4-A	Introducing changes into the tableau	Analyst
4-B	Returning to step 2-B	

Note that steps 3-B, 3-C, and 4-A are a variation of steps 1-B, 1-C, 1-D, and 2-A. The whole process has a cyclical or iterative character. The iterative process is continued until a satisfactory program is achieved. On nine farms it took three cycles to provide a satisfactory program, whereas on seven, it took more cycles, and on four, fewer cycles (Appendix C).

In each iteration (cycle), management exerts its judgment and changes the assumptions regarding the constraints, activities, and coefficients. The analyst in turn changes the formulation, and the machine provides a new, corresponding program. Put differently, management provides its judgment, the accountant provides data, and the analyst with the machine carries out the computations.[12]

To summarize, the trial-and-error procedure enables management to check and revise its hypotheses and assumptions while gaining insights in exploring the problem.

A linear-programing solution supplies two types of information: a program that indicates the suggested changes from the existing product mix, and shadow prices that indicate the marginal value of the constraints (or activities not included). By and large, the crucial information for interpretation is the set of shadow prices.[13] They indicate and evaluate the effective constraints causing bottlenecks in the system (or negative values of activities not included). In other words, each shadow price indicates the potential change in income that can be achieved if the factors determining the constraint (or corresponding to the given shadow price) are changed.[14]

Consider a farm that purchases water for irrigation from a regional company and is confronted by a monthly quota of water. The shadow prices (money terms per unit of water) of the monthly quota of water for the first run were: April—0.06; May—0.11; June—0.14; July—0; August—0.32 (Goldschmidt *et al.* 1965). The bottleneck here is the August quota. Management should search for alternatives that will add water in August and thus increase the farm's income. One way is to get extra water in August (that is, to increase the "supply" of the restricted resource). Another way is to consider the possibility of reducing the amount of water required by the crops in August, especially by the main consumers (that is, to reduce the "demand" for the restricted resource). In practice, several means for getting additional

[12] When the staff and facilities for dealing with linear programing exist, running a problem through the computer is a simple and inexpensive process. The lower the costs of the computations are, the more iterations (cycles) can be justified.

[13] For an elaboration of this subject, see Puterbaugh, Kehrberg, and Dunbar (1957).

[14] It should be noted that if one sets the constraints tight enough, the linear-programing solution will correspond to the existing product mix. See Simon (1964) on this point.

(increased "supply" and/or reduced "demand" of) water can be checked and accordingly be formulated into the linear program. The formulation takes place by changing some coefficients.

In the example, management considered a possibility of constructing a reservoir in which water can be stored for some period of time. Accordingly, some coefficients have been changed. As a result of these changes, the second run indicated a higher income for the farm ($85,843 compared to $80,783). The shadow price for the August quota has been reduced to 0.18 (from 0.32). The potential increase in the annual income served as a basis for computing the profitability of constructing the water reservoir.

The example illustrates the role of the shadow prices in pointing out production bottlenecks in a system, the possible constraints (coefficients) that might be released (changed) at some cost, and the resulting improvement in income that might result from the changes. It also illustrates the actions in phase 3 of the iterative planning process outlined above. In actual planning only the major bottlenecks were considered, and, thus, only a few iterations; that is, few reruns were made on the computer.

Rough experiments conducted during the application of linear-programing analysis indicated that improvement in income declines rapidly with additional iterations (cycles), after the main bottlenecks have been dealt with. Accordingly, the policy was to search for changes that increase income above the current one, though not necessarily the highest one achievable.

The trial-and-error procedure enabled the planner to surmount some of the inherent limitations of linear programing—for example, cases of nonlinearity, mutual exclusiveness, nondivisibility, nonconvexity, and personal preferences.

There are a few auxiliary advantages of the described planning process, in which management, analyst, and accountant work together. All the data and assumptions can be cross-checked and their reliability verified.[15] Most of the expectations and assumptions are made explicitly rather than implicitly, as is done in conventional planning. The par-

[15] The process would also force all levels of management to meet together, if this is not done otherwise.

ticipation of an objective analyst has an educational value; as the Hebrew proverb says, "A visitor for a moment discovers every deficiency."

Of course, there are disadvantages. Joint participation may be cumbersome and time-consuming and may require exposing internal data and management relations to an alien analyst.

4. Implications for the Use of Marginality in Business and the Firm's Objective Function

In this book it is assumed that the firm's objective is to maximize the present value of its income—or, as conventionally stated, to maximize profits. Although this is a common assumption in economic theory, additional goals such as survival, growth, prestige, or utility and welfare of various groups are mentioned in the literature and by business executives. Moreover, some authors suggest other alternatives such as satisficing[16] or managerial discretion.[17] One line of argument is that marginal analysis, which is crucial for maximization of income, is not used by business concerns.

Many authors claim that businessmen really do not try to maximize profits. As a result they do not need the tools of marginal analysis. If this is true, the OAAS will not have much practical use. One can argue: If marginal analysis is not used by businessmen, and even simple techniques such as direct costing are not in extensive use, why bother with such sophisticated techniques as linear programing or the OAAS for practical use in business? The experience gained in applying linear programing indicates that by providing the proper tools, managers are able and willing to incorporate marginal analysis and to improve on income. As indicated earlier, the use of linear-programing analysis

16 "Satisficing" means the willingness to settle for a satisfactory profit level without further search for the profit-maximizing alternative (Simon 1959).

17 Consider some alternative goals such as sales maximization (Baumol 1965, ch. 13), maximization of rate of growth (Baumol 1962), managerial expense preference (Williamson 1963) or managers' income maximization (Monsen and Downs 1965). In each of these cases, the firm's income is not the primary goal; nevertheless it acts as a constraint on the goal chosen for maximization. The existence of a trade-off between income and other goals clearly exists in all cases.

caused a change in management's concepts, and terms like marginal cost and opportunity cost became part of their jargon.

The farms to which linear programing has been applied have numerous objectives; one of them is profit, but it is not necessarily the most important one. This means that the application of linear programing took place in firms that have multiple goals. Still, the objective function of the linear-programing model was formulated as maximum income.

Some of the goals known to be important have not been considered because they are not subject to quantitative analysis. Nevertheless, a Pareto criterion for welfare judgment has been assumed. Thus, whatever objective the firm has, when all the goals are set at an arbitrary level, the firm would prefer more income to less. The extra income can be sacrificed, if management so wishes, to achieve more of one or several of the other goals.[18] Based on this assumption, all the goals but income have been defined as secondary goals. Since it is impossible to simultaneously optimize more than one function, income (contribution) has been defined as the objective function in the linear-programing formulation. The secondary goals were considered as constraints.

The optimum solution obtained from linear programing indicates whether there is a conflict between the secondary goals and the income goal (by indicating the effective constraints imposed by these secondary goals), and what the shadow price of these goals are. Thus, a common denominator to all the goals, in money terms, evolved. This monetary yardstick has been used in some cases as a choice criterion for decisions concerning "allocation" of goals. In other words, this formulation provided a yardstick for application of the Kaldor criterion for welfare judgment, assuming that the various goals are set by different groups in the organization.

This experience indicates that the assumption of income maximization is operational even when the firm has a multiplicity of goals, and hence does not act solely to maximize income.

[18] In other words, in Cyert and March's terms (1963), a larger cake is always preferred, to be divided among the various parties who set the goals of an organization. Moreover, increasing income is not necessarily at odds with increasing some other goals. For a formal model providing for such a situation, see Ijiri (1965, ch. 3).

It can be argued that for a regular firm, a resource is never limited in an absolute sense. It is almost always possible to acquire more of the resource at some price. This implies that the shadow price of the resource equals the market price at the margin. Thus, only the secondary goals (not necessarily all of them), formulated as constraints, will have shadow prices that do not have market prices. But in practice, management imposes restrictions on the extent of some resources used. For example, because of policy considerations, management restricts the amount of capital to be used. This is not an outside constraint but can be viewed as a secondary goal—security or survival. In other words, all or most of the constraints can be viewed as secondary goals. Dorfman (1960, p. 609) notes: "John Dewey taught us long ago that means and ends, constraints and objectives, might roughly be separated for purposes of discussion but were so intimately intertwined that they were fundamentally indistinguishable."

Part Three
Basic Concepts

XII
A QUASI-DECENTRALIZED MODEL

The measurement of income and performance for the various segments of a business firm is crucial in management. One can find a dichotomy between attitude and practice, however, regarding this point. On the one hand, the firm is viewed as a single entity. Any attempt to check the profitability of one of its segments is considered artificial. This attitude (conceptually and practically) is taken by many farm-management analysts. On the other hand, many large firms consist of several operating units, each of which is considered (practically as well as analytically) as independent except for the central management function.

The main objective of this study is to develop an information system which will allow decisions and control of resource allocation according to accepted economic principles. For this purpose it is necessary to construct a system in which the firm's operations are decomposed into both individual segments and periods. For each period and segment, cost and income are measured. The traditional cost-accounting system is designed to facilitate such a decomposition, by distributing (allocating) all costs to periods and segments. This distribution is based typically on "discretionary procedures," which may hamper both decision making and control in an economic context. A different conceptual model is suggested here in which the firm's operations are decomposed (in both spatial and temporal contexts) so as to minimize the arbitrariness of this distribution.

Two organizational forms for business are usually recognized in both literature and the real world—centralized and decentralized. Review of the literature (see Appendix D) implies that neither state exists in the real world. Rather, operating firms are characterized by a state somewhere between complete decentralization and centralization. A quasi-decentralized model is therefore suggested as the basic conceptual framework for analysis.[1] It is a conceptual framework rather than a mathematical model.

First, the firm is considered as quasi-decentralized in an organizational framework of decision making and planning. The concept is then extended to serve as a frame of reference for the OAAS. Finally the concept of quasi-decentralization is applied in temporal context, where each period in a chain of periods is considered similarly to a segment in a so-called centralized firm (spatial context).

The functioning of this quasi-decentralized model may be thought of as analogous to the functioning of the economy. In a spatial sense, given a perfectly competitive market, Adam Smith's "invisible hand" leads each unit to act, while striving to maximize its own profit, toward the best interest of the whole economy. If externalities and increasing returns to scale do not exist, macro- and microefficiency coincide. In a temporal sense, Dorfman, Samuelson, and Solow's intertemporal "invisible hand" (1958, ch. 12) leads each unit to act, while striving to maximize current profits, toward long-run asset-value maximization. If current prices and current rate of change are considered, long-run and current efficiency coincide.

1. Application to an Organizational Form of Decision Making

In order to present the quasi-decentralized model, the application of this concept to an organizational form of decision making must be presented. This application rests on the empirical research of linear programing analysis in business, as described in Chapter XI.

[1] The term "quasi-decentralized" is borrowed from Whinston (1964*a*, p. 441).

A review of the subject of centralization and decentralization as organizational forms of business indicates that each is a relative rather than an absolute state in organization. Further, the review indicates that centralization is required for optimal resource allocation and that decentralization is required for effective motivation of managers. Thus, even the so-called decentralized firm, in order to use resources efficiently, has to be partially centralized. On the other hand, the so-called centralized firm delegates some authority de facto and thereby is partially decentralized. One can view the firm and in turn the process of management as decentralized in the delegation of operational decision-making power and as centralized in the control of scarce resources and decisions with respect to meeting the firm's central objectives.

In every firm the individual segment, whether division, department, or production line, is independent to some extent since its manager must make decisions. On the other hand, each segment is restricted in its decisions in some manner by central management. Therefore, the segment is considered as quasi-independent. Since the organization is neither centralized nor decentralized, we may call it quasi-decentralized. In a decentralized firm, the independence of the segment is dominant. In a centralized firm, on the other hand, central management and its control are dominant. The quasi-decentralized model fits both cases. The special facet of this model is the effort to incorporate the advantages of both decentralized and centralized forms of organization.[2] An attempt is made to connect the organizational theorist's concept to the economist's conditions for optimization.

In order to plan or make allocation decisions in a more nearly centralized firm (using linear programing or any other procedure) three types of data are required: input-output coefficients for each production process, income or cost figures for each process, and level-of-resource and other production restrictions. The managers of the production processes are best acquainted with the first type of data. The

[2] The degree of centralization or decentralization should and indeed does differ among firms. An "optimum" balance between these extreme forms is a matter of organizational considerations. For an analyst seeking to allocate the resources of the firm in an optional manner, the organization of the firm is considered as "given."

second type of data—cost and income—is or should be provided by the accounting system. Even if the accounting system is designed to provide technical coefficients, part of the information on these coefficients must come from lower-level managers, since they are familiar with the technological processes and restrictions. In short, data and information originating from both central management and lower-level managers (department managers) should be considered while planning the firm.

Linear programing can be used to meet the operational conditions for optimal resource allocation. A straightforward application of the simplex method, however, assumes implicitly that the firm is centralized. A special procedure of applying linear programing is suggested, based on the author's experience. This experience indicates two relevant points. First, the planning process is a kind of trial-and-error procedure, like most other decision-making processes (see Chapter XI, Section 3). The first solution in the planning process is a provisional one, providing a list of shadow prices (for the restrictions and the nonincluded activities) as well as a tentative production plan. Subsequently, management may change its assumptions, restrictions, and formulations. Recomputation provides a new program, which in turn supplies further information given the new set of assumptions and restrictions. This process continues until an "acceptable" program is achieved. Second, an analyst has to guide and carry out the planning process in cooperation with management. The synthesis of the analyst's tools and analytical power with the manager's experience, judgment, and decision power provides the best planning results.

While applying this planning process, the departments' managers take part by providing the data and participating in the trial-and-error procedure. Even in a centralized firm, managers at all levels make decisions. By participation in the planning process the manager learns about the economic effects of his actions on the firm and the interrelations of his department with other segments of the firm. This knowledge will serve as a guideline for his actions and decisions, given that the control structure (management evaluation) is in line with the decision framework.

Presumably the participation of lower-level managers in the planning process will motivate them toward better performance. Although this opinion or conclusion is in dispute, Vroom (1965, ch. 4), citing various experiments including his own, concludes in the affirmative.[3]

To summarize, the organizational planning process outlined in this section provides a mechanism for optimal resource allocation because the firm is considered as one unit. This holds for both centralized and decentralized firms.[4] The relative autonomy of the segment's manager

[3] Zannetos (1965, p. 51) cites results of studies that suggest "more decentralized and participative decision making." On the other hand, A. Charnes and A. C. Stedry (in Bonini, Jaedicke, and Wagner 1964, p. 189) and Vroom (1965) cite studies with other results. See also Anthony (1965, pp. 49–50).

[4] The planning process as mentioned in the text may also be applicable to a more nearly decentralized firm. In a decentralized firm the planning process takes into consideration both the autonomy of the division's managers and the firm's overall objectives and considerations (corporate restrictions and interdivisional dependencies). The former point assumes decentralization; the latter, centralization. The application of the quasi-decentralized model as a framework for planning, in which each division is considered as quasi-independent, seems to provide a workable solution. The planning process suggested here implies the use of linear programing, where the whole firm is considered in the linear-programing formulation as centralized, and the treatment of each division as a quasi-independent unit. In short, the "decentralized" division is considered as a part in a "centralized" program.

An analyst or a group of analysts is assigned to carry out the planning process. The analyst will carry out the planning in the same manner as if each division were an operating firm. Two additional conditions must be met: the division's managers, knowing that the firm's overall considerations and restrictions exist, must agree to them as a necessary restriction while carrying out planning for the division, and the programs for all the divisions must cover an identical time period.

The analyst has to participate in the formulation of the problems to be solved and help in establishing the constraints and activities. This formulation should be carried out both for the firm at large and for each division. As a second step the analyst pools all the necessary data and carries out the computations. The computations for arriving at an optimal solution can be made either by inserting each division's data as a block in one linear-programing tableau and solving by means of the simplex method, or by using a decomposition method, if the size of the matrix becomes too large. The method for arriving at an optimal solution is purely a computational problem.

The solution for each division is returned to the division's manager as a suggested program with the list of shadow prices based on the division's data, assumptions, and restrictions and the firm's overall considerations and restrictions. The shadow prices for each of the firm's constraints reflect the objectives of central management and must be reviewed by them. This is the first step in the trial-and-error procedure of planning. The managers, both divisional and central, (especially in a decentralized firm) is maintained, and motivation of the department's manager (in a centralized firm) is thereby provided. In addition, the outlined planning process ensures exposure of the lower-level managers (of divisions or departments) to the firm's overall goals and problems. The author's experience indicates that this point was of major importance within this kind of framework when linear programing was used for planning the product mix on large farms.[5]

The attractiveness of the model lies in incorporating the advantages of both a decentralized organization (motivating managers, leaving decisions to those with the most intimate technical knowledge, economizing in the transmission of information) and a centralized organization (reconciling goals, easing the transfer of resources, overcoming externalities, avoiding harmful results of "market bargaining").

The widely accepted idea that the main problem in organizational behavior is to ensure that each manager is doing his best cannot be accepted, because adding optima from every segment will not necessarily produce an overall optimum. If the quasi-decentralized model is applied as a framework for developing the firm's information system (the OAAS), it will help to ensure that each manager is doing his best in his segment so as to serve the goal of the firm as a whole.

2. Application to an Accounting System

A conceptual framework is needed to specify the type of information required for effective management, especially for decision making and control. In other words, we may examine the application of the quasi-

---

will now consider the information, introduce changes in the assumptions, and allow recomputations.

The whole process may take several iterations as outlined above. In this trial-and-error procedure the divisions' managers take an active part. The final division's program is both "micro" (division) and "macro" (firm at large) optimal, and the division manager can think of his section of the general program as "his own program." (Other operational models are suggested by Baumol and Fabian 1964 and by Whinston 1964*b*. See Appendix D.)

[5] This organizational form of planning also provides a multiple check on the data and the assumptions used because two levels of management participate in the planning process, with coordination and judgment supplied by an objective analyst. Thus, the procedure provides the means of comprehensive control over the reliability of the data and of the basic analysis.

decentralized model to accounting. The framework to be presented here should work in any firm, no matter what the firm's degree of decentralization, although for simplicity the discussion assumes a multiproduct, centralized firm.

The firm and its segments are viewed in a manner similar to the formulation required for the use of the linear-programing technique. Consider a linear-programing tableau where each activity is viewed as an entity (vector) and, at the same time, as a part of the whole firm (set of vectors). Now, each activity "competes" with others for limited resources (constraints). Any segment in the accounting report may be considered like an activity in the tableau. Each segment is an entity but restricted by interdependencies and overall constraints of the whole business.[6] The quasi-decentralized model helps to approach this objective.

To make decisions and exercise control, in either a large or a small firm, it is necessary to know what contribution each segment is making to the firm's overall objective. Hence, the income of each segment should be measured. This can be done only if the firm's operations are decomposed into individual segments in the analytical framework. Since the ideal situation—to consider each individual segment as an independent division—cannot be fully achieved, it is suggested that each segment be viewed as quasi-independent.

The firm may be thought of as a black box which trades commodities

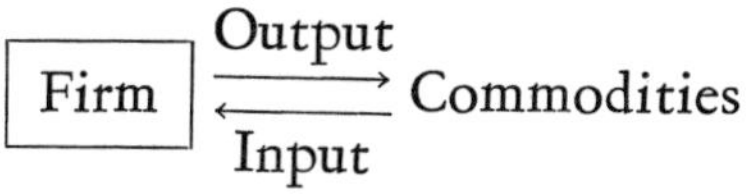

in the market. "Commodities" here means anything that is either an input or output. Since commodities have prices, it is assumed that the income for a discrete time period can be measured.

The firm in turn is composed of segments, each of which can also be viewed as a black box.

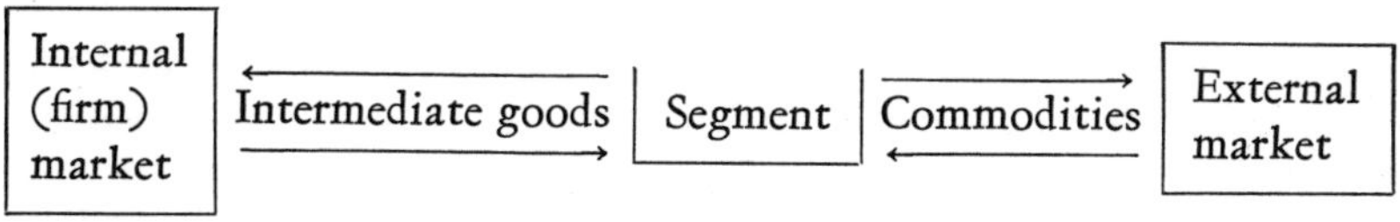

[6] See also Churchill and Stedry (1966, p. 4) on this approach.

The segment "trades" commodities in the external market and "trades" intermediate goods within the firm (that is, in the "internal market").

If there were a way to consider all the intermediate goods as commodities, a perfect decomposition would be achieved, and the model described earlier would emerge. The objective is to consider intermediate goods as commodities whenever possible. The more this can be and is done, the more the ideal model is approached. The more intermediate goods are considered as commodities, the more closely the segment can be treated as an independent firm and the more the income figures are reliable for decisions and control purposes.[7] This implies that prices should be assigned to these intermediate goods. In other words, assigning proper transfer prices will enable the decomposition of the firm into quasi-independent units.

Utilizing the linear-programing formulation to describe a firm provides another approach to decomposing the firm. A schematic form of a linear-programing tableau prepared for three activities is presented in Figure 8. In the tableau, each activity stands as an entity and the dependencies (including the intermediate goods) are formulated as restrictions.

The accounting report may be viewed in a similar way. Suppose each activity in the tableau is considered as a segment in the accounting report. Each segment earns income (similarly to the Cj coefficient) and is subject to restrictions. In the linear-programing formulation, all the activities must be aggregated into one unit (the whole firm), whereas in the accounting report the firm is decomposed into individual units (segments). Therefore, in the accounting report the objective is to untangle the restrictions and partition the dependencies as much as possible. Since some of the restrictions cannot be untangled, each segment in fact is restricted and thus quasi-independent.

The discussion above may imply a contradiction. On the one hand, the outstanding characteristic of the linear-programing solution is that it takes into consideration all the restrictions and activities simultaneously. In the suggested model, on the other hand, the opposite is done—each segment is considered as a separate unit. The two models

[7] Even a sovereign independent firm never is really independent. The very existence of externalities and government interventions provide evidence to this fact.

Figure 8. A schematic linear programing tableau

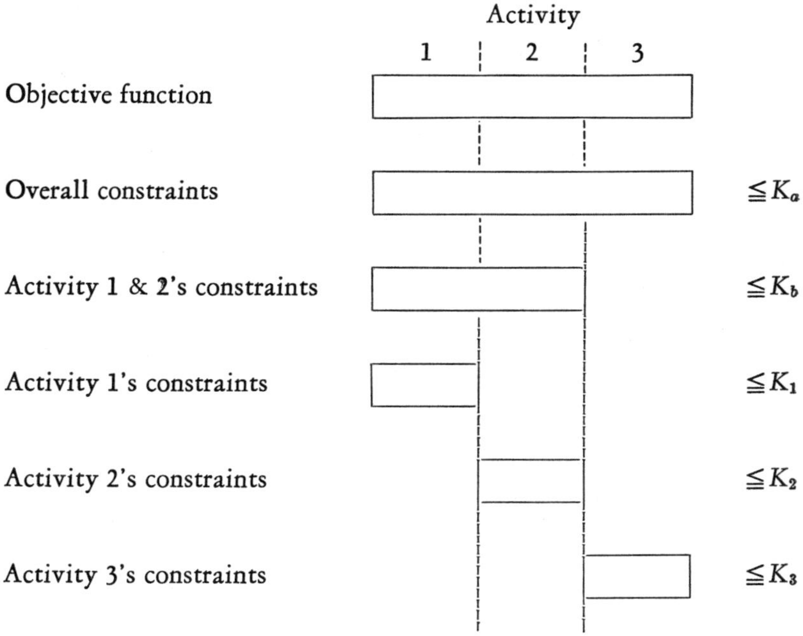

do not contradict each other, but rather should be used in a complementary manner.

The application of linear programing to programing the product mix of a firm is conditioned by the availability of detailed data for each activity. The accounting system, which supplies the data, should be designed so as to provide the necessary data. This can be achieved if the suggested quasi-decentralized model is used as a framework around which the accounting system is constructed. Moreover, the ex post accounting analysis should be carried out in a framework which is similar to the ex ante programing analysis.

The position taken above implies that the quasi-decentralized model is applicable to accounting when a firm uses the linear-programing technique in analysis. Nevertheless, the applicability also holds when nonformal programing or decision procedures are used. Application of the model has also important implications for control.

The firm is composed of various segments and production processes which are usually interdependent.[8] Partitioning these dependencies is the main problem which the analyst faces if he wants to decompose the firm into individual segments.[9]

There are essentially two kinds of dependencies that are created by the firm's overall policies (including long-range plans and secondary goals) and the physical production patterns or relationships.[10] The dependencies caused by the latter are termed here "technological dependencies." The technological dependencies linking segments include: (1) limited quantities of versatile resources, or facilities such as land, capital and plant, for which segments compete; (2) productive services such as maintenance, electricity, and research, which are not directly attributed to segments; (3) joint products—several outputs from a common input, such as oil products in a refinery or milk and calves from cows; (4) intermediate goods—the output of one activity becomes the input for another activity such as batteries for cars or green fodder for cows; and (5) externalities—actions in one segment affect another's production, such as bees fertilizing cotton blossoms or noise reducing output.

Brief analysis of each dependency shows how it can be considered in the analytical model. Overall policies of the firm can be viewed as general restrictions and thus are treated in the same manner as limited resources (point 1 above). This leaves only technological dependencies to be considered. And these technological dependencies can be reduced to two kinds—those involving intermediate goods (point 4) and general restrictions (point 1). These two dependencies provide the skeleton around which the suggested quasi-decentralized model is constructed.

[8] Instead of viewing the firm as grouping activities, Stedry (1960, ch. 5) suggests viewing the firm as grouping factors. External economies and diseconomies are replaced by cooperation and rivalry in factor use.

[9] Frequently the firm is viewed as vertically integrated—steel mill and car manufacturing, for example, or fodder crops and livestock—or horizontally integrated—car and truck manufacturing, or cows and poultry. The partitioning line can be viewed as being "perpendicular" to the direction of integration. Practically speaking, the kind of integration is not of importance; the main problem is to partition the dependencies among the segments.

[10] A third kind, market imperfections, is disregarded by assumption. The dependency may be caused, for example, when competing goods produced by the firm are sold, or an input for several activities is bought, in an imperfect market.

Productive services (point 2) are considered in the same manner as conventional production processes. As such, these services become quasi-independent units just like production activities. In some cases, the service activity can be considered as a process which is imposed on the firm by management and therefore looked upon as a restriction (research, for example).

The problem of joint products (point 3) can be viewed as follows. The common input or process is considered as a limiting resource in regard to the products which are produced from it. In some situations the common input or process (cows) on the one hand, and each of the final products (milk and calves), on the other hand, are considered as quasi-independent units.

Externalities (point 5) can be considered as either intermediate goods or restrictions. Externality refers to the situation where the production outcome or the technology of one activity is affected by actions taken in another activity. In particular, externality exists when some decision variables are not entirely under the control of the person whose decision is being considered. The distinction between an externality and an intermediate good can be made simpler by considering an intermediate good as more or less "tangible" and as produced intentionally for transfer. Hence it can be thought of in the same way as a commodity produced for the market. An externality, on the other hand, is produced "unintentionally" while production takes place, and often it is less "tangible" than a regular intermediate good. When the externality can be valued, it is treated in the model as an intermediate good. For example, noise in one department may hamper production in the neighboring department. If the reduction in productivity can be measured, the noise should be considered as an "intermediate good" with a negative value. Similarly, if the cotton blossom causes an increase in honey yield of $0.20 per acre of cotton, the blossom nectar can be considered as a regular intermediate good that is transferred by the bees from the cotton to their hives. On the other hand, if the externality cannot be valued or is a nonseparable externality (see Appendix D), the externality is considered as a restriction (that is, like a limited resource).

By elimination or reduction, the whole list of dependencies has been reduced to two kinds: restrictions (limited resources,[11] policies, common inputs in joint products and externalities in some cases) and intermediate goods (including the remaining common inputs and externalities).

To summarize, the firm can be viewed as composed of segments that are interdependent because of mutual restrictions and "exchange" of intermediate goods. The objective of the analytical model is to partition these dependencies into intermediate goods which are "traded" among the segments. In this way each segment is viewed as a contribution center. Each segment has its own costs and revenues, and thus income may be calculated. Since some dependencies cannot be partitioned, they become restrictions. Thus, the individual segments are considered as quasi-independent—that is, independent in one sense, restricted in another sense.

The decomposition of the firm into quasi-independent units can be carried out only if transfer prices are assigned to intermediate goods. Two types of prices are used: market prices when a market is available for the intermediate good and determined values when a market does not exist. This implies that "partitioning" of the linear-programing tableau (the broken vertical lines in Figure 8) is either objective (when a market exists) or artificial (when a market does not exist).

As a final point, the extent of carrying out the decomposition depends on the type and number of the dependencies,[12] and on the benefits and costs of the additional information.

The application of the quasi-independent model to an accounting system has just been outlined. For measuring periodic income, however, the whole planning horizon must be partitioned into periods, within which income is measured.

3. Quasi-independent Period in a Sequence of Periods

A troublesome area in managerial economics and accounting is the problem arising because of the continuous nature of a firm's actions

[11] A limited resource can be considered as an activity that provides service to other segments.

[12] The more dependencies there are, and the more the dependencies cannot be untangled, the more artificial the decomposition is. This observation also holds for the extent to which decentralization can be carried out in firms.

and the need for periodic evaluation of these actions. It is necessary to measure cost and income for a discrete period of time. But the very act of partitioning the flow of actions into time intervals is arbitrary in nature. The production process is continuous over a long period of time, and the cycles of production, or the various short period processes, start and end at different dates. For many production processes there might be an ideal period for analysis purposes but for the whole firm there is no single ideal period to be considered.

The arbitrary nature of the partitioning of the flow of actions can be partially surmounted by the suggested conceptual model. Each period is viewed in the analytical framework as a quasi-independent unit in a sequence of periods. This is analogous to the model outlined in the previous section, where each segment is viewed as a quasi-independent unit in the firm. Just as each segment is operated so as to maximize the firm's total period income, the operations in each period are carried out so as to maximize the objective of the going concern in terms of maximum present value of income.

In the former model, where spatial decomposition took place, each segment was viewed as a black box trading commodities and intermediate goods. The actions during a calendar period may be viewed similarly.

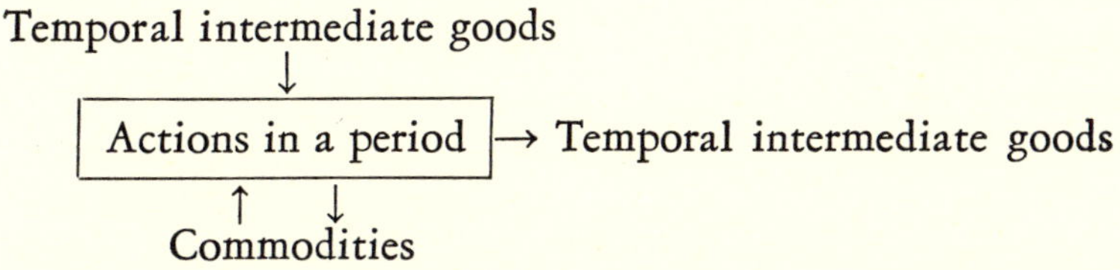

The characteristics of the internal "trade" for intermediate goods in the present model differs somewhat from the "trade" in the former model. The interperiod "trade" is carried on between two consecutive periods, and only in one direction. The output of period $t - 1$ is the input of period t. "Trade" consists mainly of temporal intermediate goods (assets) rather than of commodities. In spite of these differences, the analogy is meaningful and important for the present development.

If period income is to be measured, temporal intermediate goods must be considered as commodities. This is one of the main concerns in accounting practices. Prices must be assigned to these temporal intermediate goods. The more these prices are based on economic principles, the more the period income figures are reliable for economic decisions and control purposes. The suggested model attempts to approximate such a situation.

This problem may be illustrated by utilizing a linear-programing formulation of a long-range plan for the firm. A schematic form of such a tableau prepared for a three-period plan is presented in Figure 9. To

Figure 9. A schematic temporal linear programing tableau

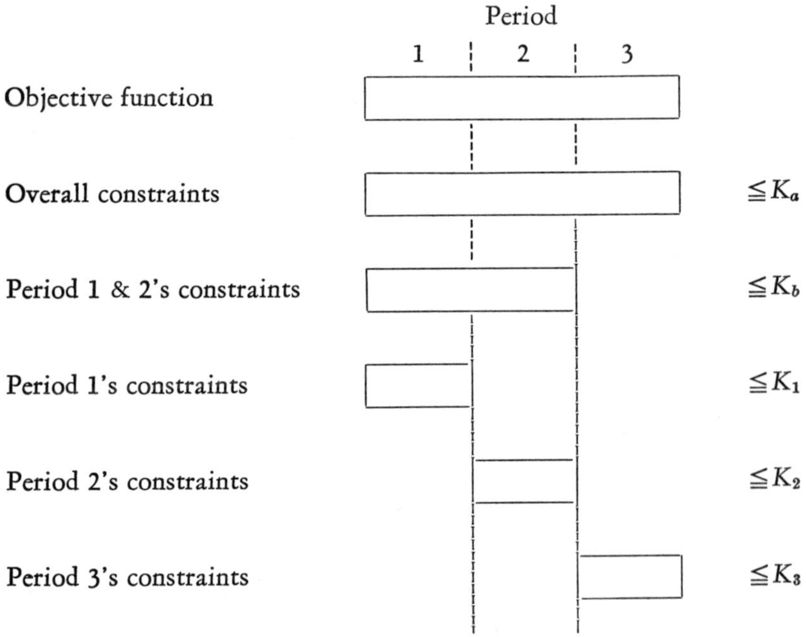

make this model operational, the value of cash flows subsequent to the horizon (the value of the assets at the horizon) have to be determined.[13] This means that these assets must be valued if an objective analysis is to be made. In the linear-programing formulation the objec-

[13] See Weingartner (1963, ch. 8) on this subject.

tive function is to maximize the income flow at the horizon, which in turn maximizes the present worth, on the condition that interest is charged periodically.

In the present analysis, the aim is to partition the "period blocks" in the linear-programing tableau into quasi-independent units, each composed of a period. If the horizon chosen is the end of a period, the linear program reduces into the black box formulation. This means that if the temporal intermediate goods (assets) are priced (valued) on economic principles and interest is charged, maximizing the period's income is equivalent to maximizing the present worth of the firm. This statement holds if long-range considerations, imposed as restrictions, are observed (see Chapter XIV).

The temporal quasi-decentralized model is completely abstract, unlike the spatial quasi-decentralized model, which is somehow tangible and even applicable as an organizational form. While each segment or group of segments has a manager, a "period" does not have a manager; rather a manager manages the firm or segment over a sequence of periods.

The management process is viewed from another perspective. At the beginning of a period a manager accepts the responsibility to operate a segment of the firm. At the end of the period he turns this segment in and gets the same segment back, but in a new period. In other words, in the temporal quasi-decentralized model, the quasi-independent period "buys" assets at the starting date from the former period and "sells" assets at the ending date to the next period. Being responsible for both the old and the new periods (or a whole sequence of periods), the manager will be reluctant to transfer income among the periods, as long as the transfer of income does not increase the present value of the future income stream. Moreover, the manager should have as an objective the maximization of income for each period (subject to restrictions imposed by long-range considerations).

Adhering to this objective, the transfer price of goods transferred from one period to another has to be specified so that income is not transferred among periods. This means that the income is generated, earned, and reported concurrently with the production process. This concept, which implies measuring income as it is generated, is alien both to accounting and to many economic calculations.[14] However, this concept serves as a main premise in the OAAS as developed in Chapter XV.

The perpetual actions of a going concern can be viewed as composed of individual periods, which are interdependent because of long-range restrictions and the existence of assets. The objective of the analytical model is to partition time dependencies into "goods" which are "traded" among periods. Assigning proper transfer prices (values) to the "goods" permits the income of the period to be measured, and thereby each period is in a sense independent of other periods. Still, some of the long-range restrictions cannot be partitioned and priced. Thus a quasi-independent period emerges.

Just as in the spatial model, two types of prices are used: market prices and determined values. Because market opportunities for temporal intermediate goods are rare, determined values developed from market prices are mainly used. This argument implies that the "partitioning" in the sense of the linear-programing tableau (the broken vertical lines in Figure 9) is mostly artificial. Without this kind of partitioning, however, annual income cannot be measured.

[14] While accounting measures the income when it is realized, usually at the end of the production process, in economic calculations for decisions the income is estimated at the outset, before the process starts.

XIII
A GENERALIZED MANAGERIAL INFORMATION SYSTEM

Decision making is one of the main functions of management. Unfortunately, a wide range of ideas and even ambiguities exist regarding the relationships between information systems and management functions, in both the literature and business itself. Even subjects or terms like "management," "decisions," "planning," and "control" convey different connotations to different people.

The objective of this chapter is to provide the background necessary for an understanding of the new accounting system. No attempt is made to provide a thorough analysis of the subject of decisions, planning, and control.[1] On the contrary, some problems are treated superficially. Specifically, the objectives are to clarify various points concerning management functions, relying heavily on former studies, to suggest a generalized information system in which the OAAS is anchored, relying on the systems approach,[2] and to try to indicate the interrelations and connections between the ideas in this study and some of the managerial techniques more widely accepted in business and literature.

[1] For an analysis of this subject, see Anthony (1965).

[2] The term "systems approach" "suggests a meaningful integration of activities" (Black 1967, pp. 8, 41). There are two complementary ways of looking at a systems approach (Boulding 1956, p. 200): each unit under analysis may be viewed as a part of a larger body, or the empirical universe may be analyzed by means of applying various disciplines.

Decisions are related to future actions and are based on expectations. However, most information must come from the past. Any move that management decides upon is determined mainly by ex post variables. This may be illustrated by comparing a business firm to a boat. Vision ahead is completely blocked so that the navigator can look out only from the stern; he can see only where the boat has been. He has to provide the best information he can to the captain, who must decide on the boat's future course. The captain instructs the helmsman and the engine room crew about their actions. In the analogy, the navigator corresponds to accountant or analyst, the captain corresponds to the manager, and the helmsman and crew correspond to the foreman and laborers. The joint actions of the crew on the boat are conditioned by the transmission of information.

A managerial information system can be conceived of as a "system of systems" or as an interrelated set of systems. Thus, for example, each of the following techniques—accounting, budgeting, and linear programing—can be thought of as a system, and together they should constitute a system of systems. Each system should be judged in terms of its fitness to the whole system rather than as standing independently. In this context attention is directed naturally toward gaps between the individual systems and between theoretical models and practical techniques.

Such an information system, if it is to work, must provide for the conceptual bridging of the gap between accounting, based on ex post information, and production economics, which requires an ex ante analysis. To improve the process of managing a firm, the functions and responsibilities of the cost accountant, analyst, and controller must be related to the requirements of the manager through an information system generally accepted as necessary by all parties.

1. A Framework for a Managerial Information System

To construct an information system for management purposes, the management functions need to be defined and those activities which require information or produce information or both must be delineated.

The term management has many connotations and there are numerous classifications of the management functions. On the one hand, some authors base their breakdown of management functions on Fayol's thesis—namely, planning, organizing, commanding, coordinating, and controlling. On the other hand, some consider decision making in its broadest sense as synonymous with managing.[3] In any case, the main functions revolve around decision and control—the functions upon which this chapter centers.

Decision and control can be subdivided into the following activities:[4] establishing goals and policies; searching for information; establishing expectations; evaluating alternatives; deciding—selecting among alternatives; implementing the results of the decisions; coordinating the actions of members of the organization; observing, recording, and reporting the results of the actions; evaluating the former activities; and recognizing and defining problems.

Each of these activities requires and/or generates information. The process of management can be thought of as a continuing cycle involving these activities as well as some others. Thus these activities provide the skeleton around which an information system may be constructed. Such an information system can be considered and depicted as a cycle through which information flows.[5]

Any attempt to construct a framework for an information system for a firm may be subject to an arbitrary and mechanistic presentation. In order to simplify the discussion which follows, however, such a framework is depicted in Figure 10. The diagram helps to illustrate the various activities, designated as phases in the system, the location of each phase and its interrelations with other phases, and the direction of the flows of information.

Unfortunately, this classification, like other classifications or diagrams for complex systems, is not simple. Rigidly adhering to this scheme does not adequately describe how the system should function in a business firm. Moreover, an information system should be adjusted to meet the special needs of each firm. Some actions should be taken simultaneously and/or informally, and some even should not be carried out at all.

[3] Simon (1960, p. 1) and Forrester (1961, p. 93), for example.

[4] See Heady (1952, pp. 465–466) and Anshen (1963, p. 23). For the decision-making process, see Cyert and March (1963, pp. 84–86) and Drucker (1967).

[5] See Welsch (1964, ch. 1) and American Accounting Association (1966, p. 50).

This presentation does, however, make several important contributions. It incorporates the various managerial activities into one system. It singles out the activities of searching and developing expectations. It makes a distinction among long-range planning, programing, and

Figure 10. A generalized framework for a managerial information system

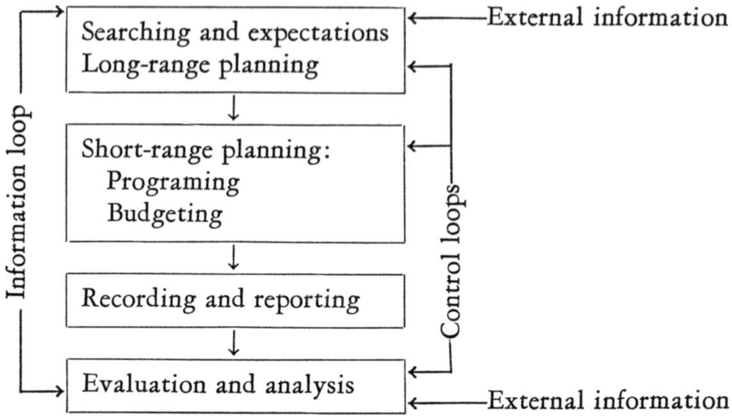

budgeting.[6] It provides for the possibility of evaluating and controlling the actions of individuals at all levels in the organizational hierarchy. It provides for feedback information to be used in planning and control. And it considers the system as a cycle in which the final stage is, in a real sense, the first stage of the new cycle.

The discussion below describes briefly the function of, the needs for, and the special aspects of the various phases outlined in Figure 10. The following material is not new. The various components are described, however, in order to give a complete presentation of the system. The classification and definitions here serve as premises in later discussions and throughout the book.

Searching and Expectations. Search is the activity of looking for relevant information and alternatives. Expectations, on the other hand,

[6] The system is similar to the recent Planning-Programming-Budgeting System (PPBS) designed for the U.S. government, though there are important differences in definitions and content.

are subjective notions of things to come.[7] This phase of the system is required for planning or decision making.

Economic theory assumes the environment to be "given." It teaches only how an optimum decision can be made, given that environment. The manager, however, has to acquire knowledge about both the existing and the expected environments. This implies, according to Simon (1959, p. 269), that other properties of an economic man such as learning, estimating, searching, and information processing have to be considered.

Expectations describe management's present attitude toward the future values of economic variables. A distinction is made between uncontrollable and controllable variables. The uncontrollable variables, such as the state of nature (climate), general economic environment (price and demand level), and competitors' actions, have to be predicted and examined. The controllable variables, such as coefficients of a new production process, have to be estimated. The new coefficients are "alien," and they never have been experienced by the firm; thus management only estimates what they may be in practice. Both forecasts and estimates have to be based on information which either exists inside or outside the firm and for which a search must be made. In other words, "information is always created, not taken" (Churchman 1961, p. 54). Information based on forecasts and estimates is used to form expectations in regard to certain variables or their values.

A search for new information and alternatives (internal and external to the firm) depends heavily on management ambition. But certainly it is initiated or stimulated when for example, a failure to earn satisfactory income (and/or utility) is experienced,[8] a relatively high income can be earned by eliminating a bottleneck, the probability of finding

[7] See Katona (1958, p. 59). For other authors' definitions see Bowman (1958, pp. 3, 12, 77, 189). The term "expectation" as used here does not hold the connotation of mathematical expectations or expected value as employed in statistics.

[8] This reasoning can be explained by the maxim "Necessity is the mother of invention." However, experiments reveal that the search ability declines when the necessity is very high (Krech, Cruchfield, and Ballachey 1962, pp. 34–37). In business, an inefficient firm with very low profits cannot afford to spare managerial ability for search, since management barely controls the existing situation.

better alternatives is high, or concern for prestige induces a continuing search for improvements or for innovations.

The search activity brings about a change in expectations regarding only a portion of the variables relevant to the firm. The rest of the firm's variables or their values are expected to continue unchanged. This implies that related ex post data can be used for ex ante decisions and programing. In other words, except when an explicit change is introduced (because the expectations suggest the need for it), the rest of the data can flow directly from the reporting phase to the planning phase. The search phase only screens the data; part of them is passed on without change and the other part is modified or discarded and new data are introduced.

Usually expectations are formulated as hunches and not through some more formal procedure. To make this phase more reliable, expectations should at least be formulated explicitly and recorded. Programing seeks to build a model of reality, and as such, it has to be built on a set of explicit assumptions. The expectations formulated by management may serve as part of the basic assumptions for decision or programing activities.

Planning. "Planning is the process of preparing a set of decisions for action in the future, directed at achieving goals by optimal means" (Dror 1963*b*, p. 50). Unfortunately, terms like "planning," "programing," and "budgeting" are often used interchangeably, and there is ambiguity regarding these activities in both the literature and in practice.[9]

A distinction is made here between long- and short-range planning. Each of these activities is composed of two stages—solving the planning problem (that is, planning for change) and preparing a plan—a budget, for the solved problem (that is, action planning).[10] Long-range planning, programing, and budgeting are defined and described below. The definition and discussion of the two stages of the long-range planning are provided in Chapter XIV, because of exposition considerations.

[9] Dror (1963*a*, p. 50) claims that the study area of planning is underdeveloped. Rossotti (1965, p. 16) claims that planning is in an experimental stage.

[10] See Ansoff (1960, pp. 231–232) and Rossotti (1965).

The various planning activities are by no means mutually exclusive. In practice they should, at least partially, be carried out simultaneously. Nevertheless, each has some special aspects that should be observed. Each of these planning activities involves decision making, where decision making is an informal process of choosing a course of action in line with the firm's objectives.

Long-Range Planning. A long-range plan can be defined as management's statement on choices concerning future actions of the firm over the complete planning horizon. Such a plan is always subject to revision or replanning. The planning process includes setting goals and policies regarding the firm's operations, choosing lines of production and resource acquisition, and, in turn, translating these into actions. The going-concern assumption and the objective of maximizing the firm's income require that events some distance in the future be considered. This means that management should carry out, explicitly or implicitly, a long-range plan. For the plan to be effective, management should prepare an explicit plan for a certain time horizon, say for a five-year period. The horizon itself is in part what management decides it to be.

The long-range plan is based on information about the present situation and expectations. Since those variables do change over time, new information requires reformulation of the old plan into a new and better one that will also cover a "new" horizon. Setting the date for replanning is also a decision that has to be specified. A practical solution is to develop a procedure for a rotating plan in which every so often a new long-range plan for a definite time horizon is developed. For example, every year preceding the act of programing, the last year's five year plan could be revised and extended for another year. As such, it would provide an important part of the expectation phase in the information system.

Programing. A program is considered to be the outcome of a formal process of reaching an optimal course of action for a given time period. The task of programing is to allocate designated, limited resources among alternative uses so as to maximize an objective function. Thus, it provides for a formal procedure of decision making on resource allocation. Programing considers simultaneously the combination of activities, the scale of these activities, and the appropriate technology for production. In short, it deals with the optimum combination of both inputs and production processes.

Any programing or decision process consists (explicitly or implicitly) of three steps: defining and formulating in a quantitative manner the objective of the firm, alternative feasible courses of action (activities), and restrictions (limited resources, externally imposed restrictions, long-range considerations, and secondary goals); assembling the data (input-output, cost and income coefficients) originating from the reporting and expectations phases; and comparing alternatives and determining the optimum program for this set of assumptions and restrictions. The quality of the program—that is, its reliability and level of income (additional income above the existing plan)—depends mainly on the reliability of the data, the extent of search activity made before and during the programing process, and the programing technique used.

Budgeting. A budget is defined here as a plan detailing a period's operations and actions in physical and monetary units. Such a budget is normally based on management decisions or the programing solution. It may be used by management to coordinate operations (input-activity-output relations) and to serve as a bench mark for evaluating performance. Note that budgeting is distinguished from programing.[11] While the program allocates the limited resources and determines the product mix given certain restrictions, the budgeting activity provides the more specific details for implementing and executing the program (decisions).

A simple example illustrates the distinction between the two techniques. Programing determines the optimum combination of machinery and labor for producing a given product and indicates whether an intermediate good can be produced by the firm instead of purchased and whether the level of raw material inventory can be reduced. Budgeting, on the other hand, determines the amount of labor required each period and schedules the production of the intermediate good and the ordering of raw materials.

[11] Usually, this distinction is made neither in the literature (Sweet 1964, p. 8) nor in business (Sord and Welsch 1958).

Both programing and budgeting are carried out at the beginning of each production period. By determining the activities to be included in the production plan, the programing phase allocates resources according to some economic criteria. The budgeting phase, on the other hand, translates the decisions or program into a workable plan; that is, it determines and schedules the spatial and temporal distribution of the inputs among given activities. In programing, the organizational borders are ignored. They must be considered, however, in budgeting. The programing phase may deal only with nonrepetitive and nonroutine decisions and leave the repetitive ones to the budgeting phase. In short, the budget states when and where an operation in the firm will take place.

Recording and Reporting. The activities of recording and reporting provide for the measurement of performance results and changes in the environment. Recording and reporting consists of two stages: the supply of input-output data by the segments to the information center or the accounting department and the accumulation and summation of these input and output data for each segment. Reporting is a current operation,[12] which is done in physical units and/or monetary terms.

The recording and reporting phase facilitates the feedback loops in the system by automatically reporting the recorded data and performance results to the involved unit in the organization. An information loop is designed to provide for the flow of necessary basic data throughout the system in a cyclical manner (see Figure 10). Thus the results flowing from the execution of previous planning plus changes in environment are transmitted via the evaluations and analysis phase to the searching and planning phases. Control loops, on the other hand, are designed to provide summary data that is used for evaluation activities.

2. Control and Evaluation of Planning and Performance

Planning and implementing plans do not automatically culminate in the realization of a firm's objective. Evaluation of the operations is also

[12] The frequency of the reporting depends on the ability to introduce adjustments in the production process, the probability of detouring from the budget, the extent of the possible damage of such detour (losses if the reporting is less frequent), and the cost of the reporting.

required. Both planning and evaluation activities can be classified as a control action, where control means obtaining correspondence between objectives and results. Such a statement implies that the information system does not function only along the main axis as depicted in Figure 10 but should also allow for deviations and should provide for information feedbacks.

Authorities differ in their conception of what "control" is or should be. What follows is the author's conception, and the one which is used in this study.

Control. Control is defined as the process of assuring that the behavior of the members of an organization is consistent with the organization's objective. In other words, control should induce effective behavior in decisions and actions among members of an organization, where effectiveness means the degree of organizational goal attainment. According to Arrow (1964*a*, p. 398):

> [Control] divides itself naturally into two parts: the choice of "operating rules" instructing the members of the organization how to act, and the choice of "enforcement rules" to persuade or compel them to act in accordance with the operating rules. Various other terms for these two problems have appeared in the literature; [an accepted form is reference] to the operating rules as control-in-the-large and the enforcement rules as control-in-the-small. It should be noted that enforcement, here as elsewhere, includes both the detection and the punishment of deviations from the operating rules.[13]

Operating rules are provided by the planning and decision-making activities in the proposed information system; the enforcement rules come from the evaluation and analysis activities (see Figure 10). Both are considered here, but not punishment for deviations. The very act of having enforcement rules (that is, the fact that deviations will be evaluated) has psychological effects and thus should motivate members of the organization, even if the results are not used directly to reward or penalize individuals.

[13] Commonly, control stands for enforcement rules.

The notion of control is used here in three contexts. First, implementation of plans is obtained by instructing subordinates and detecting deviations from instructions. Deviations of actual performance from the plan can be used in evaluation of individuals' actions. This is "management by exception."

Second, control may be considered in the context of decisions. A set of operating rules indicates how to allocate resources so as to maximize the firm's objective. This is accomplished by using improved decision-making techniques, such as production economic concepts or linear programing, and by providing correctly specified data for use in this process. Enforcement rules are developed by measuring performance in terms of the objective function: by trying to detect deviations between what could have been done and actual accomplishments and by detecting multiperiod trends in performance. This notion of control is the backbone of this study.

Third, in order for these kinds of operating rules to be effective, expectations must be developed and controlled. For this control an operating rule is achieved by instructing managers to develop expectations explicitly and record them. An enforcement rule is associated with detection of deviations of actual events from expectations.

The evaluation and analysis phase, as depicted in Figure 10, provides for enforcement in the control sense. This phase is broken into three different evaluation activities in Figure 11. These control subsystems are presented in a somewhat mechanistic format (as is true for the presentation of the whole information system in Figure 10). Nevertheless, it helps to illustrate the framework in which control is or should be exercised in a firm.

Evaluation is the process of appraising performance in terms of the deviation of actual operations from plans, or of actual events from expectations, and in terms of the degree of goal attainment. While the first context can be provided by comparing the actual outcomes with the plans (budget) or expectations, the second is a complex subject and hard to make operational.

The evaluation and analysis activities provide attention-directing information, a form of feedback information. This information indicates

Figure 11. Three generalized control subsystems in a managerial information system

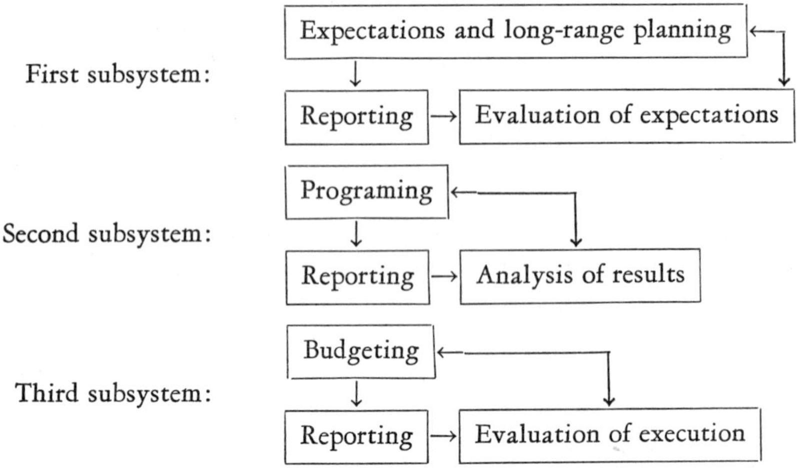

when and where there is a problem and may suggest the direction necessary to achieve improvement. It also provides data for further planning.

The second control subsystem is the primary framework around which this study is centered. It is designed to provide the required information to answer three questions (Simon *et al.* 1954, pp. 2–3) in regard to resource allocation:

Score-card questions: "Am I doing well or badly?"
Attention-directing questions: "What problems should I look into?"
Problem-solving questions: "Of the several ways of doing the job, which is the best?"

The score-card information is supplied by the reporting phase, the attention-directing information by the analysis phase, and the problem-solving by the programing phase. The score-card and attention-directing information are needed to facilitate future decisions and motivate managers.

The procedures for controlling the programing process can be viewed as similar to other production processes. The "inputs" into the process are, first, a set of assumptions regarding the restrictions, activities, and coefficients and, second, the data. The "output" is an optimum program. The process itself, involving the computations and comparisons of alternatives, can be viewed as a black box because the programing process takes place regardless of the technique used. For a set of assumptions and data, there is a unique optimum solution. The linear-programing technique, for example, will provide such a solution. The techniques actually in use by management should be evaluated and perhaps changed, since powerful programing techniques are available in the analyst's arsenal (see Chapter XI). The inputs to the program, rather than the programing process itself, have to be evaluated periodically. The assumptions are checked and evaluated by means of the first control subsystem. The data and the actual results of operations are evaluated by means of the "analysis" phase. Thus programing is controlled in two subsystems: the expectations made before planning took place (the first subsystem), and the actual results of the operations (the second subsystem).

Evaluation of Expectations. Expectations provide the assumptions used in programing. The phase during which expectations are evaluated is designed to check these assumptions, analyze them, and provide feedback information on the performance of the expectation activity. As such this is the key means of evaluating decisions.

Such evaluations usually are not practiced formally in business and only recently have they been discussed in the literature.[14] Ordinarily, people rationalize their actions and find justifiable reasons for the decision they made in the past. This is consistent with the theory of dissonance, which "predicts that, following a decision, a person will attempt to convince himself that the chosen alternative is even more attractive (relative to the unchosen one) than he had previously thought" (Festinger and Aronson 1960, p. 215).

If one wants to learn from past experience and improve expectations, he has to record his expectations and compare them with the actual outcomes. The very act of recording expectations and the knowledge that these expectations will be checked and analyzed later will improve

[14] See Modigliani and Cohen (1961), Morris (1964, pp. 119–121), and Dopuch and Drake (1964, p. 17).

the process of formulating expectations. This in turn should bring about better decisions. Such a procedure will motivate managers at all levels to perform better and will provide higher-level managers with information on expectations carried out by managers at lower levels. Edwards and Bell (1961, pp. 55–56) state:

> Genuine managerial skill should be reflected in a consistently good correlation between expected and actual events, not only for those events related to the adopted plan but also for those events associated with discarded alternatives. If events are consistently unfavorable, management is optimistic. If deviations are erratic and large, profits and losses are probably the result of luck. Management selects a course of action on the basis of expectations related to many alternatives. If the realization of the managerial expectations is generally erratic, it could select the best alternative only by pure chance. . . .
>
> An awareness of the nature of errors in expectations on all levels is a first step toward improving managerial ability, and the accumulation of this kind of information should aid in improving the decision-making process itself.

One way to evaluate expectations is to check the discrepancies between the long-range plan and the shorter-range program because the latter is based on more recent information. This is in effect a means of checking the realization of the long-range plan and thereby of checking expectations.

Evaluation of expectations is of major importance in regard to capital investment because capital outlays must be controlled, because investment decisions involve both forecasting of uncontrollable variables and estimating new coefficients of production, and because the actual results occur during a long period, long enough for the initial expectations to be forgotten. An additional task of this phase is to check whether the method and procedures used to generate these expectations are effective. In order to formalize the expectation action, it is suggested that expectations be recorded in a "diary of expectations" as an auxiliary feature of the formal accounting system. The actual events should be recorded alongside the recorded expectations developed in the past.

Analysis of Results. In the analysis-of-results phase, the operations of each segment during the past period are measured, reviewed, and analyzed. Thus, this phase serves as the mechanism for overall evaluation for either a segment or the whole firm. The task of the evaluation activity is to appraise performance in terms of the degree of goal attainment, where the goal is income maximization. There is a problem here—the objective cannot be quantified; how then should the performance be evaluated? An attempt should be made to appraise the performance in such a way that appraisal will motivate the managers to decide and act so as to maximize the firm's objective. This can be partially done by providing managers with information that indicates where and how operations should be changed in order to improve in achieving the firm's objectives. Such information should also provide motivation for the managers in pursuing these changes.

One of the objectives of the analysis phase is to check what other results could have been achieved under the same conditions, by analyzing foregone opportunities. Since this cannot be done in a simple or straightforward method (see Chapter II and IX), a common procedure for carrying out an analysis is to compare and check differences between the results of actual operations and the original plans, results from former periods, results from similar operations, or standard norms from other firms or engineering data. The reasons for differences should be analyzed. An important evaluation procedure is to examine the trend in results of operations, mainly in terms of income, over a series of periods.

The actual results of operations within a firm in terms of income figures depend on the decisions on resource allocation made originally, the economic and physical environment, and the level of performance in using technology and inputs. Practically, the effect of each factor cannot be measured. Still, the information system has to supply as much information as possible to improve management's judgment on these factors. In other words, because of the multiplicity of forces affecting them, the results of the operations cannot be evaluated in a purely objective manner.

Evaluation of Execution. This phase is included in the third control subsystem (Figure 11), which is designed to control execution. This subsystem is widely discussed in the literature under the headings of budget and control or standard costing. It is also in extensive use in industry.[15]

This phase provides for control of performance and evaluation of individuals, assuming that the operations should conform to the budget. But this assumption does not hold when the performance of a manager who makes and then carries out decisions is evaluated. This is because a manager introduces changes in the budget, and the results depend on several factors as indicated above.[16]

This phase should be used as a control on managers who do not make decisions. Evaluation is accomplished by analyzing deviations of the actual results from those budgeted. Thus, this kind of evaluation is a typical case of "management by exception." The variances are analyzed currently (according to the frequency of the reporting), and they provide attention-directing information for the managers at the supervisory level. In this phase the data has to be screened, so that management will get significant information. The report on the degree of deviations from the budget is forwarded to the corresponding level of management to correct activities within segments. Emphasis is on making the responsible units pay attention to those deviations about which something can be done and which are worth correcting.

Summary. A framework for three management control subsystems has been presented (Figure 11) and discussed in this section. Although the presentation is somewhat mechanistic, it helps to illustrate the subject matter. In the first subsystem the focus is on expectations and planning; in the second it is on planning and execution; in the third it is on execution. The first subsystem is formalized by means of long-range planning, recording the expectations, and keeping a "diary of expectations." The second subsystem is formalized by means of programing the production mix, developing the OAAS, and keeping a "diary of reallocations" (see Chapter XIV). The third control sub-

[15] Gordon (1964, p. 6).

[16] Therefore, strict conformance to a budget may be at odds with the firm's primary objective.

system is not discussed in this study because it is widely discussed in the literature and commonly used in business.

3. The Flow of Data and the Interrelation of Ex Post and Ex Ante Information

In the two previous sections a complex information system was outlined. The various parts or phases of the system are closely interrelated; none can be considered as existing independently. The difficulties involved in defining and explaining the operation of each phase separately point up the interrelations between the various activities. These interrelations can be seen in the sequence of phases as depicted in Figure 10 and in the following list. (1) Expectations are a part of long-range planning. (2) The long-range plan includes the period for which a program is developed. (3) Programing and budgeting are tightly connected. (4) The objectives and methods of analysis determine the type of reporting; hence, the report can be seen as a part of the analysis. (5) The evaluation and analysis activities automatically provide part of the search activity.

For the system to function efficiently, the same kinds of data should flow through the system, and hence the whole system "speaks the same language." Simultaneously, the individual techniques of analysis should be based on the same concepts and utilize the same types of data.

First, consider the flow of the basic data along the main axis of the information system as depicted in Figure 10. The reported data passes through the evaluations and analysis phase and the expectation phase. Part of the data is forwarded unchanged; another part is discarded or revised. Supplemented by external data, the flow continues to the planning phase. In other words, the raw accounting (ex post) data often provide a surrogate for the data on expectations used by the decision maker.

Available information from the past is used in deciding future actions. This means that ex ante activity (for instance, programing) is based on ex post information (for instance, cost accounting). In turn, the ex ante activity is checked and analyzed using an ex post report. This means that a clear line between ex ante and ex post types of analysis does not exist. The traditional view and practice is that two branches of knowledge facilitate these types of analyses—namely, microeconomics (ex ante analysis) and accounting (ex post analysis). Based on accounting principles, budgeting, recording, and reporting have been developed and applied extensively in industry (standard cost accounting). On the other hand, programing techniques have been developed and applied by economists and operations research analysts, making use of a set of production economics concepts. However, elements of both techniques should be interwoven into one system, as is done in this book.

One of the objectives of this study is to facilitate the activities of "reporting" and "analysis" in the second control subsystem as depicted in Figure 11. These activities are provided conventionally by cost-accounting techniques. Since these activities should be in line with the programing function, however, a special accounting system is necessary.

The accounting technique is a reporting technique (ex post) that provides much of the data for ex ante analysis. Thus, the question to be asked in the analysis phase is: What would have happened if some action had not been carried out? In other words, it is desirable to make an after-the-fact, ex ante analysis. This is done partially in the OAAS.

The use of the same cost and income figures (and also technical coefficients) in both the program and the budget may be questioned. The prevailing procedure in budgeting is to establish a set of figures (coefficients) as standards that management wants to be achieved. Naturally, this requires an additional set of data. There are various opinions as to what level of performance the figures in the budgets should represent. Should the standards represent average ("expected actual") or a higher level of performance? If the former approach is applicable, the same data can be used for programing and budgeting, and thus, a substantial economy in the required data can be achieved.[17]

[17] In applying linear programing (see Chapter XI), the same data used in the program was further used for the budget. In 1966 this procedure was introduced as a regular routine on a digital computer. The computer provided the optimal program and, optionally, the budgeted details for the monthly use of resources by each activity.

XIV
THE TIME PERIOD IN PLANNING AND THE USES OF OPPORTUNITY COST

The preceding chapter presented a framework for an information system that is operational over one production period. To make this framework operative, the management of a firm must also prepare a long-range plan for the firm and make decisions about changes that occur during a production period.

A distinction can be made between three kinds of plans in regard to the time period involved. The general plan for the firm is a long-range plan, say for five years, which might be replaced each year by a new plan for the next five years. Plans are also set up for periods of, say, one year. These programs are detailed and are usually arrived at in a formal manner. The third type of plan is ad hoc decisions on reallocation. For these short-term decisions, no formal technique is used; they are commonly based on the judgment of the manager.

1. The Relevancy of the "Short Run" and "Long Run" to Decisions

When time is considered in an analytical context, the terms "short run" and "long run" are often used. Unfortunately, these terms are frequently misused or misunderstood. Despite a few demurrers,[1] the dis-

[1] Alchian (1959, p. 33).

tinction between the terms is clearly made in economic theory. According to Baumol (1965, pp. 263–264):

> The long run is a period of sufficient duration for the company to become completely free in its decisions from its present policies, possessions, and commitments.
>
> The other extreme case, the very short run, is that where the firm has a minimum of free choice.

In actual life, decisions are related only to the short run since for any decision which is analyzed there are previous commitments—that is, there are always some fixed restrictions. Thus, in the real world management never confronts a true long-run situation. For various kinds of decisions, however, different variables should be considered. Suppose that a program is prepared for one year. Then only certain relevant variables would be considered. For a shorter period, say a quarter, a different set of variables would be studied, usually a smaller set. Even a plan for a longer span, say five or ten years, has to consider commitments and fixed factors; hence it is still a short-run plan although it has longer range—longer period implications.

A common problem stems from reversing the content of the definition of the long run—that is, in the long run all costs are variable. Let us present and comment briefly on two common misinterpretations. One statement is of the kind: "In the long run fixed costs are escapable."[2] This statement ignores Jevons' logical principle of "bygones are bygones." But it is impossible to escape from costs that have been committed. Call these costs sunk costs or any other name, they are irrelevant for economic analysis, which is directed toward resource allocation in future periods. Another statement is of the kind: "For long-run management decisions, full costs (both variable and fixed costs) should be used."[3] But for any decision, only the costs that the firm can avoid or save in the future count. Thus, the full-cost figure is not relevant. A similar statement is: "For long-run pricing policies,

[2] For an example of this kind of statement, see Lewis (1949, p. 9).

[3] For an example of this kind of statement, see Caspal and Eisgruber (1966, p. 7).

full cost should be considered."[4] The meaning of the term "long run" should be specified explicitly. The conventional full-cost figures do not necessarily imply total cost, or all the cost items which are relevant to the time period under consideration. This is because the conventional full-cost figures do not include some cost items, such as implicit interest, and they may be determined by means of "discretionary procedures" of cost distribution (allocation).

There is a classical distinction between short-run operational decisions and long-run decisions usually involving investments.[5] Investment is considered as an outlay that will generate income for several years, while operational expenses are those which are normally recovered in a period shorter than a year or one production period.[6] Conceptually, however, this distinction should be questioned.

Are decisions concerning inventories of the first or second type? Although such decisions have both longer and shorter period implications, they can be easily classified as type 1—that is, operational decisions—because any inventory can be thought of as being bought, processed, and sold during the production period. Decisions concerning various types of assets, such as trucks and livestock, can be considered as current operational decisions.[7] Since any asset may be considered as an inventory, the treatment of existing assets and many of the investment decisions can be analyzed in the framework of a given period.

[4] Statements of this kind are made by Brummet (1957, pp. 125–127) and Fog (1960, p. 80).

[5] For example, Shillinglaw (1961, pp. 498–506).

[6] This distinction is made also in controlling managers' actions. Cordiner (1956, p. 61), the president of General Electric, criticizes this procedure: "I believe that too much of a fetish has been made in the past of capital expenditures. A manager can lose a lot more money on inventory, foolish pricing policy, careless personnel staffing, or poor production scheduling. . . . In General Electric, capital expenditures in 1955 amounted to $153 million, but we bought $1,500 millions of materials and had a payroll of $1,200 millions."

[7] Let us illustrate this point with reference to investments in stocks. Suppose two investors purchase the same portfolio of stocks. One of them "plays the market," the other keeps the portfolio as such. Both are making current decisions. The first decides to buy new stocks every now and then (and to pay the broker's fees); the second decides always to buy the stocks he has (refraining from broker's fees).

Conventionally, when investment is considered, the cash flow is discounted, whereas the cash flow for regular operations is not discounted. In other words, interyear cash flows are discounted and intrayear cash flows are not. This procedure can be explained by the prevailing low rates of interest in the United States, which make intrayear discounts almost meaningless. When the rate of interest is high, however, the situation differs (see Chapter X).

Some production processes extend for a period longer than a year (for example, ship building). The fact that the cost of capital differs among firms and the length of time differs among operations makes the distinction between the two kinds of decisions—yearly operations and investments—less meaningful.

In conventional accounting several kinds of operations such as maintenance, training, and advertising are considered as current expenses, although they may have effects over a period of years. Nevertheless, it is difficult to differentiate "investment" from the "current expense" in costs of this kind.[8]

In short, the usual distinction between the long run and the short run may be meaningless or ambiguous for purposes of decision making. In the typical decision framework only the short run exists. Similar criticism holds for the distinction between investment and operational decisions. However, a useful distinction can be made between decisions that will affect only the current production period and not change the long-range plan, and decisions that will affect the current period and require the long-range plan to be changed as well. A given problem may have alternative solutions, some of which are of one type, some of the other. In either case, the solution depends on the long-range plan. For example, there is "excess" inventory of finished goods. They can be sold now (the first type of decision) or storage facilities can be built, allowing later sales (the second type). The long-range plan with respect to the use of these goods influences both decisions.

To overcome some of the problems indicated by the preceding discussion, the following features are suggested for use in analysis: (1) A definite planning horizon should be established so as to have a specific period of time under analysis. This will always be shorter than the

[8] See Sorter and Horngren (1962).

long-run concept.[9] (2) One period, say a year, as a fraction of the whole planning horizon, provides the basis for the main analytical model to be used. (3) Only avoidable costs of existing and future operations are considered in analyses. (4) Fixed or nonavoidable costs are considered as auxiliary information which may be required in some cases. (5) No clear-cut distinction between investment decisions and current operations is made. (6) The program for a production period considers both current operations and investments in new assets. Thus, all new investments are viewed in the context of avoidable costs. (7) The objective function is to maximize income (revenue minus cost) for a production period subject to the firm's secondary goals and other restrictions.

This format has some apparent limitations and defects, especially in regard to point 6. Nevertheless, it can be applied to actual business problems and should provide better solutions than most existing approaches.

2. The Relationship between Long- and Short-Range Planning

The going-concern assumption and the objective of maximizing the present value of income require considering events some distance into the future. This means that management should develop, explicitly or implicitly, a long-range plan as suggested in Chapter XIII. In the previous section it is argued that only a short-run type of analysis can be made. This does not contradict the need for a long-range plan, since this kind of plan also falls into the category of short-run analysis—the plan is for a firm that has already made some production commitments. By definition, a program is the result of a choice relating to one production period—that is, a short-range plan for the coming period. A long-range plan is the result of choices relating to a sequence of production periods up to the planning horizon. The problem to be analyzed is the relationship between the long-range plan (plan) and the short-range plan (program). Let us first review briefly three approaches to this problem.

A plan can be viewed as a framework for, or constructed from, the

[9] Stigler (1966, p. 108) defines the short run as "a period shorter than the long run."

programs for future periods. This approach can be demonstrated in the form of a linear-programing tableau. A schematic form of such a tableau for a three-year plan is presented in Figure 9, Chapter XII. In this model, a simultaneous solution for the sequence of periods up to the planning horizon is achieved. This type of formulation is especially applicable to investments and capital budgeting problems, when both capital constraints and other kinds of constraints are incorporated into the model. The approach also has some limitations with respect to the qualification of expectations and uncertainty about the future, estimates of the cost of capital (which, if high, discounts future outcomes heavily), and estimates of development policies and firm objectives with respect to growth.

Application of such a linear-programing model requires that several problems be dealt with. The values of the coefficients in each year t can be described by a probability distribution whose parameters (mean and variance) depend on t. The dependence of the mean on t implies collection and estimation of a vast quantity of information (coefficients), which in turn require high expenditures of time and effort. The dependence of the variance on t requires a special algorithm for obtaining a solution. Another problem is the conceivable size of the matrix. Although this problem can be surmounted by the decomposition method, the author is not aware of a study indicating a decomposition solution for a stochastic linear-programing model. Both of these situations contribute to making such a model unacceptable for practical purposes at present.

The second approach has been suggested by Modigliani and Cohen (1961):

> The decision problem confronting the entrepreneur at a given point of time is most usefully regarded not as that of selecting the best possible plan of operations over the horizon, but rather as that of *selecting the best possible first move only*. By "best possible," we mean, of course, the move that is best, not merely with reference to the first period, as though it were the only period, but with reference to the entire maximization problem over the horizon (p. 20).

They show that some of the future components and information are irrelevant to the first move or "practically irrelevant" in the sense that "they are not worth bothering about" (p. 26). Still, they suggest that some future components be incorporated "for the purpose of deciding the first move, not for the purpose of deciding later moves" (p. 55). When that time arrives, "the actual level of these components will be determined not by the level planned at an earlier date, but by the level which appears best in the light of information available at the later date" (p. 55).

A third approach is provided by Bellman's dynamic programing model (1956). In this model the computations and the solution start at the final stage, then a second-to-last stage is solved, and so on until the solution for the first stage or current period is determined.

Modigliani and Cohen's argument implies that a plan that is a general outline is required to serve as a frame for the programing activity. It is well known that the efficiency of production within a period may be at odds with long-run efficiency. For example, low income for a time may be useful if the discounted additional income from a future action is higher than the lost income from the mutually exclusive present action. Thus, the period's program should be in line with the plan. In the process of planning, the basic assumptions and policies of a firm, which are seldom stated explicitly, should be assessed. The plan should project a general outline of what management believes and aims for in regard to the firm's future moves and situation. It has to specify, for example, the policies regarding the scale of operations, lines of production, and acquisition of resources. Correspondingly, it should specify the resource requirements, especially capital, land use, labor and management training, and research. The task of the planner is to be critical in challenging the existing assumptions and policies and imaginative and systematic in formulating new alternatives.

A reconciliation of the two approaches indicated above—namely, Modigliani and Cohen's and Bellman's—is necessary in order to arrive at a long-range plan. The planning activity starts by considering a production period at the horizon. This will provide the general direction of the firm's progress. This stage can be seen as the strategic plan.

The next step will be to specify the necessary actions to be taken by the firm throughout the planning horizon—that is, between the planning date and the horizon. In this stage the policy decisions are translated into action, and therefore can be seen as action planning. Both the strategic planning and the action planning compose the long-range planning. This is, to some extent, analogous to the programing and budgeting phases, respectively, as outlined in Chapter XIII.

The plan should provide directions or restrictions on the program for the current production period. Any program can be established for the next quasi-independent period, with the overall plan imposing restrictions on it. These restrictions can be viewed as secondary goals, which are dictated by long-range considerations.[10]

Some remarks on the two planning stages are required. Strategic planning involves many variables, most of which are hard to quantify. The amount of data involved is limited and it requires the exertion of judgment by top management. Action planning, on the other hand, requires lots of data and it requires the participation of lower-level managers. In practice, strategic planning is usually done implicitly, whereas action planning is carried out more often explicitly.[11] Management experience, intuition, and judgment play an important role in strategic planning. Therefore, it is suggested that the planning process should deal with "one aspect at a time" (Anthony 1965, p. 67) or that it should be "process oriented" (Ansoff 1960, p. 240). The planning process concerning the period's program, on the other hand, should deal with the whole firm simultaneously or should be "outcome oriented."

Another possible way in which a formal approach to planning might proceed is briefly suggested below. This suggestion is based on empirical experience with linear programing, which indicates that linear-programing analysis requires a thorough analysis of the firm, on the one hand, and enables great flexibility so as to include management judgment in the planning process, on the other.

Consider two linear-programing formulations, one for the coming

10 Objectives such as survival and growth can also be seen as a part of the long-range plan.

11 See Anthony (1965, p. 38).

year and one for year *n* on the planning horizon.[12] If management assumes that no change or a proportional change in all the variables will take place during the years until year *n*, the same solution holds for both the coming year and year *n*. If the above is not assumed and/or management decides on changes, any anticipated or conceivable changes can be incorporated into the variables of the linear-programing formulation for year *n*. The solutions will indicate the optimal product mix for the coming year and for year *n*. But these two will certainly differ from each other and might even be at odds, since a different set of variables is used for each formulation. In order for the current program (for the coming period) to be optimal considering the planning horizon, the plan (providing the program for the year *n* and outlines for the rest of the years) should be solved first. Next, the current program should be determined in the light of the restrictions imposed by the plan.

An important function of the plan is to outline the main investment and finance decisions and to specify the cost of capital. Because it is difficult to differentiate between current operations and investments, investment opportunities, not necessarily major ones, may be included in each production period's program. The period's program, thus, is constructed of (1) restrictions, including those for capital, that are imposed by the present situation and the long-range plan, and (2) activities, which include investment opportunities.[13] Although this procedure is not simple, it is still applicable to minor investments. Any decision on current operations may require some investment, and any investment will affect current operations.

Two important implications stem from this discussion. First, the yearly program cannot be thought of as a true optimum, but rather as a suboptimum. An optimum can be achieved only if all the production periods up to the horizon are considered simultaneously, but such a planning procedure is not applicable for use in practice. Second, as

[12] Since the plan provides a general direction for the firm, it seems that the decision concerning which year to choose for the horizon is not crucial.

[13] Investment opportunities should be formulated in a manner consistent with the other activities. For example, the present-value figures for the alternative investments should be multiplied by the appropriate capital recovery factor (see Chapter IV, note 23) to provide annual figures.

a consequence a set of shadow prices for the temporal constraints and the temporal intermediate goods that are transferred among periods cannot be determined. This observation has an important implication for the pricing of temporal transfers.

3. Ad Hoc Decisions on Reallocation

The short-range planning activity is composed of programing and budgeting. The program is designed to allocate resources for a discrete time period. Reallocation may be necessary during the period, however, if changes in the economic and physical environment so dictate. The relations between the reallocation activity and the program are analogous to the relations between the program and the plan as outlined above.

Reallocation is required because of constant or frequently recurring changes in environment. This is especially true for agricultural production. The ideal situation can be conceptualized in the form of a feedback effect in the information system. A change in environment would be reported to the planning center, and the latter would consider possible changes in the present program. In practice, this might be too slow a process, and decisions would be made on the spot, when the direction of necessary change seems obvious. Since such ad hoc decisions on reallocation are taken in any event, no matter how formalized the information system is, it is suggested that these decisions be recorded in a somewhat formal manner.

Reallocation decisions are defined as ad hoc allocation decisions taken in response to a change in physical or economic environment during the production process or accounting period. Any kind of decision or programing may affect the firm for a long period, but generally the ad hoc reallocation decisions are the least binding. Still, these decisions, as any other, should be based on the principle of optimal resource allocation. Interestingly enough, the author's experience indicates that except when the decisions are forced or made under pressure, reallocation decisions based on common sense are likely to be optimal decisions. The more formal decisions, on the other hand, more often have not been optimal. The reason presumably lies in the circumstances in which the decision (or programing) is made. For a reallocation decision, made to solve ad hoc problems, the problem is usually simple, since only a few factors are variable. The manager uses some information and his logic to decide; recorded data are not consulted. On the other hand, the yearly program is complex, since many factors are variable and large amounts of data need to be consulted. Often such a program is carried out by the accounting department. The accountant, who will make as good a program as possible with the accounting techniques at his disposal but who is not equipped with decision-making techniques, will not develop an optimal program.

Before taking a reallocation decision, the manager estimates implicitly or explicitly the outcome of various alternatives and decides to reallocate the limited resource or facility to the segment that will pay the highest income per unit of the reallocated resource. An example may be helpful.

Consider a change in weather conditions that causes a need for additional irrigation water for cotton. Since water is limited, it can be drawn from other crops that consume water—for example, corn. The corresponding estimated damage from lack of water is $5,000 for cotton and $3,000 for corn. The rational manager reallocates the water from the corn to the cotton, to save $2,000 ($5,000 — 3,000). The opportunity cost of water to the cotton is $3,000.

The reallocation decision "punishes" one segment (corn) and "rewards" another (cotton). Provisions for this aspect should be made while analyzing the results of the operations. A formal procedure for recording ad hoc decisions, termed a "diary of reallocations," is suggested as an auxiliary feature of the formal accounting system. A diary of reallocations should include a procedure for recording the estimated opportunity costs of the limited resources whenever a reallocation decision is made.

The diary of reallocations is a device for controlling reallocation decisions. Having to record his estimates will force the manager to make explicit estimates before deciding and may thereby improve the decision. Furthermore, the availability of the recorded data can be used for after-the-fact learning and evaluation.

Sometimes the need for reallocation may be the result of a poor budget. The fact that limited resources may be reallocated to a segment with a high income may influence the manager of such a segment to prepare a poor budget, since the manager knows in advance that if some trouble arises during the production period, it will be resolved in his favor. The existence of such a diary should eliminate many excuses for inefficiency in operations and/or in preparations of the budget in a firm where changes in the environment are frequent.

For the diary to be effective, the financial results of the reallocation action should be reflected in the financial accounts of the segments involved. Let us consider three possible solutions. One is to credit and debit the involved segments. Thus, $3,000 will be credited to the corn segment for the damage for which the corn manager is not responsible and $3,000 will be debited to the cotton segment. But note that the cotton manager is not responsible for the damage either: the cotton needs the extra water because of a change in the weather, and the firm cannot purchase this extra amount. So why should he be charged for this event?

Another possible solution is to credit the corn segment and not to debit cotton. This solution is compatible with the proposed procedure of not charging internal opportunity costs to the segments, as is indicated at the end of the next section. But crediting the corn segment requires the debiting of some other account—this might be called the "management account."

A third solution is to neither debit nor credit the segments,[14] but rather to carry the accounts as an auxiliary part of the information system. This solution, which is the simplest and most straightforward one, is the one suggested here.

4. The Uses of Opportunity Cost and Shadow Price

The well-known terms opportunity cost and shadow price are crucial economic concepts in a decision-making framework. Consequently, they are used regularly throughout this study. The purpose of this section

[14] Let us make an analogy of this case to the economy at large. The first solution can be seen as a regular trade between two independent units. The other two solutions resemble a welfare economics problem, since the reallocation is enforced by central management on two quasi-independent segments. The reallocation decision with the third solution meets the Kaldor criterion; the second solution mets the Pareto criterion.

is to clarify these terms and to indicate the interrelations between them and the OAAS.

A few definitions are necessary at the outset: (1) Income is the difference between revenue and costs that are relevant to the analysis. (2) Attainable contribution is the difference between revenue and avoidable costs. (3) The opportunity cost of any productive service is the maximum amount of income it could earn elsewhere (Stigler 1966, p. 105). (4) The shadow price of a constraint, often called the dual evaluator in a linear-programing context, indicates the change in the firm's income (attainable contribution) that can be achieved if the constraint were relaxed or tightened by one unit.[15] All the foregoing assume an optimum program for the product mix, where all the avoidable (similar to variable) costs are charged to the activities. The opportunity cost is considered in two kinds of analyses: ceteris paribus (one variable at a time adjusted, all others held constant), and mutatis mutandis—simultaneous adjustment of all variables. The shadow price is a typical result of the latter kind of analysis. Both types of analysis are or should be used in managing a firm.

When linear programing is not used in management, the ceteris paribus variety of analysis is usually of importance. An example may be helpful to illustrate the use of opportunity cost in both kinds of analysis. The example serves also for further elaboration of the concept and its use.

Consider a firm producing three different products—A, B, and C—from a given type of raw material. The supply of the raw material is restricted to 150 tons per period. Assume for the sake of simplicity that raw material is not wasted; that is, from each ton of raw material one ton of either product A, B, or C can be produced. Suppose a certain type of equipment is limited to 500 hours per period. Only products A and C use this equipment. No other restrictions on production exist. The attainable contribution for the three products is: product A, \$30 per ton; product B, \$20 per ton; and product C, \$15 per ton.

The raw material is limited and thus has an opportunity cost. The

[15] Or the shadow price of an activity indicates the reduction in income resulting from the introduction of one unit of the corresponding activity into the program.

opportunity cost of raw material for producing C or B is $30 per ton, since any ton of material can produce $30 if allocated to A. Product A is the best alternative use of raw material. On the other hand, the opportunity cost of raw material for producing A is $20 per ton, since any ton of material, if not allocated to A, can produce $20 if allocated to B, which is the next best alternative to A. Thus, opportunity cost can be redefined as the loss of one activity's attainable contribution when a productive service is considered to be shifted to the second activity,[16] where the first activity is the best alternative use.

Consider the next restriction—equipment capacity. It limits A to 100 tons. Thus, the opportunity cost of raw material of $30 per ton holds for only 100 tons. The next product to be considered is B, which does not compete for service of the equipment. Fifty tons will be allocated to B. The opportunity cost of raw material for C is $20 per ton, too high a cost for including C in the program.

Now suppose that the price of C is increased and its attainable contribution rises to $21 per ton. The attainable contribution of C is higher than the opportunity cost for the last 50 tons, which is $20 per ton. In other words, C appears to be more profitable than B. However, C requires the same kind of equipment service as A. Use of equipment also has an opportunity cost. One ton of C requires one hour of equipment time, while A requires 5 hours per ton; that is, one ton of C will substitute for 0.2 tons of A in terms of equipment time. Introducing one ton of C into the program will cause the following substitutions:

Reduction of B by 1 ton	−$20
Reduction of A by 0.2 tons	−$ 6
Increase in B by 0.2 tons	+$ 4
Total opportunity cost	−$22

This figure, which can be considered as the opportunity cost (in a mutatis mutandis sense) of raw material, should be compared with product C's new attainable contribution of $21 per ton, to see if C should be introduced into the program.[17]

[16] See Heady (1952, p. 207).

[17] Such a procedure as well as similar ones are used in analyses called "programme planning" (see Chapter XI, note 9).

The optimal program, after the change in product C's price is still: A, 100 tons, and B, 50 tons. The shadow prices of the dual solution are: raw material, \$20 per ton (stems from B); equipment, \$10 per 5 hours (stems from +1 ton A, −1 ton B); product C, −\$1 per ton (stems from +1 ton C, −1 ton B, −0.2 tons A, +0.2 tons B).

Let us extend the discussion and analyze briefly some auxiliary terms which may be required in similar analyses. If a unit of a limited resource is diverted to another use, the shadow price indicates the opportunity cost of this resource. On the other hand, if an additional unit of this resource can now be obtained, the shadow price indicates the marginal income productivity of that unit of this resource. Marginal income productivity, when equivalent to shadow price, indicates the change in the firm's income that can be achieved if a unit of the corresponding resource were added. Thus, the marginal income productivity of raw material is \$20 per ton for this set of restrictions. Note that if the term "revenue" is substituted for the term "income" in the last definition, it meets the definition of the well-known term marginal value productivity.[18] The actual difference between these two terms lies in the specification of the avoidable costs related to the resource. When all the avoidable costs are charged to the activities (as is practiced in the OAAS), the marginal income productivity of a resource results; when these are not so charged, the marginal value productivity results.[19]

Suppose there is an excise tax of \$1 per ton of product. This cost item, being avoidable, is subtracted from the attainable-contribution figure. Hence, the marginal value productivity of raw material must be \$21 per ton to give marginal income productivity of \$20.

Another term that is used in analysis is the income productivity of a resource. This is defined as the attainable contribution that a resource

[18] Marginal value productivity is commonly defined as the marginal revenue multiplied by the marginal physical product of the corresponding productive service.

[19] Marginal income productivity (*MIP*) equals marginal value productivity when the avoidable costs (*AC*) related to a given resource are zero, or not charged to the activities. If the avoidable costs are charged, then $SP + AC = MVP$, for a given resource. Let $SP = Zj - Cj \equiv MIP$ of the resource; since $\text{MIP} + AC = MVP$, $SP + AC = MVP$.

can produce if allocated to a certain productive activity. In other words, the income productivity equals the attainable contribution of an activity computed per unit of limited resource. Thus, the income productivity figures in the example are:

Product	*Raw material (per ton)*	*Equipment (per hour)*
A	\$30	\$6 (\$30 per 5 hours)
B	\$20	None
C	\$15	\$15 (\$15 per 1 hour)

The opportunity cost of a resource is also the income productivity of that resource in its best alternative activity.

There are two implications to be drawn from this discussion. The attainable-contribution figure is the "raw material" from which each of the parameters is calculated. The attainable contribution of an activity (1) when computed per unit of activity (ton of product), provides the Cj coefficient for the corresponding activity in a linear-programing formulation, and (2) when computed per unit of a limited resource, it provides the income-productivity figure. Since the attainable contribution of each activity is required for decisions on resource allocation or for programing, the OAAS is designed to supply the surrogate figures for it.

The shadow prices are determined simultaneously with the optimum program, as a by-product of the linear-programing solution, whereas the income productivity and in turn the opportunity cost (in a ceteris paribus context) are used as factors in arriving at a final (close-to-optimum) program, when linear-programing is not used (point 2 above). In addition, the income productivity is used as the Cj coefficient when linear programing is in use (point 1 above). In other words, income productivity and opportunity cost (in a ceteris paribus context) are inputs, and shadow price is an output of the programing process.

Opportunity cost, as defined earlier, is the maximum amount of income one unit of an input could earn elsewhere. This "elsewhere" can be outside or inside the firm. Accordingly, a distinction is made between external and internal opportunity costs (see Chapter V). This distinction is of crucial importance in the OAAS. The external opportunity cost is taken as "given" to the firm, and thus it is included as an avoidable-cost item in the OAAS. The internal opportunity cost, on the other hand, is determined within the firm on the basis of the OAAS income figures. It can be said that the external opportunity cost is treated as an input and the internal opportunity cost as an output of the OAAS.

Assuming conditions of perfect competition, the external opportunity cost is used as an input in the programing process. The internal opportunity cost, on the other hand, is used as an input to and is also an output of the programing process as indicated above. Under market imperfections, the external opportunity cost, like the internal, is both an input to and an output of the programing process. It is "input" in the sense that it is used in programing. It can be seen as an "output" since the scale of the operations determine the prices. Still, the external opportunity cost is "given" to the firm and thus should be included in the OAAS.

The list of shadow prices, which indicate the internal opportunity cost, provided by the dual linear-programing solution, has an important use in the decision framework. The shadow prices convey information on possibilities for increasing income by valuing the constraints (see Chapter XI).[20]

Some authors suggest that the shadow prices of the constraints should be charged as costs to the various segments in the accounting framework, mainly for control purposes.[21] Such a practice has a good deal of merit since it is logical to base the measurement of performance on the same set of prices that are used in the allocation process (programing). This argument holds especially for transfer prices when more than one segment is affected by the price that is used. There are, however, some inherent complications.

The sum of the shadow prices of the constraints equals the attainable contribution of the optimum program. This implies that if the shadow

[20] Note that the shadow price is relevant only on the margin. However, its stability may be computed easily from the linear-programing solution. Moreover, the total value of a constraint, activity, or coefficient to the firm can be determined easily by solving the problem twice—with and without the item.

[21] See Smith and Barnard (1960), Dopuch and Drake (1964), Samuels (1965), and Bernhard (1968).

prices are charged to the activities in the framework of the budget (which is based on the linear-programing solution), the income of the whole firm and each activity (segment) will be zero.[22] The accounting reports can be designed accordingly. The shadow prices will be charged to the segments, and the deviation of the results from zero will provide a device for evaluating performance. This procedure requires establishing accounts for every binding constraint, accounts which will indicate the economic rent imputed to the constraints. This has some meaning when the constraints represent resources, but it has less meaning when the constraint stands for such things as a market quota for a product.

The set of shadow prices is meaningful and purposeful only while the allocation of resources takes place. After the allocation takes place, the set of shadow prices loses its meaning since a new set emerges. Hypothetically, in every point of time, a new set of constraints exists and a new set of shadow prices emerges.

Practically speaking, a new set of shadow prices emerges whenever reallocation takes place. When the shadow prices of the program are charged to the segments, income is zero; when the shadow prices of the reallocated resources are charged, some segments will experience a negative income. This will be the case when the segment to which the resource is allocated by the reallocation decision is debited by the shadow price (opportunity cost) of the resource.

Because of the problems inherent in charging the shadow prices as costs to the various segments, it is suggested that the shadow prices be recorded separately, as an auxiliary feature of the formal accounting system, rather than incorporated in the OAAS. This suggestion is strengthened by the fact that at present not many business concerns have shadow-price figures at their disposal. The list of shadow prices, together with the "diary of reallocations," will provide an important basis for control over allocation and reallocation decisions.

[22] For a conceivable way to eliminate this outcome, see Arrow (1964*b*, pp. 325–326).

XV
INFORMATION FOR CONTROL OF DECISIONS AND THE CONCEPTS OF THE OAAS

The purpose of this chapter is twofold: to outline the reasons for developing the OAAS and the needs for such a system and to discuss the main concepts underlying the OAAS. In order to develop an accounting system one has to specify what the uses of the data will be, or what the user needs. The objective of the OAAS is stated in terms of the uses it should serve: facilitating decisions and directing and motivating the decision maker. For the sake of simplicity, emphasis is given to the method of analysis used in the OAAS concepts and procedures, rather than to their compatibility with organizational lines of management responsibility. In other words, the discussion indicates only how to provide data that are appropriately chosen and measured for decisions.

As mentioned in Chapter XIII, the concept of control is not clear. Moreover, control is a complex management function. This is especially true of control of decisions. The process of control divides itself into operating rules and enforcement rules. According to Arrow (1964*a*, p. 400): "The operating rules under a centralized system take the form, 'do this or this,' while under a decentralized system they rather take the form, 'do whatever is necessary to maximize a certain objective function.'" In other words, in a centralized firm top management controls the operations by implementing the plans, and the enforcement rules are devised to detect deviations from the plans. This means that management evaluates only the executions. In a decentralized firm, on the other hand, top management has to evaluate the degree of goal attainment. Top management cannot know if the firm's objective has been maximized by a lower-level manager's decisions and actions, since that objective cannot be quantified. Nevertheless, an attempt should be made to maximize it. Hence, the enforcement rules should be such as to motivate the manager to decide and act in line with the firm's objective.

The implication here is that in a decentralized firm top management should control decisions, whereas in a centralized firm top management controls actions. Since any so-called centralized firm is quasi-decentralized (see Chapter XII and Appendix D), effective management requires control of both decisions and actions.

In the information system suggested in Chapter XIII (see Figure 11) there are three control subsystems; two of these are designed to control decisions. The first subsystem evaluates the expectations and the long-range plan that provide the assumptions on which the period's decisions depend. In the second subsystem the actual results of the firm's actions are evaluated and analyzed. Since the results of the firm's actions are affected by the decisions themselves as well as by their execution and the environment, one cannot really evaluate objectively the reasons for the outcome of past decisions. Nevertheless, for effective management, a continuing effort should be made to control decisions.

The following steps are suggested in controlling decisions for a given production period. First, record expectations and evaluate them in a formal manner (see Chapter XIII). Second, use improved decision-making techniques (for example, a set of production-economic concepts, linear programing—see Chapter XI). Third, provide managers with correctly specified data for decisions. Fourth, evaluate the results of the firm's actions by the same criteria that are used in making decisions. (This will enable after-the-fact learning of what could have been done. In turn, this process should direct and motivate the decision maker). Fifth, evaluate, record, and report shadow prices established from linear programing, when used, or opportunity costs used for reallocation decisions (see Chapter XIV). The third and fourth steps are made possible by use of the OAAS and are discussed below; the first and fifth are made possible by auxiliary diaries.

1. Information to Facilitate Decisions

Economic theory teaches us that for rational decisions, the decision maker must know three types of function: the supply functions for the firm's inputs, the demand functions for the firm's outputs, and the firm's production functions. Knowing these functions, the decision maker seeks to equate marginal costs with marginal revenue, and to determine quantities of outputs and the associated levels of input use. Economists tend to assume that the firms do know these functions, decide according to economic rules, and hence have the capacity to be in, or be close to, equilibrium.[1]

The information system should provide the decision maker with the information that will enable him to approach equilibrium, if his firm is out of equilibrium, and to react rationally to exogeneous change. In practice it is difficult to differentiate between these points since the firm never really reaches equilibrium, and the environment changes constantly.[2]

In business concerns, the decision maker certainly has some notion of the shape of the specific functions which his firm confronts. The more complex the firm is, however, the more the decision maker has to rely on the information system for estimating variables entering the decision framework.

In this book it is assumed that the supply and demand functions are

[1] There are many reasons for a firm's not striving for or being able to achieve an optimum, as Simon (1959) indicates. Moreover, a real optimum is practically unachievable because of uncertainty and multiplicity of goals. The profitability and growth of most firms may be cited as evidence that firms try to behave rationally. Most firms, however, can improve on their existing decision processes and, in turn, on their income. The results of the use of linear programing by firms (Chapter XI) provides testimony that this is true. Presumably the use of other techniques or procedures, such as the OAAS, will allow similar results.

[2] Assuming that firms in general strive toward equilibrium through trial-and-error experience, there is no doubt that supplying management with better information (as, for example, through the OAAS) can shorten the costly learning and adjustment process.

completely elastic and that the production function (and, in turn, the cost function) consists of linear sections. The former implies that only one price figure (the market price) for any input or output is available and should be reported by the information system. The assumption on the shape of the production function implies that if the information system provides data on every section of the function, the shape of the firm's production function is specified and average variable cost equals marginal cost. Providing information on each linear section of the whole production function is very expensive and unnecessary as well. It is only necessary to report the data pertinent to segments of the firm that are distinguishable from a technical or organizational point of view and where each segment is composed of one or a group of linear sections. In this case the average variable costs do not always equal marginal costs. The accounting system should provide those data that apply at the margin for each segment—that is, the data relevant to the marginal linear section of the production function.

Each segment of the firm uses two types of factors of production: variable inputs, which are essentially unlimited in quantity at market prices, and limited resources. Since the variable inputs have a constant unit price, the accounting system should report the total costs of the variable inputs (variable costs) procured by the segment. The following data on the limited resources are required: the level of use of the various resources by each activity, the amount of each resource available for use, and the external opportunity cost of the resources, whenever it exists. Historical costs of these limited resources are ignored in the decision-making process.

It should be noted that two types of data are required: financial (costs of variable inputs and external opportunity costs, on the one hand, and revenues, on the other) and technical (amount of limited resources and the level of their use). The subject of collecting, recording, and analyzing technical coefficients is beyond the scope of this study, which merely assumes that such a procedure is technically feasible. The OAAS deals only with the problem of how to specify the financial data—that is, cost, revenue, and income figures.

Under conventional accounting the firm is considered as a black box where cost enters and revenue exits. The task of the accounting system is to measure the cost and revenue as they are accrued and to compute the difference—the profit or loss. Under conventional cost accounting, the firm is decomposed into segments, but the same type of financial data is provided; that is, the accrued cost and revenue and the resulting profit or loss are provided for each segment.

The common practice of reporting full cost is of no help to the decision maker. These figures may only mislead him. Variable costs provide him with better information. If these costs are not reported, however, the full-cost figures must be decomposed to obtain the variable-cost figures. As long as the firm produces only a few products, when a manager asks, "Would a certain action be worthwhile?," he may dig into his records and get a reasonable answer to his question. In a large, multiproduct firm, such "digging" into the records is almost impossible.[3]

Variable-cost figures are provided as average figures, a procedure implying a linear production function, a procedure that may or may not be true. Commonly both full-cost and variable-cost figures do not include all the cost items, such as implicit interest charges, or the actual cost incurred, because inventories and depreciation are charged at original cost.

2. Information to Motivate the Decision Maker

Since the so-called centralized firm is actually quasi-decentralized, managers should be motivated to decide and act in line with the firm's objective. Whatever procedure is used to evaluate or induce managers, the accounting reports are often the major source of information. Hence, it is natural to expect the manager to act so as to improve the reports on his behalf, and in fact he behaves in this manner, even when this action is at odds with the firm's objective.[4] As Benston (1963, p. 354) concludes, "the careful use of accounting reports can directly

[3] A statement by a company representative illustrates this point: "Before direct costing was adopted, it was necessary to recompute burden absorption *through twenty cost centers* to determine how much a given order would add to the company's profit. As a consequence, analyses were made only for major decisions" (National Association of Accountants 1961, p. 28; emphasis added).

[4] See Chapter II, note 5.

contribute toward effective motivation by expressing goals and by supplying knowledge of performance."

For effective motivation, the accounting reports should be compatible with the decision-making process. In other words, the accounting report, which provides the basis for enforcement rules (in the control sense), should be in the same terms as the decision framework, which provides operating rules. If control is to be practiced, the basic question is not "How do we control?," but rather "What do we measure in our control system?" (Drucker 1964, p. 289). The OAAS provides a partial answer to this question.

The subject under consideration has been raised recently in the accounting literature under the topic of responsibility accounting.[5] According to Gordon (1963, pp. 6–7), there are two widely accepted principles in responsibility accounting. First, an individual should be charged only with those costs over which he has control.[6] Charging nontraceable overhead costs to a segment for which a manager is responsible is a good example of violating this principle. Second, accounts should be established for each segment so as to motivate individual managers.

If the accounting report is to motivate lower-level managers, some additional characteristics are required. According to Gordon's first principle, only controllable costs should be charged to a segment. For example, if electricity is not charged on the basis of usage, there is no incentive to economize in its use. An important controllable cost is interest on liquid assets. In the OAAS, interest is charged to the users of these assets. This procedure is helpful for both decision and motivation purposes.[7] The traditional cost-accounting practice, on the other hand, does not incorporate interest charges and thereby understates the costs of production. This in turn provides an implicit subsidy

[5] Stedry (1960, p. 12) claims that the problem of "motivation" is ignored, by and large, in cost accounting and budgeting. According to Horngren (1962*b*, p. 6) the terms "responsibility accounting," "profitability accounting," and "activity accounting" are used interchangeably in the literature.

[6] Of course, an outline or agreement as to which items should be considered controllable by the involved manager is required.

[7] The need to define interest as a cost was indicated very early by Clark (1923, p. 38). Charging interest in an accounting framework is a common rule among agricultural economists.

for the heavy user of capital assets and thereby may result in a misallocation of resources.

It can be argued that a segment's manager should have a "broad enough" attitude to put the firm's benefits ahead of the benefits to his segment, as Greer (1962, p. 6) suggests. If this is expected of him, it is unjust and ineffective to set up an evaluation of his performance that does not do this as well. The use of "discretionary procedures" regarding internal pricing and cost distribution, when practiced by the accountant, encourages the development of political skills in internal negotiations of managers at lower levels, among themselves and with the accountant. This skill does not contribute anything to the welfare of the firm. Moreover, central management may be evaluating the managers' ability to negotiate rather than their ability to control economic variables.[8]

It is argued above that the kind of accounting reports used in a firm influence the decisions and actions of its managers. Interestingly enough, the reports also affect the rate of learning of the people involved.[9] The OAAS is designed to report the right information to be learned and, presumably, makes this learning process more effective.

To summarize, the OAAS data should serve two management functions: decision making and measuring performance to motivate the decision maker. In other words, the ex post data should provide for evaluation of past decisions that were based on ex ante consideration. As such, they serve as surrogates for decisions about the future. Because of this situation, the OAAS can be viewed, at least partially, as an after-the-fact, ex ante analytic procedure.

3. Premises and Means

The basic problem in meeting objectives and requirements of the

[8] One of the findings of Simon *et al.* (1954) after interviewing more than four hundred executives in seven decentralized companies was that "where factories or departments were highly interdependent, and the 'profits' recorded on paper were affected by accounting methods, the general tendency was to complain about the accounting procedures when profits were low, rather than to assume that the operations needed improvement" (p. 42).

[9] See Ammons (1956).

OAAS is the measurement of income for the firm and its segments. Edwards and Bell (1961, p. viii) note:

The problem of income measurement has been an especially perplexing one in part because economists have approached it with essentially subjective concepts derived from expectations concerning future events, while accountants have insisted on objectivity and the measurement of actual, unfortunately often historic, events. The apparent impasse between these two points of view has led many to resign themselves to the impossibility of reconciliation, and thus has tended to widen the gap between the two disciplines. Yet, except for the difference in perspective, the two often deal with related problems and rely on similar data.

As indicated earlier, our study rests on the philosophy that accounting may be thought of as a "subset" of economics or at least as a discipline that intersects with economics over a range of topics. Assuming that economic principles are relevant to a business concern, accounting procedures should be adjusted so as to be compatible with economic principles. The concepts and operational rules provided through the OAAS are based on both economic theory and accounting procedures so as to enable the analysis of decisions and actions by a firm and its segments.

The procedures and rules that constitute the framework of the OAAS are based on a set of three premises and five means.[10] Premise 1 assumes that income is generated concurrently with the production process, in both temporal and spatial contexts. In the temporal context, income is estimated for an accounting period and recognized at the end of the period, even when the associated revenue has not yet been realized.[11] In the spatial context, income is estimated

[10] In developing an accounting system one should not forget that, on the one hand, "accounting is concerned with economic attributes and measurements" (Paton and Littleton 1940, p. 32) and that, on the other hand, "economic information is, in any event, notoriously inaccurate" (Baumol 1965, p. 37).

[11] A number of authors suggest a similar approach. Fess and Ferrara (1961) suggest using a "value added" concept, which means that "income is considered earned as utility is added to the factors of production" (p. 600) and thus "inventory valuation is based on cost plus value added to date" (p. 599). Philips

for every segment of the firm which produces marketable intermediate goods. Income is recognized at the end of the period, even when the intermediate good is not sold. Premise 2 assumes that the particular use of data should dictate the kind and form of the data which are generated or collected. Hence, the kind of accounts kept should be determined by the use to be made of the data. In premise 3, usefulness of the data is preferred to objectivity,[12] if these are mutually exclusive. In other words, utility of data in analysis has a higher order of preference than objectivity if both requirements cannot be attained simultaneously.

The five means incorporated in the OAAS are as follows: income, revenue, and cost are figured and reported regularly for a designated time period; the firm is decomposed into individual segments with an income statement prepared for each; costs are not distributed to periods or segments, where distribution means allocation of costs on the basis of some discretionary procedure; implicit cost and realizable revenue for each designated period, in addition to explicit cost and realized revenue, are debited and credited, respectively, to the segments; production economics concepts, such as marginal analysis and opportunity cost, are incorporated into the accounting system. The first two means are a response to the first premise and are related to the quasi-decentralized models developed in Chapter XII. The third means is a response to the second premise. The last two means are responses to

(1963*a*) suggests using the concept of "accretion income": "Income is an increase in economic power which can be verified with reasonable objectivity. [It] relies primarily on market values as measures of economic power" (p. 16). Horngren (1965) suggests recording "recognized" gains in value, but labeling them "unrealized": "In this way, the devotees of 'economic' income and 'accounting' income can both be served" (p. 333). Jaedicke and Sprouse (1965, p. 41) state: "It is generally acknowledged that income is attributable to the entire process of business activity, not just to a single point of time, such as the movement of sale." Chambers (1966, p. 250) states: "On the going concern principle . . . , amounts accrued but unpaid may be carried forward as liabilities (and, therefore, charged against revenues of the past period)."

[12] Objectivity is often referred to in the accounting profession as verifiability. Ijiri and Jaedicke (1966, p. 476) define objectivity as "the consensus among a given group of observers or measurers."

all three premises. These premises and means differ from those associated with conventional accounting practices, but the objectives of the OAAS dictate their use.

Accrual of Income (Premise 1). The first premise contradicts the well-established accounting principle of realization.[13] Assuming that the objective of the firm is to maximize the present value of income, the firm is better off when its durables and inventories (including goods in process and intermediate goods) gain in value, and not just at the moment they happen to be sold. This holds both when the durable or inventory can be sold in the form of durable liquid assets, marketable inventories, and intermediate goods, and when they cannot be sold because they are nonliquid assets, goods in process, or nonmarketable intermediate goods. The problem is how to measure the change in value over time. The OAAS provides a plausible solution to this problem. Hence, the OAAS can be considered more as a valuation or pricing procedure than a costing procedure.

The OAAS is based on the quasi-decentralized model where periods and segments "trade" intermediate goods. Whenever a market exists, the market price provides the basis for valuing or pricing the transferred goods. This contradicts the well-established accounting principle of objectivity.[14] When a market does not exist, the value or price is based on an estimate of a price that would prevail if a market existed for the transferred good.

In conventional accounting, profits are recognized only when revenue is realized—that is, at the final stage of the production process, when the product is sold. In economic analysis, on the other hand, both cost and revenue are figured in terms of present value and are assumed to accrue at the outset of the production process. This holds

[13] Unrealized losses are recognized in conventional accounting practices. Why not unrealized gains? Nonrealized market prices are used as supplementary factors in conventional accounting—for example, in valuation of inventories on the basis of "cost or market, whichever is lower," precious metals, by-products, or donated assets and noncash acquisitions (American Institute of Certified Public Accountants 1953*a*, pp. 31, 34, 38).

[14] Under many circumstances "market values can be measured with greater objectivity than costs" (Philips 1963*a*, p. 23). See also May (1952, p. 439). Chambers (1966, p. 243) claims that "assessment of prices in the market . . . would be no more subjective than every scientific estimate made on data of the same kind."

in both temporal and spatial contexts. The OAAS tries to reconcile these conventions by adhering to the first premise. The three conventions as they are carried out by the accountant, the economist, and the OAAS analyst are illustrated below by means of three examples.

An investor buys at the beginning of a period $1,000 worth of stock. Suppose the economic value of the stock—that is, the present value of the corresponding future cash flow to the investor—is $1,200. The net present value, which can be considered as the economic income, is $200, and therefore the stock is purchased. During the period, he receives $50 in dividend payments. At the end of the period the market value of the stock is $1,100. The economic value (to the investor) at the end of period is $1,200. The net present value now is $100; therefore he does not sell. Under conventional accounting procedures, the income for the period is $50 in dividends. In the OAAS, the period income is $100 ($50 in dividends and $100 in increased market value, minus $50 interest (5 per cent on $1,000).

As a second example, consider a job order of producing 100 steers (see the data provided in Chapter IV, Section 9). The ex ante economic value—that is, the net present value of this job—when calculating for the beginning of the process, is $12,240 (see Table 6). When computed for the end of the process, this income equals $14,000. The ex post income, as reported by the conventional accounting system, is zero for 1965 and $22,900 in 1966—a total of $22,900. In the OAAS, ex post income is $10,930 for 1965 and $3,070 for 1966—a total of $14,000. (See Table 7.)

This example illustrates several points. First, temporal decomposition is required if income within a production period is to be measured. Second, a transfer price should be assigned to the "temporal intermediate good" if the period's income is to be meaningful. Suppose that the process in the example is a part of a segment, the income of which is to be measured. The conventional report underestimates income for 1965 and overestimates it for 1966. Third, the income potential of the steer on December 31, 1965, which is an economic concept, is taken into consideration in determining the transfer price for the OAAS. On the other hand, the income is reported (in the OAAS) in a form similar to conventional accounting conventions.

The third example concerns firm A, which is composed of two

production departments: cows, which produce milk (and calves), and ice cream which is processed in the firm's plant and sold on the market. The firm's annual income amounts to $35,000 (see Table 1, Chapter III). The scale of the operation is limited by the number of cows, which in turn is limited by the size of the barn.

The economist will claim that the shadow price of the barn is $35,000. The accountant, on the other hand, will claim that the ice cream department has a profit of $35,000. The accountant assumes implicitly that the milk is transferred from one segment (cows) to the other (ice cream) at production cost. Under the OAAS the firm is decomposed into two contribution centers—cows and ice cream—and income is computed for each.

The Kind of Data to Be Divided (*Premises 2 and 3*). An "important difference between the accountant's and the economist's point of view . . . is that the accountant on the whole is interested in what is or what has been, whereas the economist is interested in what might be" (Boulding 1962, p. 50). The economist, in making decisions for future events, uses estimated data that cannot be precise (it can be provided in the form of a probability distribution). The accountant, who is concerned with historical description, uses factual data, which is precise in the sense that it can be checked and that it represents something that has actually happened. In business decisions only the future counts; the past is irrelevant except for that ex post information that can be used in predicting the future. This observation implies that the decision maker should ask, "Could we have done better?" [15] and "What do we need to know in order that we could do better?" (Boulding 1962, p. 52). The OAAS is designed to provide a partial answer to these questions by signaling the existence of opportunities.

Faced with a choice between reporting only actual events and events that might have been, the author has chosen the latter, but not to the complete exclusion of the former. This is compatible with the second premise, and it implies that such concepts as opportunity cost, implicit

[15] Demski (1967) suggests a procedure for answering this question when linear programing is applied to both ex ante data and ex post data pertaining to the same period, and for analyzing the discrepancies among these and the observed results are analyzed.

cost, realizable revenue,[16] and marginal analysis should be incorporated into the system.

Consider the third example above. The transfer price of milk is the price existing in the market. This price is considered as a realizable revenue by the cows segment and, in turn, as an implicit opportunity cost by the ice cream segment. For answering the question, "Could we have done better by reducing the number of cows?," the following information is required: the sacrifice of revenue—$.12 per unit of milk; the reduction in cost of variable inputs per unit of output or production; the opportunity rate of interest; the amount of the released capital that is invested in the cows; and the opportunity cost of the barn. The variable cost and the interest rate that hold on the margin are of concern, rather than the average figures for the whole segment or the whole firm.

The manager of a firm has to make estimates, and in fact he makes them, explicitly or implicitly, before making a decision. The viewpoint taken here is that these estimates should be made explicitly and that this should also be done for implicit decisions of the "no change" kind. Therefore, these estimates should be incorporated into the OAAS reports.

For example, in order to answer the question, "Could we have done better by reducing the number of cows?," the analyst has to value the cows. This estimate of the expected sale price involves a subjective judgment by the analyst or manager. Under conventional accounting practices, the assets are valued in terms of acquisition cost and are adjusted for that part of original costs already charged to past operations.[17] The portion to be charged to current operations is determined by means of a "discretionary procedure"—that is, a subjective judgment made by the accountant. Therefore, the valuation is discretionary.

[16] These are often considered as "intangibles," which according to Churchman (1961, p. 59) "cannot be accurately measured, at least in dollar terms. . . . If 'intangible' means 'partly a matter of judgment' then all figures of the [profit and loss], and indeed all scientific results, are intangibles. All measurement involves judgment."

[17] This is the outcome of depreciation accounting. Officially, however, depreciation is described as "a process of allocation, not of valuation" (American Institute of Certified Public Accountants 1953*b*, p. 25).

Put differently, conventional accounting deals with the distribution of fixed costs in both temporal and spatial contexts. Thus the acquisition cost of assets is distributed by means of depreciation accounting to periods and segments. Overhead and common costs are likewise distributed to segments and products. The choice of the method is subjective, and therefore the act of distribution of costs is "discretionary."

Faced with a choice between making subjective estimates of data (market value of assets, for example), and making subjective choices of methods to distribute costs (for example, choice of depreciation formula for valuing the asset), the author has chosen the former. This is compatible with the third premise as outlined earlier. Thus, in the OAAS, assets are valued on the basis of their market value or replacement cost, and overhead or common costs are not distributed to segments or products. In other words, subjective estimates are preferred over discretionary procedures because of their relevance to decisions and their potential appeal by managers.

The very fact that the OAAS has to provide data for decisions implies that no one cost, value, or income figure can be considered as "best" for all types of decisions (see premise 3). Thus, for example, a different set of figures is required if the scale of the operation is considered or a liquidation of a segment is examined. This point is amplified by the fact that the OAAS is designed to provide data for motivating management as well. Although the motivation of the manager should be in line with the decision framework, the two types of data will not always coincide.

Conclusions. Any conceivable accounting method cannot be completely foolproof. There is no one best method or set of criteria for determining prices, costs, income, and performance. For a particular use of the data, one method of determining the figures is usually better than another. Therefore one should provide not one set of "cut-and-dried" rules for the preparation of data, but rather conceptual procedures and rules to be applied according to the case at hand. The OAAS should enable this kind of improvement in the operational management process.

It may be argued that the suggested procedures are elaborate and may be costly. This argument is indeed correct. But the ultimate criterion should be the effectiveness (benefits over costs) of the technique rather than its cost per se.

Under the OAAS the accountant has to make judgments, mainly in valuing assets and determining transfer prices.[18] This requires better education on the part of the accountant. On the other hand, by providing management with correctly specified data for their decisions, not only should decisions be improved, but management's time should be saved. As Vatter (1967, p. 138) notes, "managers need and expect help, not homework, from accounting reports."

[18] Traditionally, the accountant is a "cost-minded" person. Under the OAAS he should become more "opportunity-minded."

XVI
MANAGEMENT DECISIONS, DATA REQUIREMENTS, AND THEIR SUPPLY BY THE OAAS AND CONVENTIONAL ACCOUNTING

Economic theory indicates what variables should be considered in a decision framework, but it does not indicate how values for these variables are estimated in practice, when the decision maker wants to apply the economic rules. The manager of a firm has to search for appropriate data, collect it, and analyze it. Values for the necessary variables must be estimated from past experience. Usually the firm's accounting system provides specific data relevant to past operations.

Although decision making is an important management function, there are additional functions that management has to perform in order to fulfill the firm's objectives. Decisions must be put into practice and management must oversee production. These functions, often referred to as control and coordination, also require data that are provided, at least partially, by the accounting system.

The needs for data in a firm are diverse. The problem is to establish data requirements and specifications for the various managerial purposes. In order to analyze this problem, the expected uses of the data must be specified, primarily in the context of decision making.

In this chapter, data needs are compared with information made available by both conventional accounting practices and the OAAS procedures presented in this book. A simple, hypothetical firm is used as a frame of reference. Restricting assumptions are imposed on the firm so as to simplify the discussion. Some of these assumptions are then relaxed and a more complex firm is assumed as the discussion progresses. In this process the procedures necessary for obtaining the information for decision making in a regular firm as assumed in the Introduction are evolved.

1. A Single-Product Firm

Our hypothetical firm, firm G, produces Y units of a single product. Two types of inputs are utilized in the production process: X_1 units of fixed capital assets (a building and a set of equipment) and X_2 units of variable inputs (labor and raw material used in fixed proportions). The firm is a going concern; that is, it is expected to operate permanently, and its objective is to maximize income (revenue less costs). It confronts a completely elastic demand function for its products and a completely elastic supply function for its inputs. In other words, the prices of the inputs (P_x) and of the output (P_y) are given.

The firm's production function is: $Y = f(X_1, X_2)$. The objective of the firm dictates that the manager should produce at that level where marginal costs equal the price of the product; that is, where the following holds:

$$\frac{\delta Y}{\delta X_2} = \frac{P_{x_2}}{P_y}.$$

In order to know whether he is operating in equilibrium, the manager needs two types of information. The first is the prices P_y and P_{x2} and the shape and form of the production function, or P_y and the marginal cost curve. These are required for decisions on the scale of operations (scale decisions). The second is the price of the product (P_y) and average variable costs, or total revenue and total variable costs for a given period. These are required to decide whether or not to continue production or to stop it (liquidation decisions). These two types of data are required for decisions on resource allocation, as production economics suggest.

It has sometimes been argued that the businessman does not have to know this information in order to operate in equilibrium. Friedman (1953) notes that a good manager of a firm, just as a good billiard player, need not know the exact mathematical formulation of his actions, even though the economist and the mathematician can formally describe the actions of both. Natural selection by the market economy will leave in business only those firms that are operated by good managers. This is indeed true and holds for firm G. By providing a manager with the right information, however, he will certainly approach equilibrium in shorter time, and thus save costly trial-and-error experiments.

Firm G is owned by an absentee owner and operated by a hired manager. The owner (and also the manager) has to know how much income is available for personal use before deciding how much should be used (dividend decisions). For this purpose data are required on total revenue and total costs for the period.

To summarize, the following financial data on the existing production process are required, pertinent to a given period: the marginal cost curve, total costs, total variable cost, and total revenue. In addition, information on the volume of production during the period is necessary for calculating average figures.

Since national law requires that the manager of the firm prepare an annual income statement, an accountant is hired for this purpose. The accountant, with available financial records, is also asked to provide estimates of the data required for management decisions on resource allocation. On the assumption that the future will be somewhat like the past, the accountant measures and estimates figures on past operations to be used as surrogates for data pertaining to the future.

The firm is functioning in a dynamic world. Hence the manager (and the owner) has to consider the firm's actions in the future. He has to make forecasts about future prices, changes in technology, and so on. He has to search for this kind of information as well as for alternative production processes. With this material, and with the aid of the accountant's financial data on past operations, the owner and the manager have the basic information for decision making. (In our example other types of information regarding uncertainty and tax considerations are ignored for simplicity).

2. Cost Specifications

Both conventional-accounting and OAAS procedures are designed to estimate costs, revenue, and income. The main problem lies in estimating costs of production, even in a firm with as simple a system of production as firm G's. There is a conceptual difference between the two accounting systems. The emphasis in conventional accounting is on "correct" calculations of costs, whereas in the OAAS it is on correct specification of costs. Operationally, the main difference between the two systems is as follows. In conventional accounting, only actual accrued costs are considered as cost items, and only realized revenue is recorded. In the OAAS, on the other hand, implicit costs and realizable revenue are also considered as cost and revenue items. In conventional accounting, indirect costs are distributed (allocated) to goods and goods are transferred in the accounting framework at full costs. In the OAAS, costs are not distributed and goods are transferred at their market values.

Interest Charges. Suppose all the capital of firm G is provided by the owner and there is no debt. Since there are no interest payments, interest is not included as a cost in conventional accounting. In the OAAS, however, implicit interest is charged. Firm G holds capital assets and inventories of raw material. Interest is charged on both; hence both fixed and variable costs are higher in the OAAS. Thus conventional accounting practices underestimate the costs of production when the use of capital and/or the equity ratio are high.

Depreciation. Assume an economy with a stable price level. The capital assets of firm G serve for several periods. In order to arrive at a period-cost figure, the initial investment in these assets is distributed in conventional accounting to the individual periods by means of depreciation. The choice of the depreciation method is discretionary. Thus, acquisition costs and date, and the depreciation method, determine cost for the period. In the OAAS, on the other hand, the assets are valued at the beginning and the end of the period on the basis of market price. The difference between these values is considered as depreciation (or appreciation). Neither the acquisition cost nor the date affect cost for the period.

Consider the case where the value of the building does not change during the accounting period and the value of the equipment drops considerably because of an innovation. In the OAAS no depreciation is recorded for the building and large depreciation charges for the equipment. In conventional accounting, regular period depreciation charges for each are recorded.

Thus, the direction of difference between the two costing procedures is unpredictable. Only when an asset serves beyond its expected life span—that is, when it is written off the conventional accounting books—does the OAAS cost exceed the conventional accounting figure.

Changing Price Level. Consider a period of inflation. For valuing both fixed assets and the inventory of raw material, conventional accounting uses acquisition costs and the OAAS uses current market prices. The corresponding values are higher in the OAAS than in conventional accounting.

While the value and, in turn, the cost of inventories may be higher in the OAAS, the same cannot be asserted with respect to period depreciation costs. Thus, in the OAAS appreciation may be experienced, whereas, in conventional accounting, depreciation based on low acquisition cost will be charged.

In order to remove the price-level effects, the increase in assets' value can, and for some purposes should, be reported separately, a subject that is beyond the scope of this study.

External Opportunity Cost. Suppose firm G produces its product in two stages; that is, an intermediate good is transferred from stage 1 to stage 2 of the production process. Suppose further that the intermediate good is a commodity that is traded on the market. The firm, however, does not participate in this market. In conventional accounting, either the two stages are considered as one production process or each stage is considered separately and the intermediate good is transferred from stage 1 to stage 2 at full costs. Since the firm has an opportunity to sell the intermediate good in the external market, this good has an external opportunity cost, a cost item that is included in the OAAS. The inventory of the intermediate good is transferred at its market price. In the OAAS, the market price is considered as an avoidable cost for stage 2 and as realizable revenue for stage 1. Note that under this procedure both stages may produce income. The transfer price in the OAAS will be higher than in conventional accounting whenever costs are lower than the market price.

Suppose there is no market for the intermediate good. In the OAAS the two stages are considered as one production process (for decision purposes), and each stage is considered separately and the intermediate good is transferred from stage 1 to stage 2 at "pseudo market price" (for evaluation purposes).

3. Surrogating Marginal Costs

Assume that the exact shape of firm G's production function, $Y = f(x_1, x_2)$, is not known over the full range of Y. Hence, there is no direct way to derive the marginal cost curve. The accountant tries (implicitly or explicitly) to surrogate for the marginal costs by means of actual cost figures. In conventional accounting, marginal costs are often surrogated by variable costs. When the shape of the production function is close to linear, this may be a good approximation of marginal costs. However, this practice raises two questions: Are all the cost items that are relevant to marginal analysis included in the variable cost figure? What happens when the production function is not linear?

Conventional variable costs do not include implicit costs and external opportunity costs. Thus, current market prices of raw materials, market prices of the intermediate goods, and interest charges on inventories are not included in the variable-cost figure. These items are relevant for marginal analysis and decisions and are avoidable if the decision is to reduce the level of production. These cost items are included in avoidable costs, a figure that is designed to surrogate the marginal costs in the OAAS.

Thus, conventional accounting practices underestimate marginal costs. In addition to this omission, the very convention of classifying costs into two classes, variable cost and fixed cost, often causes biased estimates of marginal costs, as is illustrated below.

Liquid Assets. Conventionally the costs related to capital assets are considered as fixed. Suppose any unit of the set of equipment of firm G can be sold on an active secondhand market whenever the firm wants. This means that the period costs related to this equipment—change in its market value during the period and interest on its value—are avoidable. These items are considered as avoidable costs in the OAAS. And conventional accounting's variable costs are lower than OAAS avoidable costs when some of the assets are liquid.

Seasonal Use of an Input. Suppose labor is hired for the whole year. A binding contract enforces paying labor even when unemployed during a slack season. Suppose further that the price of the product (P_y) drops considerably. The manager, knowing that this drop in price is seasonal and that there is not an alternative use for labor, continues to produce. The accountant, following the convention that labor is considered as a variable cost, reports that total variable costs per unit exceed the price.

By using the concept of avoidable costs, the yearly production process is viewed as two processes: the regular process, for which the yearly labor costs are avoidable, and the process in the slack season, for which the labor costs are nonavoidable. In the latter case, labor costs are not included in avoidable costs, and thus the report is consistent with the decision-making framework.

Costs on the Margin. Suppose the price of the product rises. In response, the manager decides to produce more by introducing a second shift of workers. But labor costs for a second shift are higher than the costs for regular labor. In conventional accounting, an average variable cost figure is reported. This cost figure cannot stand for the marginal costs in this case.

In the OAAS, the costs on the margin—that is, the cost of the second shift—are considered as the avoidable cost. Once again, there are two types of avoidable costs. First, there are the avoidable costs associated with scale decisions—that is, how many workers to hire for the second shift. Here the cost of the second shift per unit of product is relevant. Second, there are the avoidable costs associated with liquidation decisions. Here total labor costs are relevant. Dividing total costs by the volume of production provides an average figure, similar to the average figure in conventional accounting. Having the cost figure on the margin and the average figure, the manager knows the general shape of the marginal cost curve—whether it is horizontal, increasing, or decreasing.

Usually, a manager learns through trial and error about the true economic dimensions of his production process. Presumably the type of cost data given by the OAAS may lead him toward a better estimate of marginal costs at different levels of output.

4. Total Costs

Economic theory indicates that the average total cost curve is required to determine the long-run average cost curve. But the true long run does not exist in a going concern, since any firm always has some possessions and commitments at any given point in time. Even decisions regarding new investments or new lines of production are short-run types of decisions. Projected additional costs related to new investments are considered as avoidable costs, before the investment takes place.

Total costs are required mainly for income measurement. Unfortunately, this figure is often used for an additional purpose—for resource allocation decisions.[1]

Surrogating Total Costs. In conventional accounting, the full-cost figure substitutes for total costs; in the OAAS, a total-cost figure is used. Earlier discussion has shown that the conventional accounting full-cost figure underestimates or overestimates costs in certain situa-

[1] Total costs, including fixed costs, are of no relevance to allocation decisions. These figures are often used in business, however (see Chapter I, note 3). The small degree to which direct costing is used in business (see Chapter V, note 3) testifies to this situation as well. Consider the following caricature:

Suppose the per unit conventional-accounting full cost of production, as firm G's accountant reports it, is $8. Suppose further that an occasional customer offers $6 per unit. The manager, knowing that fixed costs exist, is tempted to accept the offer. He consults the accountant, however, since the accountant keeps the data and he is the firm's expert on cost calculations. The accountant, preparing a so-called flexible budget, calculates the full costs resulting from the increased volume to be $7. The offer is rejected. The offer may be rejected even if the variable costs per unit of the additional volume are $4. This result may be expected when the owner evaluates the manager's performance by auditing the accounting reports. The acceptance of a job paying $6 per unit when full costs are $7 per unit does not indicate a rational decision by the manager, even though it is on economic grounds.

tions. In addition, the full costs include depreciation, arrived at by means of a discretionary procedure.

The OAAS total-cost figure, on the other hand, is based on estimates using current market prices. Thus, market prices are determined or approximated for capital assets, inventory of raw material, and intermediate goods. In addition, adjustments of market prices to reflect increased maintenance or obsolescence of the building are made. Thus, an appraised value of this nonliquid asset is determined. Since the intermediate good is transferred from stage 1 to stage 2 at market price, it is expected that the OAAS total costs of the final product exceed the conventional accounting full cost, because income may be recognized at stage 1 as well as at stage 2.

Aid in Pricing Decisions. Relax for a moment the assumption that firm G confronts a completely elastic demand curve for its product. Assume that there are market imperfections and that the firm sets the price for its product (P_y). The decision maker does not know his marginal costs, nor does he know the demand curve for his product. When reacting to market demand, he can (and indeed in actual business he does) rely at least partly on the available cost figures in establishing the price intuitively. He may use both total-cost and variable-cost figures. Because conventional accounting practices often underestimate or overestimate actual costs, these errors may also be reflected in the prices of the product. In turn, such pricing may cause misallocation of resources in the economy.

5. Income

Since firm G's objective is to maximize income, income figures are required for control purposes, where "control" means obtaining correspondence between the objective and the results. Thus, income figures are required for liquidation decisions and for evaluation of past performance. Income figures are also required for dividend decisions.

Income, when measured for liquidation decisions (that is, switching to another production process) is the difference between revenue and variable costs in conventional accounting; it is revenue minus avoidable costs in the OAAS.

A Criterion to Be Maximized. Economic theory assumes that the firm's objective is to maximize the present value of its future income. To be operational, income for a period must be measured. But here there is a danger that maximizing the income for a period is at odds with the firm's overall objective. Hence, the firm should maximize the period income subject to long-range considerations. Unfortunately, "long-range considerations" is a vague term. Even if the firm has a long-range plan, it can be stated only in general and rough form. In addition, it is difficult to evaluate the degree of compliance obtained with the restrictions imposed by this plan. This implies that any income measurement cannot serve as an unequivocal criterion to be maximized. Other performance criteria and judgment must be used as well.

Consider an alternative assumption. The firm's objective is to achieve satisfactory profits; that is, the firm "would try to 'satisfice' rather than to maximize" (Simon 1959, p. 263). This implies that if the firm's income statement indicates profits that are equal to or above a given level (absolute income or a rate of return), management's objectives are met. Neither the owner nor the manager will try to learn whether the firm approaches equilibrium. But even under these circumstances, the standard management tools of economic analysis, developed under the assumption of profit-maximizing behavior, can be applied effectively.

Because firm G is "a coalition of participants" (owner, manager, laborers, and surrounding community) "with disparate demands," it must have more than one goal (Cyert and March 1963, p. 43). Achievement of some designated, satisfactory level of income may restrict the level of achievement in some other goal of the firm. Thus, there must be a trade-off between other goals and income (profits). For decision making, income may still be maximized, subject to restrictions established for these additional goals. In this manner standard maximizing tools can be used, but they must be conditioned to meet certain additional requirements for competing nonprofit goals.

Evaluation of Operations. Economic theory provides decision rules for resource allocation. These rules are necessary but not sufficient for managing a firm. The results of carrying out these decisions and of the operations themselves should be evaluated.

Since income is the firm's primary objective, income is used to control and evaluate the firm's operations. The income figure incorporates the outcome of a whole series of decisions and actions; hence it is used in business as an overall criterion of the firm's success and its manager's performance.

The absentee owner of firm G needs an income figure that indicates the level of success of the firm as a business. The manager, not knowing the detailed nature of his production function, needs an income figure that helps him to learn about his operations in the past.

In order to evaluate the results of the operations, current income should be compared to income in former years and of other firms. Income is comparable only if all costs, explicit and implicit, are charged to operations and if adjustments for price level changes are introduced. In the OAAS, "contribution from operations" is used for this purpose. In this case, implicit interest charges are included in the total-cost figure. The conventional accounting profit figure does not include implicit costs nor does it allow for price-level adjustments. Hence, it does not provide the best figure for evaluation purposes.

Surrogating Income for Dividend Decisions. Both the owner and the manager should get a figure on that amount of income for the period that the owner can set aside for personal use, assuming that the firm will be at least as well off at the end of the period as it was at the beginning. This is Hicks' definition of income (1946, p. 172). In conventional accounting, profit is used for this purpose, where profit equals the period revenue minus accrued full costs. In the OAAS, "net contribution to owners"—that is, revenue minus total cost—is used. In this case, implicit interest charges are deducted from total costs. The main difference between the two income figures lies in the procedures for valuing assets. In conventional accounting, acquisition costs and discretionary procedures for depreciation are used in determining full costs. In the OAAS, estimates of current market values are used. Gains or losses from holding the firm's assets during an inflationary or depression period may or should be reported separately in both accounting systems.

6. A Two-Product Firm

Firm H produces two separate products. It is helpful to visualize this firm in a linear-programing context, even when the production function of a process is nonlinear, since this function can be approximated by breaking it into several linear sections. A manager considers the firm as a conglomerate of activities and often he assumes that marginal costs of individual activities are constant. Even firm G is composed of several activities in a linear-programing sense—namely, two stages of production, a second shift of workers, and production during a slack season requiring different cost components. There are some aspects regarding decisions and data requirements for firm H that differ from those required for firm G. Only the additional data requirements in firm H are discussed below.

An important aspect of firm H is the existence of several binding restrictions. Without these restrictions, firm H would produce only one product—the one with the highest return to the restriction—and thus become firm G.

Allocation Decisions. In firm H both types of allocation decision—namely, scale decisions and liquidation decisions regarding both production processes—should be taken simultaneously. The linear-programing technique is most suitable for this purpose. When linear programing is not used, one process at a time is considered, assuming that the other levels of production are fixed. Whether linear programing is used directly in analysis or not, a certain type of data is required under these conditions.

Firm H has two production processes that compete with one another for limited resources. In order to decide on the scale of both, two types of data are required: per unit revenue minus avoidable costs (attained contribution) for each process and the requirements of each process for the limited resources, given in physical units.

Internal Opportunity Cost. Revenue minus avoidable costs, when imputed to a limited resource, provides an estimate of the opportunity cost of the resource, termed internal opportunity cost. In a linear-programing analysis, this figure is provided by the shadow price of the resource. Two important variables must be specified for this crucial figure—the revenue minus avoidable costs and the level of the binding restriction. The former variable is provided by the OAAS; the latter is usually known to management. A thorough analysis, however, especially by use of linear programing, provides more information on the binding restrictions.

The internal opportunity cost of a limited resource provides information on the profitability of acquiring more of the resource (if it costs less than its internal opportunity cost), and of introducing a new process (if income is left after internal opportunity costs are charged to this process).

The external opportunity cost—that is, a market price of a good or resource—is included in the OAAS as a cost item. The internal opportunity cost, on the other hand, is not. Thus, the external opportunity cost can be considered as an "input" and the internal opportunity cost as an "output" of the system.

Overhead Costs and Common Services. Firm H incurs some cost items (termed overhead costs), such as the salary of the top manager, that cannot be traced to either production process. In the OAAS these costs are not distributed to the two processes, but rather kept in the aggregate. In conventional accounting, on the other hand, these costs are distributed. The distribution is based on a discretionary procedure. Hence, the conventional accounting full-cost figure of each product cannot be considered as an objective figure.

Suppose the two production processes use a common service, such as trucking. In the OAAS the trucking is considered as a separate activity. The trucking services are considered as intermediate goods, transferred to the two production activities at a market rate. In conventional accounting, on the other hand, accrued full costs of trucking are charged to both production processes.

Control of Operations. There are three managers in firm H, a top manager and a manager for each of the two production processes. The decisions taken by the top manager have to be implemented, and the actions of both lower-level managers should be coordinated. Budgets for the two are prepared and combined for the firm as a whole. In order to evaluate the performance of the lower-level managers, the income of each process is measured.

Two income measurements are required pertaining to each process: a value that should be maximized, identical to the income figure used for allocation decisions, and a figure that may be compared with income obtained in former years and from other processes and to norms. Comparability is achieved by charging to the process only traceable costs. Both income figures are provided by the OAAS. In conventional accounting, profit is used for both purposes.

The income of a process cannot be used as a single criterion for measuring the performance of that manager, since income is partially determined by factors not under the manager's control. One of these factors is the allocation of scarce resources by the top manager.

Returns on Investment. The criterion of rate of return on investment is in wide use in business. This criterion is often used for both evaluation purposes and allocation decisions, in the context of the firm at large or a single production process. Dorfman (1960, p. 613) notes:

> There are two fallacies tucked away in [a ratio] criterion. First, it assumes that [capital] is the only scarce resource, and encourages economizing it at the expense of all other resources. . . . Second, it is a ratio and, as economists are well aware, the objectives of an operation are almost invariable to maximize some difference . . . rather than any ratio. Profit maximization is not the same thing as unit cost minimization [or unit return maximization].

In addition, there are problems of estimating the figures for this ratio. The numerator is provided by the conventional accounting profit figure, a subject that was discussed earlier. A crude estimate of the value of capital used in production provides the denominator.

Quasi-decentralized Firm. In order to make allocation decisions, three types of data are required: input-output coefficients for each production process, income figures for each process, and level-of-resource and other production restrictions. The managers of the production processes are best acquainted with the first type of data. The second type of data is provided by the OAAS. The top manager is best acquainted with the third type of data.

If firm H were organizationally centralized, only the top manager would make allocation decisions, using accounting data. The lower-level managers should participate in the decision-making process, however, in order to ensure that all the required data are considered and to induce them to act in line with the firm's objective. Thus, a quasi-decentralized firm emerges. Maximizing the income of each process, subject to the firm's overall constraints, becomes the objective of the manager of each process.

7. A Multiproduct Integrated Firm

Consider finally firm J, which is best described by Arrow (1964*a*, p. 399):

> A large corporation contains many diverse productive activities, which have important connections with each other and yet are separately identifiable. The products of one activity are the inputs of another. . . . Some commodities have to be purchased from outside, stored, transported from one place to another, . . . and assigned to the activities using them; some activities produce final products which have to be transported, stored, and sold; other activities produce intermediate products. . . . Further, the coordination is needed not only at a single point of time but over many time periods; each activity takes time, so its product can only be used in another activity beginning when the first one ends.

Firm J integrates many activities; each activity is similar to the complete production process of firm G. While a group of firms similar to firm G are coordinated by market forces, the activities in firm J are coordinated by management, aided by an internal budget system.

A whole series of integrated activities results in a product that is sold on the market. Market forces do not affect each activity in this series, but rather the series as an integrated unit. Firm J has several of these series of activities, which manufacture several products for the market. In this aspect, firm J is similar to firm H. The maker of allocation decisions considers the whole series as one production process.

While in firm H the decision-making process is relatively simple (there are only a few variables to consider and a few alternatives to compare), the complexity of firm J makes this process more elaborate.

Hence, the probability that firm J is in equilibrium is much lower than that of firm H. The more that formal and sophisticated techniques are used for programing the firm's operations and for supplying correctly specified data, the closer firm J should approach equilibrium.

In the OAAS, the whole series of activities is broken into individual activities by means of valuing the intermediate goods at market prices. Thus, the use of OAAS will reflect market forces or the price mechanism in the functioning of the integrated process. Conventional accounting practices, on the other hand, isolate the individual activities in an integrated process from the market forces and, in turn, reduce the possibilities of using prices in allocating resources. In other words, the relative profitability of the whole series may cover up individual activities that may be inefficient and unprofitable. Moreover, the OAAS provides much of the financial data required for linear-programing analysis. Thus the use of the OAAS will hopefully make use of linear programing in analysis simpler.

The dynamic aspects of the economy and the existence of uncertainty force the managements of firms G, H, and J to decide anew on resource allocation every period. This situation requires that management search for information, develop expectations about the future, and prepare a long-range plan. In a stationary economy, once resources are allocated optimally, only coordination and control of operations are necessary. This function of management is minor in firms G and H, but of major importance in firm J.

The complex combination of production processes and organization in firm J requires two special features: emphasis on aspects such as coordination of operations, control of members of the organization, and evaluation of subordinates, and the use of a more formal and effective information system and planning techniques to supply data for and facilitate the various management functions. The so-called "budget and control" system has been developed in order to take care of the first feature. This system is used extensively in business, and is not discussed in this study. Much remains to be done, however, in developing a system concerned with providing correctly specified data for decisions, especially in respect to resource allocation.

The preceding discussion implies that firms are not in or close to equilibrium, as economists often imply. There is a need for systems and methods that are designed to help managers to improve the supply of the data required for allocation decisions, which in turn will improve firms' income. This study attempts to serve these needs. If it arouses some interest in the subject, it will have served its purpose.

Appendixes, Bibliography, and Index

APPENDIX A FULL-COST PRICING IN BUSINESS: A REVIEW

Kaplan *et al.* (1958, p. 256), studying the pricing procedures in some of the largest corporations in the United States, notes: "Production and cost characteristics of the main product played a primary role in conditioning the pricing policies adopted by several companies in the sample." If costs are to be used for pricing decisions, it is natural to expect the businessman to add a markup on total cost as a profit margin. This gives rise to a cost-plus pricing method.

There are several reasons for expecting businessmen to adopt, consciously, the cost-plus pricing method. Oxenfeldt (1951, pp. 164–165) indicates five reasons: (1) most price setters do not know the demand for their product; (2) some firms might lose by altering price whenever they believe demand changes; (3) this method is easy to use; (4) in the mind of entrepreneurs, there is a correspondence between a "fair" profit and some fixed margin over costs; and (5) the cost-plus method can be used for public relations. Similar arguments are given by other authors who have experience in consulting firms in the U.S. —for example, Dean (1951) and Tucker (1966).

Full-cost pricing has special merits in a regulated industry when the question of justifying costs is raised. Adelman (1949, p. 242) quotes the following from Government Briefs:

"An 'honest retailer' would attempt to 'price his merchandise in the traditional American way,' that is, cost, plus expenses, plus a profit." Full-cost pricing, however, is harmful to the firm, to consumers, and to the maintenance of competition, as Baumol claims in a testimony on earnings and prices (1966) pertaining to a public utility.

Sometimes it is claimed that estimates of full cost provide a guide to competitors' probable prices (Shillinglaw 1963, p. 78). This cannot really be true because the full-cost figure of a product depends on the particular techniques used by the accountant (cost distribution, valuation of assets, pricing internal transfers) (*ibid.* 1963, p. 78) and the volume of production and the technology used by each firm.

Studies of business pricing methods indicate that the cost-plus pricing method is the most common one in use. The price is based, at least partially, on full-cost information supplied by the accounting system plus a markup, where the full-cost estimate is considered as a surrogate for total cost.

The author is aware of the several surveys indicating the use of full-cost pricing by businessmen—for example, Hall and Hitch (1951), Lanzillotti (1958), Backer (1959), Fog (1960), Gibson (1963, p. 496). Oxenfeldt (1951, p. 162) and Heflebower (1955) cite additional studies. These results may indicate answers elicited by the questions, since the decision maker often is reluctant to tell or cannot spell out the real answer (Simon 1962, pp. 9–10). See also Friedman (1953, pp. 15, 31) and Kaplan *et al.* (1958, pp. 5–6, 128) on this point.

The widespread use of full costs for pricing, or the belief that they are or should be used, can also be explained by the fact that the accountant is the supplier of cost information and usually he is the sole acknowledged expert in this field of information supplied to management (for example, Simon *et al.* 1954, p. 36; and Gibson 1963, p. 497). Results of a survey by Eiteman and Guthrie (1952) indicate implicitly that the accountant's full-cost reports affect management beliefs regarding their cost curves. This situation is also indicated by remarks given by managers (for example, *ibid.* p. 838; Fog 1960, pp. 76–78; and Burns 1967, pp. 187–191).

Accountants can be characterized as cost-minded experts. As such, the accountant recognizes that his business cannot be operated for a long time if it sells its products at less than cost. In other words, only if all the explicit costs are covered by the selling price, will a full recovery of cost be achieved and no loss be recorded. This argument indicates why many accountants believe that full costs have to serve as the basis for pricing (for example, National Association of Accountants 1953*b*, p. 1672, and Heuser 1956). Moreover, accountants (and managers) claim that using other cost figures, such as variable costs, will lead to establishing prices that are too low (for example, National Association of Accountants 1951, and Fog 1960, p. 78).

No doubt, in setting prices, the decision maker should get information on marginal costs. Unfortunately, marginal cost may be difficult and in some cases even impossible to determine. For example, a problem arises when marginal costs are of the nature of a step function. A good illustration of the difficulties that one may run into by using marginal cost pricing is the ad absurdum example of "the traveler to Calais," given by Dessus (1964, pp. 42–43):

> Let us suppose that a traveler gets to the Station Paris-Nord just in time to board the Calais-bound train. If unoccupied seats are available, the cost of transporting our traveler will, in practice, be nil. But if it is necessary to put on an additional coach . . . run an extra train . . . lay a new track . . . , the cost of moving this last traveler mounts with astonishing rapidity. How, in a situation of this kind, do we estimate marginal cost?

So-called "good managers" strive to get information on variable costs, which is closer to marginal costs than full costs, to be used in pricing decisions. Thus, Backer (1959) indicates that all the twenty-five firms in his survey use full costs for pricing. The answers to additional questions, however, revealed that about two-thirds of them used also variable-cost information. Earley's survey (1956) of 110 "excellently managed" companies indicates that most of them also used variable costs for pricing. For some arguments of a businessman for pricing on the basis of variable cost, see Johnson (1962).

To summarize, full cost as a base for the cost-plus pricing method is popular in business "because to businessmen it seems the fair and safe way to price. It also is easiest to explain and justify to customers and others" (Tucker 1966, p. 43). While this is not the whole story of pricing practices, certainly full-cost figures affect pricing decisions, either directly or indirectly, by providing in some cases floors under prices.

APPENDIX B
MONTHLY RECEIPTS AND OUTLAYS FOR PRODUCING FOUR PRODUCTS IN ISRAEL*

	Product A		Product B		Product C		Product D	
Month	Receipts	Outlays	Receipts	Outlays	Receipts	Outlays	Receipts	Outlays
Oct.		59.20		53.00		7.8		85.5
Nov.		58.99		48.80		18.1		27.9
Dec.		35.18		81.35		14.3		23.8
Jan.	123.51	40.17		30.40		1.1		14.4
Feb.	247.00	57.48		35.00		12.0		31.7
Mar.				37.10		10.1		63.2
Apr.				25.40	33.5	4.5		40.6
May				27.30		8.3		44.1
June				64.50		18.4		90.0
July			46.30	58.75	48.1	18.6		110.5
Aug.			79.00	115.50	67.3	14.8	173.9	207.1
Sept.			99.20	251.40		36.1	208.7	196.9
Oct.			138.50	9.80	43.4	35.7	117.6	110.7
Nov.			153.80	13.22	72.8	22.2	177.0	109.5
Dec.			119.00	13.22	20.2		234.0	89.2
Jan.			110.80	13.22	24.1	1.8	297.2	89.2
Feb.			130.80	12.63	9.9		203.6	81.2
Mar.			232.00	12.32	25.0		167.0	5.0
Apr.			265.80	10.47				
May			317.00	10.47	25.6			
June			87.60	10.47	10.2			
July					8.9			
Total	370.51	251.02	1779.80	934.41	389.0	223.8	1579.0	1421.5
Total in U.S.$ per dunam	123.50	83.7	593.3	311.50	129.7	74.6	526.3	473.8

* Genuine data from farms in Israel are used. All figures are in Israeli units representing I£ (1 I£ = $0.33) per dunam (1 dunam = 0.25 acres). Product A is cauliflowers; product B is apples; product C is cotton; and product D is apples.

APPENDIX C SOME DATA ON THE EXTENT AND RESULTS OF PROGRAMING TWENTY FARMS IN ISRAEL*

Farm no.	Irrigated land (dunams)	Dry-farming land (dunams)	Orchards (dunams)	Fishponds (dunams)	Water (1,000 cu. m./yr.)	Labor (days/yr.)	Dairy cows	Bull calves	Ewes	Feed for cattle (10,000 f.u./yr.)
	Resources included in the programs									
1	1,920			450	1,140	5,876	120		480	396
2	2,650				1,480	11,250	200	100	750	632
3	2,000				1,242	2,539				
4	4,440		170		1,025	11,482	240			596
5	1,900			860	2,560	6,500	58	100		753
6	1,400				550	1,050	90			172
7	2,480				1,809	3,250	120			773
8	1,690				750	1,700	110			329
9	2,200				2,807	3,267	115			314
10	3,400	1,010			720	8,442	110			604
11	2,499			575	1,153	9,598	170		450	395
12	1,363					8,011	220			522
13	4,770	1,000	231		733	11,238	202	190		847
14	1,290	120	470		1,800	1,215				
15	1,690		560		810	7,585				
16	2,250				1,743	3,780			400	
17	2,725	2,110				5,963	150			419
18	1,446	1,140			500	2,614	120	100		363
19	2,500	3,600			842	10,478	151	83		428
20	2,292				691	8,249	130	75		349
Total or range	46,905				22,355	124,087	2,306			7,892

* The programs are for the year 1964–1965 or the year 1965–1966. All figures are in Israeli units: 1 dunam = 0.25 acres; 1 cubic meter = 264 gallons; 1 f.u. (Hanson's) = 2.1 pounds TDN in corn, or 2.8 TDN in better hay; 1 I£ = $0.33.

Figures concerning the programing							Income (contribution)			
Farm no.	Activities	Restrictions	Duration		Intermediate computer runs	Alternative plans	Linear programing (I£)	Conventional planning (I£)	Difference	
			Start	End					Absolute (I£)	Relative (%)
1	117	142	3/64	10/64	6	5	169,709	138,351	31,358	23.0
2	51	78	3/64	10/64	6	3	559,924	530,810	29,114	5.5
3	30	34	3/64	12/64	8	4	242,350	212,000	30,350	14.4
4	96	130	6/64	12/64	3	1	667,030	610,431	56,599	8.5
5	66	75	11/64	1/65	3	3	495,000	486,500	88,500	1.8
6	12	25	1/65	2/65	3	1	108,013	96,850	11,163	11.5
7	15	29	12/63	3/64	3	2	331,667	306,830	24,837	7.5
8	90	110	9/64	3/65	3	3	151,795	127,179	24,616	19.5
9	90	113	1/65	4/65	3	1	205,507	175,003	30,504	17.5
10	85	83	1/65	4/65	2	1	662,200	609,400	52,800	8.7
11	192	144	7/64	5/65	10	3	609,000	567,200	41,800	8.0
12	89	91	8/64	5/65	6	1	394,000	325,000	69,000	21.0
13	100	146	8/64	5/65	5	1	769,606	739,564	30,042	4.0
14	35	80	1/65	6/65	3	2	511,925	489,396	22,529	4.5
15	38	45	10/64	6/65	8	7	305,225	285,100	20,125	7.1
16	31	54	12/64	6/65	2	1	307,000	275,000	32,000	12.0
17	119	150	10/64	6/65	3	1	631,261	591,487	39,774	7.0
18	41	49	7/64	6/65	1	1	235,500	203,000	32,500	16.0
19	131	151	11/64	6/65	2	1	525,492	447,675	77,817	17.0
20	70	116	8/64	6/65	3	1	489,773	450,400	39,373	8.0
Total or range	12–192	25–151			1–10	1–7	8,371,977	7,667,176	704,801	9.2

APPENDIX D
OPTIMIZATION IN A DECENTRALIZED ORGANIZATION: A REVIEW

The framework underlying the model outlined in Chapter XII can be clarified by a review of some of the problems of decentralization—specifically, some implications of welfare economics, optimization procedures of decentralized firms, advantages of decentralization, and the degree of decentralization that exists in practice. The review implies that central management has to intervene to achieve overall optimization in a decentralized firm, that decentralization is required for motivation purposes, and that both centralized and decentralized aspects exist side by side in large firms.

At a certain level of abstraction there are similarities in the problems of efficient resource allocation and decision making within the general economy and within a decentralized firm. In a decentralized firm, the objective is to achieve an overall optimum in a way analogous to that of the whole economy. The resulting optimal decisions of each decentralized division would be in fact the best attainable in terms of the overall objective of the firm. Dean (1955, pp. 67–68) goes to an extreme in this analogy, suggesting that "the modern integrated, multiple-product firm functions best if it is made into a sort of miniature of the competitive, free-enterprise economic system."

Under perfect competition, optimum resource allocation is achieved by following the principles of equating marginal cost with marginal revenue. If some of the assumptions of the free market are not fulfilled, however, mainly when external economies or diseconomies (externalities) are present and when increasing returns to scale exist, the market-price mechanism does not suffice for achieving an overall optimum.

Externalities exist when each individual's cost function involves decision variables that are subject to control by others. Whinston (1962) distinguishes between two kinds of externalities in which the cost function is separable and nonseparable. In the first case the micro and macro conditions of optimization can be brought into reconciliation by price or pricelike devices, such as subsidies or taxes. In the second case, however, other supplements, such as physical quotas, are needed for a micro and macro condition of optimization.

These cases are referred to by Whinston as "mixed systems" in which prices form only a part of the administrative instruments used in a decentralized organization to direct optimal resource allocation. In the case of mutual externalities among two firms, the externalities would be internalized and profit would be maximized through merger. A "natural unit" for decision making would or might be realized. When the externalities are separable, internalization still enables complete decentralization within the organization. This cannot be done in the case of nonseparable externalities. The decision of each division depends on the decision of the other division. Thus, the decisions of both divisions should be made together and simultaneously.

The crucial point is that even under conditions of perfect competition, when externalities exist, profit maximization on the micro level will not necessarily lead to a macro optimum. Part of the externalities can be eliminated by employing pricing devices. But one should bear in mind that interfirm pricing is harder to achieve than intrafirm pricing.

Let us now turn to review some suggestions for intrafirm pricing procedures when externalities exist. Specifically, the review indicates some suggestions for optimal decisions in a decentralized firm.

Hirshleifer (1956, 1957) suggests that the marginal cost schedule of one division be presented to the other one for determining the quantity and price for the transferred intermediate good in a decentralized firm. For solving demand dependencies, a system of "taxes and bounties" have to be set by central management.

Arrow (1959) suggests an iterative decision-making process in which central management sets and revises price information (shadow prices of limited resources and marginal revenues when demand is dependent) and, in turn, the individual units plan and replan their operations. The process starts with tentative prices and will, under certain conditions, eventually converge to an optimal solution.

O. Lange suggested in 1938 a similar conceptual procedure for a socialist economy (Gordon 1964, p. 20). Gale (1960, pp. 85–93) suggests applying the concepts of linear programing for planning the economy in an analogical procedure. Whinston (1964*a*) follows a similar procedure. However, he suggests incorporating externalities into a nonlinear-programing, decomposable model.

Based on the decomposable linear-programing model developed by Dantzig and Wolfe (1960), Baumol and Fabian (1964) suggest an operational procedure to achieve an overall optimal resource allocation in a finite number of iterations. Further developments have been made by Whinston (1964*b*) and Hass (1968).

Like Arrow's iterative process, Baumol's and Fabian's algorithm provides for planning each division, based on shadow prices for the overall restrictions (limited resources, interdivisional dependencies) calculated by the central office. In the final step, the division pools all its proposals and averages them by weights which are given by the central office (and are also the product of the iterative process) to provide the plan to follow. Note that in this procedure, central management intervenes in the planning process and dictates weights to be used for the final solution.

As can be seen, central management must intervene in the decision or programing process, if resources are to be optimally allocated. Central management must also intervene where there is a possibility for bilateral monopoly in the "internal market" for intermediate goods in a vertically integrated firm (Bierman 1963, pp. 95–97; Hirshleifer 1964) or oligopoly in the external market for a horizontally integrated firm. Some possible intracompany competitive situations are analyzed by Ophir (1960, ch. 9).

The existence of externalities introduces uncertainty into the decision framework of the division and hampers estimation of the optimum outcome. Whinston (1964*a*) shows by an analogy to the theory of games that imposed restrictions by central management will reduce the level of uncertainty for each division.

This discussion indicates that for optimal resource allocation centralization is required. On the other hand, decentralization provides some advantages by inducing motivations, incentives, and greater responsibility on the part of managers at lower levels. This is, for example, Benston's conclusion (1963) after surveying the literature. Note in contrast Camman's idea (1929, p. 40) that giving department heads a voice in decisions "would have a tendency toward disorganization." Decentralization also has an advantage in economizing on the transmission of information. Moreover, "individual managers will inevitably know more about their own spheres of activity than higher officials" (Arrow 1964*a*, p. 400). Simon (1962, p. 6) claims that with modern computing equipment, "the decentralized procedures simply do not yield the savings in information-transmitting cost usually claimed for them." Anton (1966, p. 519) and Dearden (1967) claim the contrary.

This review implies that centralization is required for optimal resource allocation, but that decentralization is best for motivation of members of the organization. However, neither extreme exists. Absolute decentralization is synonymous with absolute independence—a situation that never exists (Zannetos 1965, p. 53). Even a sovereign firm is not completely independent. Centralization, on the other hand, literally means that all decisions are reserved to one manager, which implies a one-man business (E. F. L. Brech, in Kruisinga 1954, p. 54). Effective centralization requires that only top management decides and therefore has to be completely informed and that the remainder of the organization only executes the decisions. This situation cannot exist. For management to be completely informed, individuals in the lower echelon have to provide information. But the selection of the type of information to be sent up to the decision maker is a decision in itself (Shubik 1964, pp. 210–211; Anton 1964, p. 236). Some production processes require ad hoc decisions on the spot. This is especially true in agricultural firms, where the level of application of an input depends on prevailing biological conditions. These decisions cannot be made by central management. Therefore, decisions are made at all levels of the organization. The conclusion is that the notion of decentralization is relative and not universal; therefore one can speak about the degree of decentralization rather than about absolute decentralization or centralization.

The extremes in decentralization can be seen in the examples of a farmer who works with his family and delegates some authority to the other workers and a large corporation with almost independent divisions. About the first example, Samuelson (1956, p. 9) notes that even in the family "there is discernible a decentralization of decision making." An illustration of the second example is General Electric, where two divisions producing major appliances distribute and set prices completely independently (Cordiner 1956, p. 59).

To summarize, any decentralized firm is partially centralized, and any centralized firm is partially decentralized. This implies that the decision-making framework as well as the control structure have to be compatible with this organizational form.

BIBLIOGRAPHY

Ackoff, R. L. 1967. "Management misinformation systems." *Management Science,* Dec. 1967, pp. B–147–156.

Adelman, M. A. 1949. "The A & P Case: A Study in Applied Economic Theory." *Quarterly Journal of Economics,* May 1949, pp. 238–257.

Alchian, A. 1959. "Costs and Outputs." In M. Abramovitz (ed.), *The Allocation of Economic Resources: Essays in Honor of B. F. Haley,* pp. 21–40. Stanford, Cal.: Stanford University Press, 1959.

Alexander, S. S. 1950. Income measurement in a dynamic economy. In American Institute of Accountants, Study Group on Business Income, *Five monographs on business income,* pp. 1–95. New York, 1950.

American Accounting Association 1966. *A Statement of Basic Accounting Theory*. Evanston, Ill., 1966.

American Institute of [Certified Public] Accountants 1953*a*. *Restatement and Revision of Accounting Research Bulletins.* (Accounting Research and Terminology Bulletin No. 43.) New York, 1953.

—— 1953*b*. *Reviews and Resume.* (Accounting Terminology Bulletin No. 1.) New York, 1953.

—— 1963. *Reporting the Financial Effects of Price-Level Changes.* (Accounting Research Study No. 6, by the Staff of the Accounting Research Division.) New York, 1963.

Ammons, R. B. 1956. "Effects of Knowledge of Performance: A Survey and Tentative Theoretical Formulation." *Journal of General Psychology,* April 1956, pp. 279–299.

Anshen, M. 1963. "Organization Structure and the New Decision-Making Technology." In D. M. Bowman and F. M. Fillerup (eds.), *Management: Organization and Planning,* pp. 17–40. New York: McGraw-Hill, 1963.

Ansoff, H. I. 1960. "A Quasi-analytic Method for Long-Range Planning." In C. W. Churchman and M. Verhulst (eds.), *Management Science Models and Techniques,* II, 229–251. (Proceedings of the Sixth International Meeting, Institute of Management Science.) New York: Pergamon, 1960.

Anthony, R. N. 1965. *Planning and Control Systems: A Framework for Analysis.* Boston: Harvard University Graduate School of Business, 1965.

Anton, H. R. 1964. "The Budgetary Process and Management Control." In Bonini, Jaedicke, and Wagner (1964), pp. 227–236.

—— 1966. "Activity Analysis of the Firm: A Theoretical Approach to Accounting (Systems) Development." In H. R. Anton and P. A. Firmin (eds.), *Contemporary Issues in Cost Accounting,* pp. 515–530. Boston: Houghton Mifflin, 1966.

Arrow, K. J. 1959. "Optimization, Decentralization, and Internal Pricing in Business Firms." In *Contributions to Scientific Research in Management,* pp. 9–18. Los Angeles: University of California, 1959.

—— 1964*a*. "Control in Large Organization." *Management Science,* April 1964, pp. 397–408.

—— 1964*b*. "Research in Management Controls: A Critical Synthesis." In Bonini, Jaedicke, and Wagner (1964), pp. 317–327.

Backer, M. 1959. "A Study of the Usefulness of Accounting Costs for Product Pricing and Capital Formation Decision." Unpub. Ph.D. thesis, University of Michigan, 1959; University Microfilms No. 59–4430.

Baldwin, W. L. 1964. "The Motives of Managers, Environmental Restraints, and the Theory of Managerial Enterprise." *Quarterly Journal of Economics,* May 1964, pp. 238–256.

Baumol, W. J. 1961. What Can Economic Theory Contribute to Managerial Economics?" *American Economic Review,* May 1961, pp. 142–146.

—— 1962. "On the Theory of Expansion of the Firm." *American Economic Review,* Dec. 1962, pp. 1078–1087.

—— 1965. *Economic Theory and Operations Analysis,* 2nd ed. Englewood Cliffs, N.J.: Prentice-Hall, 1965.

—— 1966. "Historical Costs Not the Proper Basis for Determining Rates." In *Testimony on Earnings and Prices Presented to FCC.* N. p.: American Telephone and Telegraph Company, 1966.

Baumol, W. J., and T. Fabian 1964. "Decomposition, Pricing for Decentralization and External Economics." *Management Science,* Sept. 1964, pp. 1–32.

Baxter, W. T. 1967. "Accounting Values: Sale Price Versus Replacement Cost." *Journal of Accounting Research,* autumn 1967, pp. 208–214.

Becker, S., and D. Green, Jr. 1962. "Budgeting and Employee Behavior." *Journal of Business,* Oct. 1962, pp. 392–402.

Bellman, R. E. 1956. *Dynamic Programming.* Princeton, N.J.: Princeton University Press, 1956.

Benston, G. J. 1963. "The Role of the Firm's Accounting System for Motivation." *Accounting Review,* April 1963, pp. 347–354.

Bernhard, R. H. 1968. "Some Problems in Applying Mathematical Programming to Opportunity Costing." *Journal of Accounting Research,* spring 1968, pp. 143–148.

Bierman, H., Jr. 1963. *Topics in Cost Accounting and Decisions.* New York: McGraw-Hill, 1963.

—— 1966. "A Further Study of Depreciation." *Accounting Review,* April 1966, pp. 271–274.

—— 1967. "Inventory Valuation: The Use of Market Prices." *Accounting Review,* Oct. 1967, pp. 731–735.

Bierman, H., Jr., and S. Smidt 1967. "Accounting for Debt and Costs of Liquidity under Conditions of Uncertainty." *Journal of Accounting Research,* autumn 1967, pp. 144–153.

Black, G. 1967. "Systems Analysis in Government Operations." *Management Science,* Oct. 1967, pp. B–41–58.

Bliss, J. H. 1922. "Cost Methods in the Packing Industry." *NACA Official Publications,* April 1922, pp. 1–16.

Bodenhorn, D. 1961. "An Economist Looks at Industrial Accounting and Depreciation." *Accounting Review,* Oct. 1961, pp. 585–588.

Boiteux, M. 1964. "Peak-Load Pricing." In Nelson (1964), pp. 59–89.

Bonbright, J. C. 1937. *The Valuation of Property,* Vol. I. New York: McGraw-Hill, 1937.

Bonini, C. P., R. K. Jaedicke, and M. M. Wagner (eds.) 1964. *Management Controls: New Directions in Basic Research.* New York: McGraw-Hill, 1964.

Boulding, K. E. 1956. "General Systems Theory—The Skelton of Science." *Management Science,* April 1956, pp. 197–208.

—— 1962. "Economics and Accounting: The Uncongenial Twins." In W. T. Baxter and S. Davidson (eds.), *Studies in Accounting Theory,* pp. 44–55. Homewood, Ill.: Irwin, 1962.

—— 1966. "The Economics of Knowledge and the Knowledge of Economics." *American Economic Review,* May 1966, pp. 1–13.

Bowman, Mary J. (ed.) 1958. *Expectations, Uncertainty, and Business Behavior.* New York: Social Science Research Council, 1958.

Breimyer, H. F. 1961. *Demand and Prices for Meat: Factors Influencing Their Historical Development.* (U.S. Dept. of Agriculture Technical Bulletin No. 1253.) Washington, 1961.

Brown, E., and J. Sheehan 1966. *Grocery Distribution Center Efficiency Report.* Ithaca, N.Y.: Dept. of Agricultural Economics, Cornell University, 1966.

Brummet, R. L. 1957. *Overhead Costing.* (Michigan Business Studies, Vol. XIII, No. 2.) Ann Arbor: University of Michigan, 1957.

Buckley, J. W. 1966. "Management Services and Management Audits by Professional Accountants." *California Management Review,* autumn 1966, pp. 43–50.

Burns, T. J. (ed.) 1967. *The Use of Accounting Data in Decision Making.* (Ohio State University, College of Commerce and Administration Monograph No. AA 1.) Columbus: Ohio State University, 1967.

Camman, E. A. 1929. "Interdepartmental Profits." *Journal of Accountancy,* July 1929, pp. 37–44.

Candler, W., and D. Sargent 1962. "Farm Standards and the Theory of Production Economics." *Journal of Agricultural Economics,* Dec. 1962, pp. 282–290.

Caplan, E. H. 1966. "Behavioral Assumptions of Management Accounting." *Accounting Review,* July 1966, pp. 496–509.

Caspall, K. K., and L. M. Eisgruber 1966. *Functional Accounting for Farm Management Decision Making.* (Research Progress Report 216.) Lafayette, Ind.: Purdue University Agricultural Experiment Station, 1966.

Chambers, R. J. 1966. *Accounting, Evaluation and Economic Behavior.* Englewood Cliffs, N.J.: Prentice-Hall, 1966.

Chang, Emily C. 1962. "Business Income in Accounting and Economics." *Accounting Review,* Oct. 1962, pp. 636–644.

Charnes, A., and W. W. Cooper 1961. *Management Models and Industrial Applications of Linear Programming,* Vol. I. New York: Wiley, 1961.

—— 1967. "Some Network Characterizations for Mathematical Programming and Accounting Approaches to Planning and Control." *Accounting Review,* Jan. 1967, pp. 24–52.

Churchill, N. C., and A. C. Stedry 1966. "Some Developments in Management Science and Information Systems with Respect to Measurement in Accounting." In R. K. Jaedicke *et al.* (eds.), *Research in Accounting Measurement,* pp. 28–48. N. p.: American Accounting Association, 1966.

Churchman, C. W. 1961. *Prediction and Optimal Decisions: Philosophical Issues of a Science of Value.* Englewood Cliffs, N.J.: Prentice-Hall, 1961.

Churchman, C. W., and R. L. Ackoff 1955. "Operational Accountings and Operations Research." *Journal of Accountancy,* Feb. 1955, pp. 33–39.

Clark, J. M. 1923. *Studies in the Economic of Overhead Costs.* Chicago: University of Chicago Press, 1923.

Clarke, G. B. 1962. *Programme Planning.* (OECD Documentation in Food and Agriculture No. 45.) Paris: Organization for Economic Co-operation and Development, 1962.

Coase, R. H. 1960. "The Problem of Social Cost." *Journal of Law and Economics,* Oct. 1960, pp. 1–44.

Comiskey, E. E., and F. A. Mlynarczyk 1968. "Recognition of Income by Finance Companies." *Accounting Review,* April 1968, pp. 248–256.

Cook, P. W., Jr. 1955. "Decentralization and the Transfer-Price Problems." *Journal of Business,* April 1955, pp. 87–94.

—— 1957. "New Technique for Intracompany Pricing." *Harvard Business Review,* July–Aug. 1957, pp. 74–80.

Cordiner, R. J. 1956. *New Frontiers for Professional Managers.* New York: McGraw-Hill, 1956.

Cyert, R. M., and W. R. Dill 1964. "The Future of Business Education." *Journal of Business,* July 1964, pp. 221–237.

Cyert, R. M., and J. G. March 1963. *A Behavioural Theory of the Firm.* Englewood Cliffs, N.J.: Prentice-Hall, 1963.

Dantzig, G. B., and P. Wolfe 1960. "Decomposition Principles for Linear Programming." *Operations Research,* Feb. 1960, pp. 101–111.

Davidson, S. 1962. *The Meaning of Depreciation.* (Selected Papers No. 2, Graduate School of Business, University of Chicago.) Chicago, 1962.

—— 1963*a*. "Old Wine into New Bottles." *Accounting Review,* April 1963, pp. 278–284.

—— 1963*b*. "The Day of Reckoning—Managerial Analysis and Accounting Theory." *Journal of Accounting Research,* autumn 1963, pp. 117–126.

Day, H. 1966. *Profits, Learning and Convergence of Satisficing to Marginalism.* (Workshop Paper 6601 [mimeo.], Social Systems Research Institute, University of Wisconsin.) Madison, 1966.

Dean,, J. 1951. *Managerial Economics*. Englewood Cliffs, N.J.: Prentice-Hall, 1951.

—— 1955. "Decentralization and Intracompany Pricing." *Harvard Business Review*, July–Aug. 1955, pp. 65–74.

—— 1958. "An Approach to Internal Profit Measurement." *NAA Bulletin*, March 1958, pp. 5–12.

Dearden, J. 1960. "Interdivisional Pricing." *Harvard Business Review*, Jan.–Feb. 1960, pp. 117–125.

—— 1967. "Computers: No Impact on Divisional Control." *Harvard Business Review*, Jan.–Feb. 1967, pp. 99–104.

Demski, J. S., 1967. "An Accounting System Structured on a Linear Programming Model." *Accounting Review*, Oct. 1967, pp. 701–712.

Dessus, G. 1964. "The General Principles of Rate-Fixing in Public Utilities." In Nelson (1964), pp. 31–49.

Devine, C. T. 1950. "Cost Accounting and Pricing Policies." *Accounting Review*, Oct. 1950, pp. 384–389.

Dixon, S. 1966. *The Case for Marginal Costing*. N.p.: General Educational Trust of the Institute of Chartered Accountants in England and Wales, 1966.

Dopuch, N., and D. F. Drake 1964. "Accounting Implications of a Mathematical Programming Approach to the Transfer Price Problem." *Journal of Accounting Research*, spring 1964, pp. 10–24.

Dorfman, R. 1960. "Operations Research." *American Economic Review*, Sept. 1960, pp. 575–623.

Dorfman, R., P. A. Samuelson, and R. M. Solow 1958. *Linear Programming and Economic Analysis*. New York: McGraw-Hill, 1958.

Drake, O. F., and N. Dopuch 1965. "On the Case for Dichotomizing Income." *Journal of Accounting Research*, autumn 1965, pp. 192–205.

Dror, Y. 1963*a*. "Abstract Theory and Common Sense Trivialities: The Modern Study of Planning." *Public Administration Review*, March 1963, pp. 47–50.

—— 1963*b*. "The Planning Process: A Facet Design." *International Review of Administrative Sciences*, No. 1 (1963), pp. 46–58.

Drucker, P. F. 1964. "Controls, Control and Management." In Bonini, Jaedicke, and Wagner (1964), pp. 286–296.

—— 1967. "The Effective Decision." *Harvard Business Review*, Jan.–Feb. 1967, pp. 92–98.

Earley, J. S. 1955. "Recent Developments in Cost Accounting and the

'Marginal Analysis.'" *Journal of Political Economy,* June 1955, pp. 227–242.

—— 1956. "Marginal Policies of 'Excellently Managed' Companies." *American Economic Review,* March 1956, pp. 44–70.

Earley, J. S., and W. T. Carleton 1962. "Budgeting and the Theory of the Firm: New Findings." *Journal of Industrial Economics,* July 1962, pp. 165–173.

Edwards, E. O., and P. W. Bell 1961. *The Theory and Measurement of Business Income.* Berkeley and Los Angeles: University of California Press, 1961.

Eiteman, W. J., and G. E. Guthrie 1952. "The Shape of the Average Cost Curve." *American Economic Review,* Dec. 1952, pp. 832–858.

Evans, M. K. 1955. "Accounting Problems in Measuring Performance by Organizational Units." *NACA Bulletin,* Aug. 1955, pp. 1739–1748.

Fess, P. E., and W. L. Ferrara 1961. "The Period Cost Concept For Income Measurement—Can It Be Defended?" *Accounting Review,* Oct. 1961, pp. 598–602.

Festinger, L., and E. Aronson 1960. "The Arousal and Reduction of Dissonance in Social Contexts." In D. Cartwright and A. Zander (eds.), *Group Dynamics Research and Theory*, pp. 214–231. Elmsford, N.Y.: Row, Peterson and Co., 1960.

Fog, B. 1960. *Industrial Pricing Policies.* Amsterdam: North-Holland Pub., 1960.

Forrester, J. W. 1961. *Industrial Dynamics.* New York: M.I.T. Press and Wiley, 1961.

Fremgen, J. M. 1964. "The Direct Costing Controversy—An Identification of Issues." *Accounting Review,* Jan. 1964, pp. 43–51.

Friedman, M. 1953. "The Methodology of Positive Economics." In M. Friedman, *Essays in Positive Economics*, pp. 3–43. Chicago: University of Chicago Press, 1953.

Frumkin, D., and U. Gilead 1966. *Report on Short-Run Planning of a Kibbutz Farm by Linear Programming*. Tel Aviv: Inter Kibbutz Economic Advisory Unit, 1966.

Galbraith, J. K. 1936. "Monopoly Power and Price Rigidities." *Quarterly Journal of Economics*, May 1936, pp. 456–475.

Gale, D. 1960. *The Theory of Linear Economic Models.* New York: McGraw-Hill, 1960.

Garner, S. P. 1954. *Evaluation of Cost Accounting to 1925.* Montgomery: University of Alabama Press, 1954.

Gibson, J. L. 1963. "Accounting in the Decision-Making Process: Some Empirical Evidence." *Accounting Review*, July 1963, pp. 492–500.

Giles, A. K. 1962. *Gross Margins and the Future of Account Analysis.* (University of Reading, Department of Agricultural Economics Misc. Studies No. 23.) Reading, Eng., 1962.

Gillespie, C. 1962. *Standard and Direct Costing.* Englewood Cliffs, N.J.: Prentice-Hall, 1962.

Goetz, B. B. 1967. "Transfer Prices: An Exercise in Relevancy and Goal Congruence." *Accounting Review,* July 1967, pp. 435–440.

Goldschmidt, Y. 1968. "Cost Analysis and Profitability of a Service with Seasonal Character." *American Journal of Agricultural Economics*, Dec. 1968, pp. 1580–1585.

Goldschmidt, Y., D. Frumkin, and A. Shapira 1965. *Application of Linear Programming to Plan Kibbutz Farms in the Eastern Israel Valley.* Tel Aviv: Department of Agricultural Economics, Faculty of Agriculture, Hebrew University, and Inter Kibbutz Economic Advisory Unit, 1965. (In Hebrew.)

Goldschmidt, Y., U. Gilead, A. Levinger, D. Frumkin, M. Noi, and D. Shalem 1965*a*. *A Guide for Planning a Kibbutz Farm with Linear Programming.* Tel-Aviv: Inter Kibbutz Economic Advisory Unit, 1965. (In Hebrew.)

—— 1965*b*. *Application of Mathematical Programming to Kibbutz Farms: Report on the Application to Twenty Farms.* Tel Aviv: Inter Kibbutz Economic Advisory Unit, 1965. (In Hebrew.)

Goldschmidt, Y., and S. Smidt 1969. "Valuing the Firm's Durable Assets for Managerial Information." *Accounting Review*, April 1969.

Gordon, M. J. 1963. "Toward a Theory of Responsibility Accounting Systems." *NAA Bulletin*, Dec. 1963, pp. 3–9.

—— 1964. "The Use of Administered Price Systems to Control Large Organizations." In Bonini, Jaedicke, and Wagner (1964), pp. 1–26.

Gould, J. R. 1964. "Internal Pricing in Firms When There Are Costs of Using an Outside Market." *Journal of Business*, Jan. 1964, pp. 61–67.

Green, D., Jr. 1960. "A Moral to the Direct-Costing Controversy," *Journal of Business*, July 1960, pp. 218–226.

Green, D., Jr., and G. H. Sorter 1959. "Accounting for Obsolescence—a Proposal," *Accounting Review*, July 1959, pp. 433–441.

Greer, H. C. 1962. "Divisional Profit Calculation-Notes on the 'Transfer Price' Problems." *NAA Bulletin,* July 1962, pp. 5–12.

Gross, B. M. 1964. *The Managing of Organizations,* Vol. II. New York: Free Press of Glencoe, 1964.

Hall, R. L., and C. J. Hitch 1951. "Price Theory and Business Behaviour." In Wilson, T. and P. W. S. Andrews (eds.), *Oxford Studies in the Price Mechanism*, pp. 107–138. London: Oxford University Press, 1951.

Hanson, E. I. 1966. "The Budgetary Control Function," *Accounting Review,* April 1966, pp. 239–243.

Harrod, R. F. 1936. "Imperfect Competition and the Trade Cycle." *Review of Economic Statistics,* May 1936, pp. 84–88.

Hartley, R. V. 1968. "Operations Research and Its Implications for the Accounting Profession." *Accounting Review,* April 1968, pp. 321–332.

Hass, J. E. 1968. "Transfer Pricing in a Decentralized Firm." *Management Science,* Feb. 1968, pp. B–310–331.

Heady, E. O. 1952. *Economics of Agricultural Production and Resource Use.* New York: Prentice-Hall, 1952.

Heady, E. O., and W. Candler 1958. *Linear Programming Methods.* Ames, Iowa: Iowa State College Press, 1958.

Heady, E. O., and J. L. Dillon 1961. *Agricultural Production Functions.* Ames, Iowa: Iowa State University Press, 1961.

Heebink, D. V. 1964. "Postcompletion Audits of Capital Investment Decisions." *California Management Review,* spring 1964, pp. 47–52.

Heflebower, R. B. 1955. "Full Costs, Cost Changes, and Prices." In *Business Concentration and Price Policy: A Conference of the University—National Bureau of Economic Research,* pp. 361–392. Princeton, N.J.: Princeton University Press, 1955.

Heuser, F. L. 1956. "Organizing for Effective Intra-Company Pricing." *NACA Bulletin,* May 1956, pp. 1100–1105.

Hicks, J. R. 1937. "Mr Keynes and the 'Classics': A Suggested Interpretation." *Econometrica,* April 1937, pp. 147–159.

—— 1946. *Value and Capital,* 2nd ed. Oxford: Clarendon Press, 1946.

Hirshleifer, J. 1956. "On the Economics of Transfer Pricing." *Journal of Business,* July 1956, pp. 172–184.

—— 1957. "Economics of the Divisionalized Firm." *Journal of Business,* April 1957, pp. 96–108.

—— 1962. "The Firm's Cost Function: A Successful Reconstruction?" *Journal of Business,* July 1962, pp. 235–255.

—— 1964. "Internal Pricing and Decentralized Decisions." In Bonini, Jaedicke, and Wagner (1964), pp. 27–37.

Hitch, C. J., and R. N. McKean 1954. "Suboptimization in Operations Problems." In J. F. McCloskey and F. N. Trefethen (eds.), *Operations Research for Management, I*, 168–186. Baltimore: Johns Hopkins Press, 1954.

—— 1960. *The Economics of Defense in the Nuclear Age*. Cambridge: Harvard University Press, 1960.

—— 1961. "What Can Managerial Economics Contribute to Economic Theory?" *American Economic Review*, May 1961, pp. 147–154.

Holt, C. C., *et al.* 1960. *Planning Production, Inventories, and Work Force*. Englewood Cliffs, N.J.: Prentice-Hall, 1960.

Horngren, C. T. 1962*a*. *Cost Accounting: A Managerial Emphasis*. Englewood Cliffs, N.J.: Prentice-Hall, 1962; rev. 1967.

—— 1962*b*. "Choosing Accounting Practices for Reporting to Management." *NAA Bulletin*, Sept. 1962, pp. 3–15.

—— 1965. "How Should We Interpret the Realization Concept?" *Accounting Review*, April 1965, pp. 322–333.

—— 1967. "A Contribution Margin Approach to the Analysis of Capacity Utilization." *Accounting Review*, April 1967, pp. 254–264.

Horngren, C. T., and G. H. Sorter 1961. " 'Direct' Costing for External Reporting." *Accounting Review*, Jan. 1961, pp. 84–93.

Howe, M. 1962. "Marginal Analysis in Accounting." *Yorkshire Bulletin of Economic and Social Research*, Nov. 1962, pp. 81–89.

Hughes, W. R. 1962. "Short-Run Efficiency and the Organization of Electric Power Industry." *Quarterly Journal of Economics*, Nov. 1962, pp. 592–612.

Husband, G. R. 1954. "Rationalization in the Accounting Measurement of Income." *Accounting Review*, Jan. 1954, pp. 3–14.

Ijiri, Y. 1965. *Management Goals and Accounting for Control*. Amsterdam: North-Holland Pub., 1965.

—— 1967. *The Foundations of Accounting Measurement: A Mathematical, Economic, and Behavioral Inquiry*. Englewood Cliffs, N.J.: Prentice-Hall, 1967.

Ijiri, Y., and R. K. Jaedicke 1966. "Reliability and Objectivity of Accounting Measurements." *Accounting Review*, July 1966, pp. 474–483.

Ijiri, Y., R. K. Jaedicke, and K. F. Knight 1966. "The Effects of Accounting Alternatives on Management Decisions." In R. K. Jaedicke *et al.* (eds.), *Research in Accounting Measurements*, pp. 186–199. N.p.: American Accounting Association, 1966.

Jaedicke, R. K. 1962. "Accounting Data for Purposes of Control." *Accounting Review*, April 1962, pp. 187–188.

Jaedicke, R. K., and R. T. Sprouse 1965. *Accounting Flows: Income, Funds, and Cash*. New York: Prentice-Hall, 1965.

Johnson, G. 1962. "The Pricing of Consumer Goods." *Yorkshire Bulletin of Economic and Social Research,* Nov. 1962, pp. 74–80.

Johnson, R. A., F. E. Kast, and J. E. Rosenzweig 1963. *The Theory and Management of Systems*. New York: McGraw-Hill, 1963.

Johnston, J. 1960. *Statistical Cost Analysis*. New York: McGraw-Hill 1960.

Kaplan, A. D. H., J. B. Dirlam, and R. F. Lanzillotti 1958. *Pricing in Big Business: A Case Approach*. Washington: Brookings Institute, 1958.

Katona, G. 1958. "Business Expectations in the Framework of Psychological Economics (Toward a Theory of Expectations)." In Bowman (1958), pp. 59–73.

Kemp, P. S. 1966. "Post-Completion Audits of Capital Investment Projects." *NAA Management Accounting*, Aug. 1966, pp. 49–54.

Kline, C. A., Jr., and H. Hessler 1952. "The du Pont Chart System for Appraising Operating Performance" (conference proceedings), *NAA Bulletin*, 1952, pp. 1595–1619.

Kohler, E. L. 1963. *A Dictionary for Accountants*, 3rd ed. Englewood Cliffs, N.J.: Prentice-Hall, 1963.

Koontz, H., and C. O'Donnel 1959. *Principles of Management: An Analysis of Managerial Functions*, 2nd ed. New York: McGraw-Hill, 1959.

Koopmans, T. C. 1951. "Analysis of Production as an Efficient Combination of Activities." In Koopmans, T. C. (ed.), *Activity Analysis of Production and Allocation*, pp. 33–97. New York: Wiley, 1951.

Krech, D., R. S. Cruchfield, and E. L. Ballachey 1962. *Individual in Society*. New York: McGraw-Hill, 1962.

Kruisinga, H. J. (ed.) 1954. *The Balance between Centralization and Decentralization in Managerial Control*. Leiden, Neth.: H. E. Stenfert Kroese, 1954.

Langholm, O. 1965. "Cost Structure and Costing Method: An Empirical Study." *Journal of Accounting Research*, autumn 1965, pp. 218–227.

Lanzillotti, R. F. 1958. "Pricing Objectives in Large Companies." *American Economic Review,* Dec. 1958, pp. 921–940.

Lawrence, F. C., and E. N. Humphreys 1947. *Marginal Costing*. London: McDonald & Evans, 1947.

Leavitt, H. J. 1964. *Managerial Psychology: An Introduction to Individuals, Pairs, and Groups in Organizations*, 2nd ed. Chicago: University of Chicago Press, 1964.

Lemke, K. W. 1966. "Asset Valuation and Income Theory." *Accounting Review*, Jan. 1966, pp. 32–41.

Lewis, R. W. 1955. "Measuring, Reporting and Appraising Results of Operations with Reference to Goals, Plans and Budgets." In Controllership Foundation, Inc., *A Case Study of Management Planning and Control at General Electric Company*, pp. 29–41. New York, 1955.

Lewis, W. A. 1949. *Overhead Costs: Some Essays in Economic Analysis*. London: George Allen and Unwin, 1949.

—— 1961. "Depreciation and Obsolescence as Factors in Costing." In J. L. Meij (ed)., *Depreciation and Replacement Policy*, pp. 15–45. Chicago: Quadrangle Books, 1961.

Loftsgard, L., and E. O. Heady 1959. "Application of Dynamic Programming Models for Optimum Farm and Home Plans." *Journal of Farm Economics,* Feb. 1959, pp. 51–62.

Lowe, H. D. 1963. "The Essentials of a General Theory of Depreciation." *Accounting Review*, April 1963, pp. 293–301.

Lowe, Y. 1963. *The Farm and Its Economic Analysis*. Tel-Aviv: Am-Oved, 1963. (In Hebrew.)

Lutz, Friedrich, and Vera Lutz 1951. *The Theory of Investment of the Firm*. Princeton, N.J.: Princeton University Press, 1951.

Machlup, F. 1967. "Theories of the Firm: Marginalist, Behavioral, Managerial." *American Economic Review*, March 1967, pp. 1–33.

March, J. G., and H. A. Simon 1958. *Organizations*. New York: Wiley, 1958.

Marple, R. P. (ed.) 1965. *National Association of Accountants on Direct Costing: Selected Papers*. New York: Ronald, 1965.

Marschak, T. 1960. "Capital Budgeting and Pricing in the French Nationalized Industries." *Journal of Business*, April 1960, pp. 133–156.

Mattessich, R. 1964. *Accounting and Analytical Methods*. Homewood, Ill.: Irwin, 1964.

May, G. O. 1952. "Limitations on the Significance of Invested Cost." *Accounting Review*, Oct. 1952 pp. 436–440.

McDonald, D. L. 1968. "A Test of Application of the Feasibility of Market Based Measures in Accounting." *Journal of Accounting Research*, (spring 1968, pp. 38–49.

McFarland, W. B. 1966. *Concepts for Management Accounting*. New York: National Association of Accountants, 1966.

McFarquhar, A. M. M. 1962. "Research in Farm Management Planning Methods in North Europe." *Journal of Agricultural Economics*, May 1962, pp. 78–100.

Meade, J. E. 1952. "External Economies and Diseconomies in a Competitive Situation." *Economic Journal*, March 1952, pp. 54–67.

Mee, J. F. 1963. *Management Thought in a Dynamic Economy*. New York: New York University Press, 1963.

Menge, J. A. 1961. "The Backward Art of Interdivisional Transfer Pricing." *Journal of Industrial Economics*, July 1961, pp. 215–232.

Miller, D. W., and M. K. Starr 1960. *Executive Decisions and Operations Research*. Englewood Cliffs, N.J.: Prentice-Hall, 1960.

Modigliani, F., and K. J. Cohen 1961. *The Role of Anticipations and Plans in Economic Behaviour and Their Use in Economic Analysis and Forecasting*. Studies in Business Expectations and Planning; Urbana: University of Illinois, 1961.

Monsen, R. J., Jr., and A. Downs 1965. "A Theory of Large Managerial Firms." *Journal of Political Economy*, June 1965, pp. 221–236.

Moonitz, M. 1961. *The Basic Postulates of Accounting*. (AICPA Accounting Research Study No. 1.) New York: American Institute of Certified Public Accountants, 1961.

Morris, W. T. 1964. *The Analysis of Management Decisions*, rev. ed. Homewood, Ill.: Irwin, 1964.

Mueller, G. G. 1964. "Valuing Inventories at Other than Historical Costs—Some International Differences." *Journal of Accounting Research*, autumn 1964, pp. 148–157.

National Association of (Cost) Accountants 1951. "Assignment of Nonmanufacturing Costs for Managerial Decisions." (Research Series No. 19.) *NACA Bulletin*, May 1951, pp. 1133–1174.

—— 1953*a*. "Direct Costing." (Research Series No. 23.) *NACA Bulletin*, April 1953, pp. 1077–1128.

—— 1953*b*. "Product Costs for Pricing Purposes." (Research Series No. 24.) *NACA Bulletin*, Aug. 1953, pp. 1669–1730.

—— 1956. *Accounting for Inter-Company Transfers*. (Research Series No. 30.) New York, 1956.

—— 1957. *Costing Joint Products*. (Research Series No. 31.) New York, 1957.

—— 1959. *Return on Capital as a Guide to Management Decisions.* (Research Report No. 35.) New York, 1959.

—— 1961. *Current Application of Direct Costing.* (Research Report No. 37.) New York, 1961.

National Commission on Food Marketing 1966. *Organization and Competition in Food Retailing.* (Technical Study No. 7.) Washington, 1966.

Nelson, J. R. 1963. "Practical Applications of Marginal Cost Pricing in the Utility Field." *American Economic Review,* May 1963, pp. 474–481.

—— (ed.) 1964. *Marginal Cost Pricing in Practice.* Englewood Cliffs, N.J.: Prentice-Hall, 1964.

Ophir, T. 1960. *Intracompany Pricing in the Decentralized Firm.* Unpub. Ph.D. thesis, Massachusetts Institute of Technology, 1960.

Oxenfeldt, A. R. 1951. *Industrial Pricing and Market Practices.* New York: Prentice-Hall, 1951.

Paton, W. A. 1947. "Restoration of Fixed Asset Values to the Balance Sheet." *Accounting Review,* April 1947, pp. 198–200.

—— 1949. *Essentials of Accounting,* rev. ed. New York: Macmillan, 1949.

Paton, W. A., and A. C. Littleton 1940. *An Introduction to Corporate Accounting Standards.* Evanston, Ill.: American Accounting Association, 1940.

Philips, G. E. 1963*a*. "The Accretion Concept of Income." *Accounting Review,* Jan. 1963, pp. 14–25.

—— 1963*b*. "The Revolution in Accounting Theory." *Accounting Review,* Oct. 1963, pp. 696–708.

Puterbaugh, H. L., E. W. Kehrberg, and J. O. Dunbar 1957. "Analyzing the Solution Tableau of a Simplex Linear Programming Problem in Farm Organization." *Journal of Economics,* May 1957, pp. 478–489.

Regev, U., A. Levinger, and D. Yaron 1964. *Application of the Linear Programming Technique to a Kibbutz Farm* (Faculty of Agriculture Bulletin 71.) Rehovot: Dept. of Agricultural Economics, Hebrew University, 1964. (In Hebrew.)

Rickard, E. B. 1950. "A Study of Decentralization: Controllership in a Divisional Organization." *NACA Bulletin,* Jan. 1950, pp. 567–578.

Ridgway, V. F. 1960. "Dysfunctional Consequences of Performance Measurements." In A. H. Rubenstein and C. J. Haberstroh (eds.), *Some Theories of Organization,* pp. 371–377. Homewood, Ill.: Dorsey and Irwin, 1960.

Robichek, A. A., D. Teichroew, and J. M. Jones 1965. "Optimal Short-Term Financing Decisions." *Management Science,* Sept. 1965, pp. 1–36.

Ross, M. H. 1960. "Depreciation and User Cost." *Accounting Review*, July 1960, pp. 422–428.

Rossotti, C. O. 1965. *Two Concepts of Long Range Planning*. Boston: Boston Consulting Group of Boston Safe Deposit and Trust Co., 1965.

Sack, S. H. 1958. "Costing Practices of 37 Cotton Textile Firms." *NAA Bulletin*, March 1958, pp. 31–41.

Samuels, J. M. 1965. "Opportunity Costing: An Application of Mathematical Programming." *Journal of Accounting Research*, autumn 1965, pp. 182–191.

Samuelson, P. A. 1956. "Social Indifference Curves." *Quarterly Journal of Economics*, Feb. 1956, pp. 1–22.

Schrader, W. J. 1959. *A Critical Evaluation of Income Measurement by "Products" and "Periods."* (Industrial Research Bulletin No. 6, College of Business Administration, Pennsylvania State University.) N. p.: The College, 1959.

Shillinglaw, G. 1957. "Guides to Internal Profit Measurement." *Harvard Business Review*, March–April 1957, pp. 82–94.

—— 1961. *Cost Accounting: Analysis and Control*. Homewood, Ill.: Irwin, 1961; rev. 1967.

—— 1962. "Towards a Theory of Divisional Income Measurement." *Accounting Review*, April 1962, pp. 208–216.

—— 1963. "The Concept fo Attributable Cost." *Journal of Accounting Research*, spring 1963, pp. 73–85.

—— 1964. "Divisional Performance Review: An Extension of Budgetary Control." In Bonini, Jaedicke, and Wagner (1964), pp. 149–185.

—— 1967. "A Critique." In Burns (1967), pp. 123–134.

Shubik, M. 1961. "Approaches to the Study of Decision-Making Relevant to the Firm." *Journal of Business*, April 1961, pp. 101–118.

—— 1964. "Incentives, Decentralized Control, the Assignment of Joint Costs and Internal Pricing." In Bonini, Jaedicke, and Wagner (1964), pp. 205–226.

Simmons, J. D. 1964. *Long-Range Profit Planning*. (NAA Research Report No. 42.) New York: National Association of Accountants, 1964.

Simon, H. A. 1959. "Theories of Decision-Making in Economics and Behavioral Science," *American Economic Review*, June 1959, pp. 253–283.

—— 1960. *The New Science of Management Decisions*. New York: Harper, 1960.

—— 1962. "New Developments in the Theory of the Firm." *American Economic Review*, May 1962, pp. 1–15.

—— 1964. "On the Concepts of Organizational Goal." *Administrative Science Quarterly*, June 1964, pp. 1–22.

Simon, H. A., H. Gnetzkow, G. Kozmetsky, and G. Tyndall 1954. *Centralization vs. Decentralization in Organizing the Controller's Department.* New York: Controllership Foundation, Inc., 1954.

Smidt, S. 1965. "Accounting Concepts and Present Value." Unpub. MS No. 379:7, Graduate School of Business and Public Administration, Cornell Universtiy, 1965.

Smith, V. E., and C. S. Barnard 1960. "Cost Allocation and the Detection of Unprofitable Ventures." *Journal of Farm Economics*, Aug. 1960, pp. 666–675.

Smithies, A. 1965. "Conceptual Framework for the Program Budget." In D. Novick (ed.) *Program Budgeting: Program Analysis and the Federal Budget*, pp. 2–32. Washington: U.S. Government Printing Office, 1965.

Solomons, D. 1961. "Economic and Accounting Concepts of Income." *Accounting Review*, July 1961, pp. 374–383.

—— 1965. *Divisional Performance: Measurement and Control.* New York: Financial Executives Research, 1965.

Sord, B. H., and G. A. Welsch 1958. *Business Budgeting: A Survey of Management Planning and Control Practices.* New York: Controllership Foundation, Inc., 1958.

Sorter, G. H., and C. T. Horngren 1962. "Asset Recognition and Economic Attributes—the Relevant Costing Approach." *Accounting Review*, July 1962, pp. 391–399.

Sprouse, R. T. (reporter) 1964. *The Management of Property, Plant, and Equipment in Financial Statements.* (Harvard Business School Accounting Round Table, A Summary of Proceedings.) Boston: Harvard Graduate School of Business Administration, 1964.

Sprouse, R. T., and M. Moonitz 1962. *A Tentative Set of Broad Accounting Principles for Business Enterprises.* (AICPA Accounting Research Study No. 3.) New York: American Institute of Certified Public Accountants, 1962.

Stedry, A. C. 1960. *Budget Control and Cost Behavior.* Ford Foundation Doctoral Dissertation Series; Englewood Cliffs, N.J.: Prentice-Hall, 1960.

Stigler, G. J. 1952, 1966. *The Theory of Price.* New York: Macmillan, rev. ed. 1952; 3rd ed. 1966.

Stone, W. E. 1957. "Management Practices with Respect to Internal Transfer Pricing in Large Manufacturing Companies." Unpub. Ph.D. thesis, University of Michigan, 1957; University Microfilms No. 23-643.

Sweet, F. H. 1964. *Strategic Planning: A Conceptual Study.* (Research Monograph No. 26, Bureau of Business Research.) Austin: University of Texas, 1964.

Taggart, H. F. 1953. "Sacred Cows in Accounting." *Accounting Review,* July 1953, pp. 313–319.

Tarshis, L. 1947. *The Elements of Economics.* Boston: Houghton Mifflin, 1947.

Thomas, A. L. 1966. *Revenue Recognition.* (Michigan Business Report No. 49, Bureau of Business Research.) Ann Arbor: Graduate School of Business Administration, University of Michigan, 1966.

Tucker, S. A. 1961. *Successful Managerial Control by Ratio-Analysis.* New York: McGraw-Hill, 1961.

—— 1966. *Pricing for Higher Profits: Criteria, Methods, Applications.* New York: McGraw-Hill, 1966.

U.S. Bureau of the Budget 1965. *Planning-Programming-Budgeting.* (Bulletin No. 66-3.) Washington, 1965.

Vanek, J. 1965. "Worker's Profit Participation, Unemployment and the Keynesian Equilibrium," *Weltwirtschaftliches Archiv,* 1965, pp. 206–214.

Vatter, W. J. 1954. "Tailor-Making Cost Data for Specific Uses." (1954 Conference Proceedings.) *NACA Bulletin,* Aug. 1954, pp. 1691–1707.

—— 1958. "Contributions of Accounting to Measurement in Management." *Management Science,* Oct. 1958, pp. 27–37.

—— 1959. "Does the Rate of Return Measure Business Efficiency?" *NAA Bulletin,* Jan. 1959, pp. 33–48.

—— 1966. "Income Models, Book Yield, and the Rate of Return." *Accounting Review,* Oct. 1966, pp. 681–698.

—— 1967. "A Critique." In Burns (1967), pp. 135–145.

Vroom, V. H. 1965. *Motivation in Management.* N. p.: American Foundation for Management Research, 1965.

Walters, A. A. 1960. "The Allocation of Joint Costs with Demands as Probability Distributions." *American Economic Review,* June 1960, pp. 419–432.

Weingartner, H. M. 1963. *Mathematical Programming and the Analysis of Capital Budgeting Problems.* Ford Foundation Doctoral Dissertation Series; Englewood Cliffs, N.J.: Prentice-Hall, 1963.

Welsch, G. A. 1964. *Budgeting: Profit Planning and Control,* 2nd ed. Englewood Cliffs, N.J.: Prentice-Hall, 1964.

Westerdahl, W. E. 1961. "Comparing the Company with Its Industry by Ratios." *NAA Bulletin,* Nov. 1961, pp. 29–42.

Westfield, F. M. 1966. "Practicing Marginal-Cost Pricing—a Review." *Journal of Business*, Jan. 1966, pp. 67–73.

Whinston, A. 1962. *Prices Coordination in Decentralized Systems*. (O.N.R. Research Memorandum No. 99 [Ditto].) Pittsburgh: Graduate School of Industrial Administration, Carnegie Institute of Technology, 1962.

—— 1964*a*. "Price Guides in Decentralized Organizations." In W. W. Cooper *et al.* (eds.), *New Prospectives in Organization Research*, pp. 403–448. New York: Wiley, 1964.

—— 1964*b*. "Theoretical and Computational Problems in Organizational Decision Making." In *Operational Research and the Social Sciences*. London: International Conference of the Operational Research Society, 1964.

Williamson, O. E. 1963. "Managerial Discretion and Business Behavior." *American Economic Review*, Dec. 1963, pp. 1032–1057.

Wold, H., and L. Jureen 1953. *Demand Analysis*. New York: Wiley, 1953.

Wright, F. K. 1964. "Towards a General Theory of Depreciation." *Journal of Accounting Research*, spring 1964, pp. 80–90.

—— 1965. "Depreciation and Obsolescence in Current Value Accounting." *Journal of Accounting Research*, autumn 1965, pp. 167–187.

Wright, W. 1962. *Direct Standard Costs for Decision Making and Control*. New York: McGraw-Hill, 1962.

Zannetos, Z. L. 1964. "Some Thoughts on Internal Control Systems of the Firm." *Accounting Review*, Oct. 1964, pp. 860–868.

—— 1965. "On the Theory of Divisional Structures: Some Aspects of Centralization of Control and Decision Making." *Management Science*, Dec. 1965, pp. B–49–68.

INDEX